LA Lite™ Cookbook

Simple Recipes

Simply Delicious

LA WEIGHT LOSS CENTERS

LA LITE™

Cookbook

▶ *Simple Recipes*

Simply Delicious

The joy of the L A Weight Loss program is the variety of foods available to you while you're losing weight. With the L A Lite Cookbook you now have new and unique ways to prepare the wide array of food choices found in each program. Your entire family will enjoy these light and naturally delicious meals that range from steaming beef vegetable and french onion soup to succulent entrees such as soy-glazed chicken and beef stroganoff, to tantalizing desserts including chocolate truffles and apple crisps. Plus, you'll find hundreds of other recipes for drinks, entrees, vegetable preparations, ethnic meals and sweet delights. Each recipe was overseen by our head nutritionist and represents a collection of the best preparations from our centers and clients. You can be certain that all recipes work with your L A Weight Loss program as exchanges are provided for each recipe.

So enjoy and happy eating!

Exclusively distributed by L A Weight Loss Franchise Company.
All exchanges provided are specific to L A Weight Loss Program.
6-55958-35002-0

Contents

▶ *Portion sizes may vary according to plan.*
Please be certain to check your L A Weight
Loss Menu Plan for the correct portion size.

Jump Start

Breakfast is an essential part of your day. It has been shown that eating breakfast each morning may help you to have better concentration throughout the day. Also people who skip breakfast are more likely to eat more at the next meal and therefore may have trouble controlling or losing weight in the long run. It is not essential to sit down to a three course meal at breakfast, but it is important to have a small meal to get you, and your metabolism, running efficiently. The following section will give you some ideas for eating on the run and for a leisurely Sunday breakfast.

Strawberry Cheesecake Crepe recipe can be found on page 11

Basic Methods of Cooking Eggs

- **Poached** — whole eggs are simmered gently in water; a small amount of vinegar may be added to keep the egg together.
- **Scrambled** — eggs are whisked until fluffy and cooked over medium heat.
- **Fried** — whole eggs are fried in butter on a griddle; the yolks may be runny (over-easy) or cooked through (over-hard).
- **Sunny-side up** — whole eggs are fried in butter on a griddle; the egg is not flipped over in the cooking process, leaving the yolk, and sometimes the white, slightly runny.
- **Hard-boiled** — whole eggs boiled in water in the shell until cooked through with a firm yolk and white, about 20 minutes.
- **Soft-boiled** — whole eggs boiled in water in the shell until white is cooked through and yolk is almost set.
- **Coddled** — similar to a poached egg; a whole egg, without shell, is placed in simmering water in a porcelain or glass dish for 1-2 minutes until soft.

Breakfast Terms

- **Quiche** — a classical breakfast or lunch item; eggs are beat with milk or cream and typically combined with vegetables or meats and cheese; the egg mixture is poured into a savory pie crust and baked.
- **Eggs Benedict** — a restaurant favorite; poached eggs are served atop Canadian bacon and toasted English muffins; it is finished with a rich hollandaise sauce.
- **Strata** — a baked egg and milk mixture with vegetables, cheese and/or meats; the mixture is poured over layers of bread before baking.
- **Frittata** — a baked omelet of eggs and desired fillings; the omelet is cooked on the stovetop and then baked until set; sometimes pasta may be added as well.
- **Omelet** — a classical French menu item; eggs are cooked in a sauté pan and folded over any desired fillings.
- **Crepes** — a very thin pancake-like batter that is cooked in a sauté-like pan and wrapped with either sweet or savory fillings.

Food Safety

Though there is very low risk of food-borne illness with consumption of eggs, you should still make sure eggs are of high quality and fresh, and are cooked thoroughly in order to prevent salmonella. If you are concerned about consuming undercooked egg whites, you may use pasteurized liquid egg whites, or powder or pasteurized liquid egg substitute.

TIP!

Eating breakfast in th morning promotes bloo sugar level stability, bette concentration and more energy. Your body depends breakfast to keep your energy levels high througho the day.

Jump
❀ Star

Scrambled Egg

serving

SERVING SIZE: 1 ENTRÉE
COUNTS AS:
1 PROTEIN

ze according to plan

☼ Ingredients

1 or 2 egg(s), size according to plan

1 Tbsp skim milk

dash of lite salt

freshly ground pepper

nonfat cooking spray

1 In a bowl, whisk all ingredients thoroughly until they have reached a uniform yellow color.

2 Coat skillet with nonfat cooking spray. Heat skillet over medium flame.

3 Pour egg mixture into skillet.

4 As mixture begins to set at bottom and sides, gently lift cooked portion with spatula so that thin, uncooked portion can flow to the bottom.

5 Cook until egg(s) are thickened throughout, but still moist, about 3-5 minutes.

Cheesy Scrambled Egg

serving

good source of calcium

SERVING SIZE: 1 ENTRÉE
COUNTS AS:
1/2 OR 1 PROTEIN

ze according to plan

☼ Ingredients

1 whole egg

2 or 4 egg whites, size according to plan

1oz (28g) reduced-fat cheddar or swiss cheese

1/4 tsp snipped parsley

1/4 tsp snipped chives

nonfat cooking spray

1 Break egg into a medium mixing bowl; add egg whites. Mix until well blended.

2 Add cheese, parsley and chives.

3 Coat skillet with nonfat cooking spray and heat over medium flame.

4 Add egg mixture to skillet.

5 As mixture begins to set at bottom and sides, gently lift cooked portion with spatula so that thin, uncooked portion can flow to bottom.

6 Cook until eggs are thickened throughout, but still moist, approximately 3-5 minutes.

Jump
❖ Start

Puffy Omelet

1 *serving*

- SERVING SIZE: ENTRÉE
- COUNTS AS:
  - 1 PROTEIN

▶ *size according to plan*

☀ Ingredients

2 or 3 eggs, separated, size
  according to plan

1/4 cup (60ml) water

1/4 tsp lite salt

1/8 tsp freshly ground pepper

nonfat cooking spray

1. Preheat oven to 325°F.

2. With a mixer, beat egg whites, water and salt on high speed until stiff, but not dry.

3. In a separate bowl, beat egg yolks and pepper on high speed until very thick and lemon colored. Fold yolks into egg whites.

4. Coat 10-inch ovenproof skillet with nonfat cooking spray. Heat skillet over medium flame.

5. Pour egg mixture into skillet; reduce heat.

6. Cook over low heat until puffy and light brown on bottom, about 5 minutes.

7. Bake, uncovered, in oven, until knife inserted in the center comes out clean, about 10-15 minutes.

8. Fold omelet in half; slip onto a plate.

Broccoli Omelet Bake

1 *serving*

good source of fiber

- SERVING SIZE: 1 OMELET
- COUNTS AS:
  - 1 PROTEIN
  - 2 VEGETABLES
  - 1/2 DAIRY

▶ *size according to plan*

☀ Ingredients

2 or 3 eggs, size according
  to plan

1/2 cup (125ml / 78g)
  cooked broccoli, chopped

1 tsp dried onion

1oz (28g) reduced-fat
  cheddar or swiss cheese

2 Tbsp skim milk

1/4 tsp lite salt

1/4 tsp dried basil

1/2 tsp garlic powder

1 tomato cut into 6 slices

1. Beat eggs until light and fluffy.

2. Stir in broccoli, onion, half of the cheese, milk, salt, basil and garlic powder.

3. Pour into ungreased baking dish.

4. Arrange tomato slices on top; sprinkle with remaining cheese.

5. Bake, uncovered, in 325°F oven for 20-25 minutes.

Jump
❖ Star

Apple Pancake

serving

SERVING SIZE: 1 PANCAKE
COUNTS AS:
1 PROTEIN
1 STARCH
1 FRUIT

ze according to plan

☀ Ingredients

1/2 or 3/4 cup (125 or 200ml) of egg substitute, size according to plan

3 slices Melba toast, crushed

1 small apple, peeled and grated

1/2 tsp cinnamon

1 packet artificial sweetener

nonfat cooking spray

1 Combine all ingredients in a small bowl.

2 Coat skillet with nonfat cooking spray. Pour mixture into skillet. Heat until lightly brown; flip over and brown on other side. Serve.

"Talk about something new and unusual. This is definitely it. No more plain old pancakes. They are absolutely delicious."

- Michael G.

French Toast

serving

SERVING SIZE: 1 SLICE
COUNTS AS:
1/2 PROTEIN
1 STARCH
1 FRUIT

ze according to plan

meals in minutes

☀ Ingredients

1/4 cup (60ml) egg substitute

1 Tbsp skim milk

dash of sugar substitute

dash of cinnamon

dash of nutmeg

1 slice diet bread

12 small strawberries, sliced

nonfat cooking spray

1 Combine egg substitute, milk, spices and sugar substitute in a shallow bowl; mix well.

2 Add slice of bread to egg mixture and let stand until egg mixture is absorbed.

3 Coat skillet with nonfat cooking spray and heat over medium heat. Place bread in skillet and brown both sides of diet bread.

4 Place on serving dish; top with sliced strawberries.

Jump
♣ Start

Greek Omelet

1 *serving*

■ SERVING SIZE: 1 OMELET
■ COUNTS AS:
  1 PROTEIN
  1 VEGETABLE
  1/2 DAIRY

▶ *size according to plan*

meals in minutes

✴ Ingredients

2 Tbsp chopped red onion

1/4 cup (60ml / 14g) fresh spinach

2 Tbsp skim milk

1/4 tsp garlic powder

1/2 or 3/4 cup (125 or 200ml) egg substitute, size according to plan

1oz (28g) lite feta cheese

9 black olives, diced

nonfat cooking spray

1. Coat medium skillet with nonfat cooking spray; heat over medium flame.

2. Sauté onions and spinach, until onions are tender and spinach has wilted down.

3. Remove vegetables from skillet and place in small mixing bowl; cool for 5 minutes.

4. Add milk, garlic powder and egg substitute to mixing bowl. Mix well.

5. Coat skillet with nonfat cooking spray and heat over medium heat. Add egg mixture to skillet and cook over low heat until brown.

6. Flip egg mixture over and brown on other side. Turn heat to low and sprinkle with cheese and olives, cover skillet 1-2 minutes or until cheese is softened.

Bran Muffin

1 *serving*

■ SERVING SIZE: 1 MUFFIN
■ COUNTS AS:
  1/2 PROTEIN
  1 STARCH

▶ *size according to plan*

good source of fiber

✴ Ingredients

1/2 cup (125ml) egg substitute

2 Tbsp water

2 Tbsp skim milk

1 tsp vanilla

1/2 tsp cinnamon

1 Tbsp flour

pinch nutmeg

1/2 cup (125ml / 30g) unprocessed bran

1/2 cup (125ml / 72g) blueberries

3 packets artificial sweetener

nonfat cooking spray

1. In a large bowl, combine egg substitute, water, milk, vanilla, cinnamon, flour, nutmeg and bran.

2. Add blueberries.

3. Coat muffin pan with nonfat cooking spray.

4. Divide batter between 2 muffin cups.

5. Bake in 350°F oven for 15 minutes.

Jump
✤ Start

Crepes

servings

☀ Ingredients

1/2 cup (125ml / 63g) whole wheat flour

1/2 cup (125ml / 63g) white flour

1/2 cup (125ml) egg substitute

1 packet artificial sweetener

3/4 cup (200ml) skim milk

1/4 cup (60ml) water

1/4 tsp lite salt

2 tsp vanilla extract

1 Tbsp margarine, melted

nonfat cooking spray

Batter

1 Combine flour, salt and sugar substitute in small bowl. Set aside.

2 In a separate bowl, beat eggs and milk together with an electric mixer.

3 Beat flour mixture slowly into eggs.

4 Once flour is combined into eggs; slowly stir in melted butter and vanilla extract.

Crepes

1 Coat small skillet, or crepe pan, with nonfat cooking spray and heat over medium-high.

2 Scoop 2 tablespoons of batter into skillet.

3 Tip and rotate the skillet to help spread the batter, as thinly as possible, over bottom of pan.

4 Cook 30-60 seconds, or until bottom is lightly browned.

5 Carefully flip over and cook 15-20 more seconds.

6 Remove from pan. Set aside.

7 Continue to cook crepes until all batter is used. Place a piece of wax paper between each cooked crepe to prevent them from sticking together. (Cool skillet for 1-2 minutes periodically during cooking to prevent burning.)

8 Crepes can be frozen in the wax paper for up to a month.

Strawberry Cheesecake Crepe

serving

☀ Ingredients

2oz (56g) reduced-fat ricotta cheese

3 small strawberries diced

1 tsp artificial sweetener

1/4 tsp vanilla extract

1 Tbsp fat-free whipped topping

1 Crepe (see crepe recipe)

3 small strawberries, sliced

1 In small mixing bowl combine cheese, sweetener, diced berries and vanilla.

2 Mix well.

3 Place filling over one half of the crepe and fold over filling.

4 Top with sliced strawberries and whipped topping.

Jump
♣ Start

Banana Nut Crepe

1 *serving*

- **SERVING SIZE: 1 CREPE**
- **COUNTS AS:**
  - 1 STARCH
  - 1 FRUIT
  - 1 FAT

▶ *size according to plan*

☼ Ingredients

1/2 small banana

4 walnuts

1/2 packet artificial sweetener

1/4 tsp cinnamon

1 crepe (see crepe recipe on page 11)

1 Slice banana.

2 Chop walnut into small pieces.

3 Place banana slices over half of the crepe.

4 Sprinkle walnuts, artificial sweetener and cinnamon over bananas.

5 Fold crepe over filling.

6 If desired, heat in microwave 30 seconds to soften banana.

Mushroom & Spinach Crepe

1 *serving*

- **SERVING SIZE: 1 CREPE**
- **COUNTS AS:**
  - 1 STARCH
  - 1 VEGETABLE

▶ *size according to plan*

☼ Ingredients

2 Tbsp chopped sweet onions

1/4 tsp lite salt

1/4 packet artificial sweetener

1/4 cup (60ml / 18g) chopped white mushrooms

2 tsp garlic powder

1/4 cup (60ml / 8g) fresh spinach, chopped

1 crepe (see crepe recipe on page 11)

nonfat cooking spray

1 Coat small skillet with nonfat cooking spray.

2 Place onions in skillet, add salt and sweetener; sauté on high heat for 1-2 minutes until onions begin to soften.

3 Add mushrooms and garlic powder and sauté 3 minutes, or until mushrooms are tender.

4 Add spinach; cook additional 2-3 minutes, until all vegetables are cooked.

5 Place vegetable mixture over one half of the crepe. Fold crepe over filling.

6 Serve hot.

Jump
❖ Star

Mexican Omelet

serving

SERVING SIZE: 1 OMELET

COUNTS AS:

1 PROTEIN

2 VEGETABLES

e according to plan

✳ Ingredients

1/2 or 3/4 cup (125 or 200ml) egg substitute, size according to plan

2 tsp hot sauce

1/4 tsp lite salt

1 Tbsp skim milk

1 Tbsp diced green peppers

1 Tbsp diced red peppers

1 Tbsp diced white onion

1 tsp cilantro

1 Tbsp diced tomato

1 Tbsp chopped green onion

1 Tbsp salsa

1 Tbsp fat-free sour cream

nonfat cooking spray

1 Combine egg, hot sauce, salt and milk in mixing bowl. Whisk together vigorously; set aside.

2 Coat medium skillet with nonfat cooking spray. Heat over high flame.

3 Add red and green pepper, white onion and cilantro to skillet. Sauté 2-3 minutes or until vegetables start to soften.

4 Remove veggies from skillet, allow skillet to cool 2-3 minutes.

5 Coat skillet, again, with cooking spray, return to heat over medium flame.

6 Pour egg into skillet, distributing evenly.

7 Continue to cook over medium heat; use a spatula to gently lift the edges of the omelet, allowing uncooked egg to move underneath.

8 Once egg is almost cooked, with only a small amount uncooked, add the pepper mixture and tomatoes. Cover skillet with a lid and cook additional 2-3 minutes over low heat, or until egg fully cooked.

9 Use spatula to remove omelet from pan, flipping in half while transferring to plate.

10 Top with salsa, sour cream and green onion.

11 To spice things up...sprinkle chili powder over your omelet!

Matzo Brie

serving

SERVING SIZE: 1 RECIPE

COUNTS AS:

1 PROTEIN

1 STARCH

e according to plan

✳ Ingredients

1 sheet of matzo

1/2 or 3/4 cup (125 or 200ml) egg substitute, size according to plan

1 cup (250ml) warm water

nonfat cooking spray

1 Break matzo into pieces. In small bowl, soak the matzo in water for 1-2 minutes, or until soft. Drain matzo well.

2 Add eggs and salt to matzo mixture.

3 Coat medium skillet with nonfat cooking spray. Heat over medium heat.

4 Pour egg mixture into skillet. Cook until lightly brown one side; flip over and brown on other side.

5 Season with either salt and pepper, or cinnamon and artificial sweetener.

13

Jump
❖ Start

servings **12**

Buttermilk Scones

family fare

■ **SERVING SIZE: 1 SCONE**
■ **COUNTS AS:**
  1 STARCH
  1 FRUIT
  1 FAT

▸ *size according to plan*

☀ Ingredients

1 1/2 cups (375ml / 187g) flour

1 1/2 cup (375ml / 121g) old-fashioned oats

1 Tbsp sugar

3 packets artificial sweetener

1 Tbsp baking powder

1 tsp cream of tartar

1/2 tsp lite salt

1/3 cup (85ml) unsalted margarine, melted

2/3 cup (170ml) nonfat buttermilk

1/2 cup (125ml) egg substitute

1/2 cup (125ml / 78g) raisins or currants

nonfat cooking spray

1 Preheat oven to 425°F.

2 Combine flour, oats, sugar, artificial sweetener, baking powder, cream of tartar and salt in a large bowl.

3 Add margarine, buttermilk and egg.

4 Mix just until batter is moistened.

5 Stir in raisins.

6 With your hands, shape the dough to form a ball.

7 Pat out on a lightly floured surface to form an 8-inch circle.

8 Cut into 12 wedges.

9 Bake on a cookie sheet coated with nonfat cooking spray for 12-15 minutes, or until light brown.

---

 serving **1**

Breakfast Burrito

good source of calcium

■ **SERVING SIZE: 1 BURRITO**
■ **COUNTS AS:**
  1 PROTEIN
  1 STARCH
  1 VEGETABLE
  1/2 DAIRY

▸ *size according to plan*

☀ Ingredients

1 Tbsp diced green pepper

1 Tbsp chopped green onion

1/2 or 3/4 cup (125 or 200ml) egg substitute, size according to plan

1/4 tsp lite salt

1 Tbsp diced tomato

1/2 whole wheat tortilla

1oz (28g) reduced-fat pepper jack cheese

1 Tbsp fat-free sour cream

nonfat cooking spray

1 Coat medium skillet with nonfat cooking spray. Heat over high heat.

2 Add pepper and onion to skillet. Sauté 2-3 minutes, or until vegetables start to soften.

3 Pour egg into skillet, distributing evenly. Sprinkle with salt.

4 Once eggs are cooked through, turn down heat; add tomatoes, cook 1 minute until tomatoes are warm.

5 Place egg in middle of tortilla; top with cheese.

6 Roll up tortilla into a burrito.

7 Top with sour cream.

Jump
❖ Star

Sausage Patties

servings

SERVING SIZE: 1 PATTY
COUNTS AS:
PROTEIN

according to plan

family fare

☀ Ingredients

10 green onions, finely chopped

1/2 cup (125ml / 54g) bread crumbs (see recipe on page 154)

1/2 cup (125ml) skim milk

2 pounds (996g) ground lean pork

1 tsp white pepper

1/4 tsp freshly ground pepper

1/4 tsp cayenne

1 tsp finely chopped fresh thyme

1 tsp finely chopped fresh sage

nonfat cooking spray

1 Coat skillet with nonfat cooking spray and heat over medium heat.

2 Cook onion, stirring occasionally, until softened and beginning to brown. Remove from heat and cool for 10 minutes.

3 While onions are cooling, stir together bread crumbs and milk in a large bowl and let stand until crumbs absorb the milk.

4 Add onions and remaining ingredients to crumb mixture and stir with a fork until blended well.

5 Preheat oven to 250°F.

6 Form sausage patties into 1/2-inch thick patties with dampened hands and arrange on a wax paper lined tray.

7 Make into 12 patties.

8 Spray heavy skillet with nonfat cooking spray; heat over medium-high heat, cook patties, turning once, until browned and just cooked through, 4-6 minutes per batch.

9 Transfer to shallow baking pan and keep warm, covered with foil, in oven while cooking remaining batches.

Turkey Sausage

servings

SERVING SIZE: 1 PATTY
COUNTS AS:
1/2 PROTEIN

according to plan

family fare

☀ Ingredients

10 or 14oz (280 or 392g) ground turkey breast, size according to plan

1/2 tsp dried sage

1/4 tsp freshly ground pepper

1/4 tsp cayenne pepper

1/4 tsp lite salt

nonfat cooking spray

1 In large bowl, combine turkey and seasonings. Mix thoroughly.

2 Shape into 2 1/2 -3 1/2oz (70-98g) patties, size as according to plan.

3 Heat skillet, coated with nonfat cooking spray, over a medium flame.

4 Add patties to skillet and cook thoroughly on each side, or to an internal temperature of 165°F.

5 Uncooked patties may be frozen.

Jump
❖ Start

Savory
Soups&
❖Salads

Many of us think of soups as a type of comfort food; the kind of dish that warms us inside and out. Salad of course is an old meal-starter favorite. There are several varieties of soups and salads such as broth-based or cream-based soups and tossed or Caesar salads. Unfortunately, canned and pre-made soups can be very high in sodium and/or fat. Salad dressing and cheese can also add a lot of extra fat and calories. However, you'll find lots of ways to eliminate fat without sacrificing flavor and all the basic methods of preparing your own soups and salads inside.

Waldorf Salad recipe can be found on page 32

Cooking Methods

Broth or stock is one of the simplest cooking methods. This soup base starts with water and incorporates the meat or bones, as well as vegetables and herbs. The mixture is simmered for a moderately long amount of time to infuse the water with flavor; eventually, the solids are strained out of the broth or stock before use. Broths and stocks are the base of any soup and provides added flavor.

Canned stock and bouillon cubes may be used for ease, but fresh stock will provide optimum flavor. If using canned stock, choose a low-sodium variety! Bouillon cubes can be found also in a "very low-sodium" variety with less than 35mg sodium per serving; this method is quite easy and requires you only to reconstitute the broth by adding warm water.

Cream-based soups have been known to be higher in fat and calories, but there are methods to reduce the fat and calories. Cream-based soups or chowders typically start as a broth-based soup and cream or milk may be added at the end of the recipe, to allow the flavors to meld. Vegetable-cream soups are commonly pureed together for serving to achieve a velvety texture. The cream used in soups may be replaced by fat-free half and half, evaporated skim milk, regular skim or reduced-fat milk, to cut back on calories.

Other Cooking Tips

When making broth-based soups, or other soups that will not be pureed, it is important to cut or chop the vegetables and protein in uniform pieces so that it may cook quickly and in the same amount of time. You may also use leftover proteins and vegetables that are already prepared in order to shorten cooking times even further.

If a thicker soup is desired for texture, you have several options. Eggs provide a rich and creamy texture to soup, but it is easy to make scrambled eggs in the hot broth. The best method is to scramble 1 or 2 eggs in a small bowl and add a small amount of hot soup or broth, whisking together, then gradually incorporate this mixture back into the soup.

Flour may also be used in the early stages of the soup by lightly sprinkling over the vegetables as they sauté or in the final stages by adding a tablespoon of cornstarch (mixed with 1-2 tablespoon of water) into the soup or broth. To thicken pureed soups, you may want to add a half-cup of rice or potatoes or a slice or two of bread before puree in a blender or food processor.

TIP!

The cream us in soups may replaced by fat-free half a half, evapora skim milk, or regular skim reduced-fat milk, to redu the amount o calories.

Greens Dictionary

■ **Endive** — also known as Belgian endive; a small, cigar-shaped head of pale yellow-green lettuce, with a bitter taste, well paired with nuts and cheese.

■ **Frisee** — also known as curly endive; a member of the chicory family; thin, curly leaves appear to be frizzy with a slightly bitter taste; commonly found in "spring mix" salads.

■ **Romaine** — also known as cos lettuce; a common lettuce in the US, with dark green, long leaves that are coarse; inner leaves are paler in color and have a more delicate flavor.

■ **Iceberg** — this lettuce got its name from its original shipping method—growers packed the heads in ice, it was previously known as crisphead lettuce; this particular head of lettuce has one of the highest water content, 90%, of all lettuces.

■ **Looseleaf** — examples of this variety includes red leaf, green leaf and oak leaf lettuces; the leaves vary in flavor, red lettuces tend to be more sharp or bitter; the oak variety tends to be more coarse than leaf lettuce.

■ **Escarole** — also a member of the chicory family, though with a milder flavor; leaves are broad and wavy, though smaller than a leaf lettuce; most commonly mixed with other lettuces in salads due to its sharp taste; also used cooked, commonly in Italian cuisine.

■ **Watercress** — a member of the mustard family; has small leaves and thin stems, with a slightly bitter and peppery flavor; also commonly used in soups and sandwiches.

■ **Spring Mix** — also known as field greens, micro greens, or mesclun; may include a variety of baby lettuces, such as spinach, frisee, oak leaf, radicchio, etc; of growing popularity over the past few years.

■ **Butterhead** — this includes Boston and Bibb lettuces; Bibb lettuce is found to be smaller heads of lettuce with loose, true green leaves with more flavor; Boston lettuce is commonly a larger head of lettuce with leaves lighter in color and flavor.

■ **Spinach** — a dark leafy green, high in fiber, that can be used raw or cooked; approximately 1 pound raw equals 1 cup cooked; choose spinach with smaller leaves and stems, also known as baby spinach, because it will be delicate and tender.

■ **Radicchio** — also known as red chicory; appears as a red cabbage; coarse, crisp leaves with bitter leaves, commonly mixed with other greens, may be grilled to enhance flavor or used as colorful garnish.

■ **Arugula** — also known as rocket; peppery flavored delicate green leaves, similar in shape to spinach.

■ **Kale** — a type of cabbage with curly, wrinkled leaves, which are hardy and coarse; most commonly used cooked, but may be used raw as a garnish or mixed into salads with other greens.

■ **Mustard Greens** — a dark leafy green that can be found with red or green leaves; common in the Southern states; known for its sharp, peppery taste.

Savory
Soups&
❖ Salads

Chicken Stock

4 *servings*

- **SERVING SIZE: 1 CUP (250ML)**
- **COUNTS AS:**
  - 1/2 PROTEIN
  - 1 STARCH
  - 1 FAT

▶ *size according to plan*

☀ Ingredients

1 pound (448g) chicken parts

1 large onion

3 stalks celery, including leaves

1 large carrot

3 whole cloves

6 cups (1.5L) water

1/4 cup (60ml) cold water (optional)

1 egg

1 Cut onion into quarters.

2 Chop celery and carrot into 1-inch chunks.

3 Place chicken pieces, onion, celery, carrot and cloves in a large soup pot or Dutch oven.

4 Add 6 cups (1.5L) water. Bring to a boil.

5 Reduce heat, cover and simmer for 1 hour.

6 Remove chicken and vegetables. Strain stock.

7 Skim fat off the surface.

To clarify the stock for a clear soup: Combine 1/4 cup (60ml) of broth, 1 egg white and 1 crushed eggshell in small bowl. Add mixture to strained stock. Bring to a boil. Remove from heat, let stand 5 minutes. Strain again through a sieve lined with cheesecloth.

Seafood Soup

4 *servings*

- **SERVING SIZE: 1 RECIPE**
- **COUNTS AS:**
  - 1 PROTEIN
  - 1 DAIRY
  - 1 LA LITE

▶ *size according to plan*

good source of fiber

☀ Ingredients

5 or 7oz shrimp, according to plan

6 slices low-sodium turkey bacon

1 cup (250ml / 160g) onions, chopped

1 pound (448g) potato, thin-skinned, cut into 1/2-inch cubes

2 1/2 cups (625ml) low-sodium chicken broth

3 Tbsp flour

2 1/2 cups (62ml) skim milk

1/2 tsp freshly ground pepper

1/4 cup (60ml / 15g) chopped fresh parsley sprigs

nonfat cooking spray

1 In a small saucepan coated with nonfat cooking spray, add shrimp, onion, pepper and garlic. Sauté until seafood is cooked.

2 Add soup mix, milk and half & half; stir until smooth.

3 Heat well.

4 Season with hot pepper sauce (optional).

Savory
Soups&
❖ Salad

Broccoli Soup

servings

SERVING SIZE:
1 CUP (250ML)
COUNTS AS:
1 STARCH
1 VEGETABLE
1 FAT

ze according to plan

good source of fiber

☀ Ingredients

2 Tbsp olive oil

1 medium onion, sliced

1 garlic clove, smashed

1 potato (russet), peeled and diced

1/4 tsp thyme

4 cups (1L) chicken stock
(see recipe on page 20) or very
low-sodium broth

1 pound (448g) frozen broccoli,
thawed

4 Tbsp fat-free half & half

1 In a saucepan add olive oil, onion and garlic over medium heat cook until translucent, about 5 minutes.

2 Add the potato, thyme and broth and bring to a boil.

3 Adjust the heat to maintain a gentle simmer, and cook uncovered until the potato is fork tender, about 10 minutes.

4 Add the broccoli and simmer for 3 minutes.

5 Puree the soup in batches in a blender.

6 Return the soup to the pot and add the half and half.

7 Bring to a simmer, season with pepper for taste.

Cream of Spinach Soup

serving

SERVING SIZE: 1 RECIPE
COUNTS AS:
1 VEGETABLE
1 DAIRY
1 LA LITE

ze according to plan

meals in minutes

☀ Ingredients

1 L A Lite Cream of Mushroom
soup mix

8oz (250ml) skim milk

1 tsp finely minced onion

1/2 cup (125ml / 90g) steamed
fresh spinach

1 tsp fresh lemon juice

freshly ground pepper

1 Add milk into a saucepan, warm over medium heat.

2 Empty one envelope of the mushroom soup into a saucepan.

3 Add remaining ingredients and stir.

4 Heat until desired temperature, serve.

"There's no extra food. I just made the servings I needed according to my plan."

- Paula R.

Savory
Soups&
✤ Salads

Cream Chicken & Rice Soup

1 *serving*

- SERVING SIZE: 1 RECIPE
- COUNTS AS:
  - 1 PROTEIN
  - 1 STARCH
  - 1 VEGETABLE
  - 1 DAIRY
  - 1 LA LITE

▶ *size according to plan*

good source of fiber

☀ Ingredients

1 L A Lite Cream of Chicken soup mix

8oz (250ml) skim milk

6oz or 8oz (168 or 224g) according to plan, chicken breast, chopped into bite-size pieces

1/4 cup (60ml / 48g) raw brown rice

1 cup (250ml / 70g) fresh broccoli florets

1 tsp finely minced onion

freshly ground pepper

nonfat cooking spray

1. In a small sauce pan sprayed with nonfat cooking spray; sauté chicken and onion.

2. Add milk, empty one envelope of the Cream of Chicken soup into the Dutch oven; stir until blended.

3. Add broccoli and rice; cook until rice is done; serve immediately.

> "No leftovers to go bad."
> - *Paula R.*

New England-Style Clam Chowder

8 *servings*

- SERVING SIZE: 1/2 CUP
- COUNTS AS:
  - 1 PROTEIN
  - 1 STARCH
  - 1 DAIRY

▶ *size according to plan*

☀ Ingredients

1/4 cup (60ml / 5g) lite margarine

1 1/2 large onions, chopped

3/4 cup (200ml / 94g) all-purpose flour

1 quart (1L) shucked clams, with liquid

48oz (1.5L) clam juice

1 pound (448g) boiling potatoes, peeled and cubed

1 cup (250ml) skim milk

2 cups (500ml) evaporated skim milk

salt and freshly ground pepper

1/2 tsp chopped fresh dill

1. Melt margarine in a large saucepan or pot over a medium flame. Add onions and sauté until soft and translucent. Add flour, stirring constantly, for 4-5 minutes until lightly brown. Remove from heat and cool to room temperature.

2. In a separate saucepan, add clams with liquid and clam juice. Bring to a boil, reduce heat and simmer for 15-20 minutes.

3. Meanwhile, in a another pot, cover potatoes with cold water by one inch; bring to a boil and cook until fork tender, about 15 minutes.

4. Slowly whisk in warmed clam-broth mixture into flour, stirring constantly. Bring up to a boil, stirring occasionally. Reduce heat, add potatoes, skim milk, evaporated skim milk, salt and pepper and dill. Simmer 5-10 minutes, until heated through.

Savory Soups & Salad

Minestrone Soup

family fare

servings

SERVING SIZE:
1 CUP (250ML)
COUNTS AS:
1 STARCH
2 VEGETABLES

ze according to plan

☀ Ingredients

2 cups (500ml / 320g) chopped onion

2 Tbsp low-sodium tomato paste

1/4 cup (60ml / 15g) chopped fresh parsley

4 garlic cloves, chopped

1 tomato, diced

1 carrot, diced

1 celery stalk, diced

1 cup (250ml / 30g) chopped fresh spinach

1 cup (250ml / 20g) lentils, rinsed

2 bay leaves

8 sprigs parsley and 6 sprigs fresh thyme, tied together

9 cups (2.25L) low-sodium vegetable broth

2 cups (500ml / 28g) cooked pasta

freshly ground pepper

nonfat cooking spray

1. In a large stock pot sprayed with nonfat cooking spray, sauté onions until brown.
2. Add tomato paste, chopped parsley, garlic, carrots, celery and spinach and cook for 3 minutes.
3. Add lentils, bay leaves, parsley-thyme sprigs and broth and bring to a boil.
4. Lower heat and simmer partially covered for 20 minutes.
5. Add tomato and season with pepper.
6. Simmer for 10 minutes.
7. Remove bay leaves and parsley-thyme sprigs and discard.
8. Add pasta, heat through and serve.

Potato & Leek Soup

serving

SERVING SIZE: 1 RECIPE
COUNTS AS:
1 STARCH
1 VEGETABLE
1 DAIRY
1 LA LITE

ze according to plan

good source of calcium

☀ Ingredients

1 L A Lite Cream of Chicken or Cream of Mushroom soup mix

8oz (250ml) skim milk

1/2 cup (125ml / 45g) chopped fresh leeks

1/2 small potato, chopped

1 garlic clove, finely minced

1 tsp onion finely minced

1. Add milk to small sauce pan.
2. Add the soup mix, potato, leeks, onion and garlic.
3. Heat to a boil; lower heat and cook over low heat until potatoes are tender. About 5 minutes.

Savory
Soups&
♣ Salads

Cream of Mushroom **Pasta Soup**

 1 *serving*

- **SERVING SIZE: 1 RECIPE**
- **COUNTS AS:**
  1 STARCH
  1 VEGETABLE
  1 DAIRY
  1 LA LITE

▶ *size according to plan*

 good source of fiber

☀ Ingredients

1 L A Lite Cream of Mushroom soup mix

8oz (250ml) skim milk

1/3 cup (85ml / 46g) cooked pasta of choice

1 tsp onion, finely minced

1 garlic clove, finely minced

1/2 small tomato, chopped

1/4 green pepper, chopped

parsley, oregano, basil to taste

nonfat cooking spray

1 Cook pasta according to directions on the pasta package. Set aside.

2 In a small saucepan coated with nonfat cooking spray, sauté onion, garlic, tomato, pepper and seasonings.

3 Add milk and soup mix blend, heat through.

4 Pour over pasta; stir well and serve immediately.

Chicken **Gumbo**

6 *servings*

- **SERVING SIZE:**
  2 CUPS (500ML)
- **COUNTS AS:**
  1 PROTEIN
  1 STARCH

▶ *size according to plan*

☀ Ingredients

6 cups (1.5L) low-sodium chicken broth

4-6 cups (1-1.5L) water

3 pounds (1.3kg) chicken breast, boneless and skinless, cut into bite size pieces

1 1/2 pounds (672g) fresh or frozen okra, 1/4-inch slices

2 Tbsp canola oil

1/4 cup (60ml / 32g) all-purpose flour

1 tomato, seeded and chopped

1 large onion, chopped

2 garlic cloves, minced

1/2 tsp freshly ground pepper

1/4 tsp cayenne pepper

2 cups (500ml / 330g) rice, cooked

nonfat cooking spray

1 In large soup pot, over medium heat, combine chicken broth and water.

2 Meanwhile, heat skillet coated with nonfat cooking spray. Sauté chicken pieces until lightly brown, about 10 minutes. Set aside and keep warm.

3 Sauté okra over medium heat until tender, about 10-12 minutes. Remove from skillet and set aside.

4 Add oil to skillet; heat over medium flame for 2-3 minutes. Add flour, stirring constantly. This mixture is called a roux.

5 Reduce heat to medium-low and continue to cook, stirring. Cook roux, stirring, until golden brown, about 15-20 minutes.

6 Stir roux-tomato mixture into heated broth. Bring to a boil; reduce heat to low and add chicken and okra.

7 Cover and cook another 30-40 minutes, before serving. Add more water or broth to reach desired thickness throughout the final cooking process.

Savory
Soups &
❖ Salad

Pasta e Fagioli

family fare

☀ Ingredients

1 tomato, diced

1 celery stalk, diced

1 small onion, diced

2 garlic cloves, minced

2 cans (8oz / 224g each)
low-sodium tomato sauce

2 cups (500ml) low-sodium
chicken broth

freshly ground pepper

1 Tbsp dried parsley

2 tsp dried basil leaves

15oz (420g) can cannelloni
beans, drained and rinsed

1 1/3 cups (335ml / 187g)
ditalini pasta

nonfat cooking spray

1   Heat a Dutch oven coated with nonfat cooking spray
    over low heat. Sauté celery and onion until soft.

2   Add garlic and sauté briefly.

3   Stir in tomato sauce, chicken broth, pepper, parsley
    and basil; simmer for 20 minutes.

4   Cook ditalini pasta in a large pot of boiling water and
    cook for 8 minutes or according to directions on the
    package; drain.

5   Add beans and tomatoes to the sauce mixture and
    simmer for 5 minutes.

6   Stir pasta into sauce and bean mixture.

Bean Soup

good source of fiber

☀ Ingredients

4 cups (1L / 708g) Great
Northern Beans cooked

1 small onion, minced

2 small potatoes, quartered and
sliced

28oz (784g) low-sodium canned
tomatoes, diced

6 cups (1.5L) water

freshly ground pepper

nonfat cooking spray

1   In a large stock pot coated with nonfat cooking spray,
    sauté onion until brown.

2   Add remaining ingredients and bring to a boil.

3   Reduce heat; simmer for 30 minutes or until potatoes
    are tender.

Savory
Soups &
❧ Salads

Creamy Vegetable Soup

■ SERVING SIZE: 1 RECIPE
■ COUNTS AS:
  2 VEGETABLES
  1 DAIRY
  1 LA LITE

▶ *size according to plan*

☀ Ingredients

1 L A Lite Cream of Mushroom soup mix

8oz (250ml) skim milk

1 cup (250ml) cooked of any of the following vegetable choices (choose 2 vegetables, 1/2 cup (125ml) cooked each: cauliflower florets, broccoli florets, celery, 1 small tomato, spinach, asparagus, cabbage, carrot, mushrooms

1 tsp onion, finely chopped

1 garlic clove, finely minced

2 Tbsp fat-free half & half

nonfat cooking spray

1 In a small saucepan coated with nonfat cooking spray, sauté onion and garlic.

2 Add milk, fat-free half & half, soup mix; blend; heat through.

3 Add vegetables. Bring to a simmer and cook 5 minutes.

4 Serve immediately.

Sweet Potato Soup

4 *servings*

■ SERVING SIZE: 3/4 CUP (200ML)
■ COUNTS AS:
  1 STARCH
  1 VEGETABLE
  1/2 DAIRY

▶ *size according to plan*

☀ Ingredients

2 garlic cloves, crushed

1 small onion, chopped

1 tsp curry powder

3 cups (750ml) water

1 1/2 cup (375ml) skim milk

12oz (336g) sweet potato, peeled and chopped

2 low-sodium vegetable broth cubes, crumbled

nonfat cooking spray

1 In a large stock pot spray with nonfat cooking spray, sauté garlic, onion and curry powder until soft.

2 Add potato, water and broth cube.

3 Simmer, covered for 15 minutes or until vegetables are cooked. Cool.

4 Blend or process sweet potato mixture until smooth.

5 Gradually add the milk, processing until well combined.

6 Return to stock pot and heat well, do not boil.

Savory
Soups&
❖ Salad

Beef Vegetable Soup

serving

SERVING SIZE: 1 RECIPE
COUNTS AS:
1 PROTEIN
3 VEGETABLES

ze according to plan

☀ Ingredients

4 or 6oz (112 or 168g) chuck roast, size according to plan

2 cups (500ml) very low-sodium beef broth, prepared from bouillon

1/2 medium carrot, thinly sliced

1/2 large celery stalk, sliced

1/2 cup (125ml / 55g) fresh green beans, trimmed and cut into 1/2-inch pieces

1 small tomato, seeded and diced

nonfat cooking spray

dash of salt and freshly ground pepper

1 Rinse roast and pat dry; cut into 1 inch pieces. Season with salt and pepper, to taste.

2 Coat a Dutch oven with nonfat cooking spray. Add beef and cook over a medium flame until lightly browned.

3 Add beef broth; bring to boil.

4 Add remaining ingredients to pot. Return soup to a boil.

5 Reduce heat; cover and simmer until beef and vegetables are tender, approximately 20 minutes.

6 Serve immediately or store in refrigerator up to 24 hours.

Cheddar Cheese Soup

servings

SERVING SIZE: 1/4 RECIPE
COUNTS AS:
1 DAIRY
1 FAT

ze according to plan

meals in minutes

☀ Ingredients

2 Tbsp minced green onion

2 Tbsp lite margarine

3 Tbsp flour

3 cups (750ml) low-sodium beef broth

2 cups (500ml) skim milk

3/4 cup (200ml) light or reduced-fat cheddar cheese, grated

1/2 tsp freshly ground pepper

paprika and parsley for garnish

nonfat cooking spray

1 Sauté the onion in butter until softened; add flour and blend.

2 Gradually stir in the broth and add the milk.

3 Bring to a boil and add cheese and pepper.

4 Simmer until cheese is melted.

5 Sprinkle with paprika and chopped parsley.

Savory
Soups&
✤ Salads

Split Pea Soup

6 *servings*

- **SERVING SIZE: 3/4 CUP (200ML)**
- **COUNTS AS:**
  1 STARCH
  3 VEGETABLES

▶ *size according to plan*

☀ Ingredients

2 cups (500ml) split peas, uncooked

6 cups (1.5L) water

1 bay leaf

2 cups (500ml / 240g) carrots, chopped

1 cup (250ml / 120g) celery, chopped

1 cup (250ml / 160g) onion, chopped

1 tsp thyme

1/2 tsp freshly ground pepper

1 tsp garlic powder

1 Rinse and drain split peas.

2 Combine dried split peas, water and bay leaf, in a large stock pot.

3 Bring to a boil and then reduce heat and simmer for 1 hour. Stir occasionally to prevent the split peas from sticking and to make sure there is enough water. Add water if the soup looks like it is becoming dry.

4 Add carrots, celery, onions and seasoning.

5 Continue to simmer for 30 minutes or longer.

6 Add more water if a thinner soup is desired.

French Onion Soup

1 *serving*

- **SERVING SIZE: 1 RECIPE**
- **COUNTS AS:**
  1 STARCH
  1 VEGETABLE
  1/2 DAIRY
  1 FAT

▶ *size according to plan*

☀ Ingredients

1 packet low-sodium beef bouillon

1 cup (250ml) water

1/2 cup (125ml / 80g) raw white onion slices

3 slices melba toast

1oz (28g) reduced fat or part skim cheese

1 bay leaf

1/4 tsp onion powder

1/4 tsp lite salt

freshly ground pepper

dash of parsley

1 tsp butter

1 Sauté the onion in lite margarine until softened; add flour and blend.

2 Gradually stir in the broth and add the milk.

3 Bring to a boil and add cheese and pepper.

4 Simmer until cheese is melted.

5 Sprinkle with paprika and chopped parsley.

Savory
Soups&
❖Salad

Sweet Red Pepper Soup

servings

SERVING SIZE:
1/2 CUP (125ML)
COUNTS AS:
3 VEGETABLES

ze according to plan

✳ Ingredients

4 red peppers, halved and deseeded

1 red chili, seeded and finely chopped

3 garlic cloves, chopped

20 green onions, chopped

4 tomatoes, chopped

2 cups (500ml) very low-sodium vegetable stock

freshly ground pepper

1 Tbsp freshly chopped parsley or oregano

2 Tbsp freshly chopped chives or basil

1. Preheat the grill to high.

2. When very hot, place the red pepper under, skin-side up, for about 15-20 minutes or until the skin is charred and blistered.

3. Remove and place in a paper bag until cool enough to handle.

4. Heat the oil in a pan and add the chili, garlic and onions and sauté for 4-5 minutes. Meanwhile, peel and roughly chop the peppers.

5. Add the tomatoes and stock and simmer for 10 minutes, then add the roasted peppers.

6. Cover and cook over a low heat for about 5-10 minutes, then remove from the heat and allow to cool.

7. Puree the soup in a food processor until smooth.

8. Return the soup to a clean pan and gently warm through.

9. Season to taste and serve. Sprinkle with fresh herbs of your choice.

Egg Drop Soup

serving

SERVING SIZE: 1 RECIPE
COUNTS AS:
1 PROTEIN
1 VEGETABLE

ze according to plan

✳ Ingredients

2 cups (500ml) very low-sodium chicken broth, prepared from bouillon

1/4 tsp lite salt

dash of white pepper

5 green onions, sliced

2 or 3 eggs, according to plan

1. In a medium saucepan, add chicken broth, salt and pepper. Bring to a boil; reduce heat.

2. In a small bowl, lightly beat eggs. Stir in onions.

3. Pour egg mixture slowly into broth, stirring constantly with a fork, until the eggs form strands.

Savory
Soups&
✤ Salads

Garden Vegetable Soup

1 *serving*

- SERVING SIZE: 1 RECIPE
- COUNTS AS:
  3 VEGETABLES

▶ *size according to plan*

good source of fiber

☀ Ingredients

3 green onions, chopped

1/2 medium carrot, chopped

1/2 celery stalk

2 garlic cloves, minced

1/2 cup (125ml / 35g) green cabbage, shredded

1/2 cup (125ml / 56g) zucchini, sliced

1/2 tsp dried basil, crushed

1/2 tsp thyme

freshly ground pepper

1 small tomato, diced

2 cups (500ml) very low-sodium chicken broth

nonfat cooking spray

1 Coat a medium saucepan with nonfat cooking spray. Add onion, carrot, celery and garlic.

2 Cook, stirring occasionally, over medium heat for 15-20 minutes, or until carrots begin to soften.

3 Stir in cabbage, zucchini, basil, thyme and pepper. Cook for 5-10 minutes longer, or until cabbage is tender.

4 Stir in tomato and broth. Bring to a boil. Reduce heat; cover and simmer for another 10 minutes, to allow flavors to meld.

5 Serve immediately.

Chicken Caldo

1 *serving*

- SERVING SIZE: 1 RECIPE
- COUNTS AS:
  1 PROTEIN
  3 VEGETABLES

▶ *size according to plan*

☀ Ingredients

6 or 8oz (168 or 224g) boneless, skinless chicken breast, size according to plan

freshly ground pepper

3 green onions, chopped

1 garlic clove, minced

2 cups (500ml) water

1/2 large celery stalk, sliced

1/2 medium carrot, sliced

1/2 cup zucchini, sliced

1/2 cup cabbage, chopped

1/4 tsp lite salt

1/8 teaspoon freshly ground pepper

1 Rinse chicken and pat dry. Cut into bite size pieces. Season with pepper, to taste.

2 Place chicken, onion and garlic in a medium saucepan.

3 Cover with water; bring to a boil.

4 Reduce heat; simmer for 30 minutes, or until chicken is tender.

5 Add remaining ingredients; simmer for another 20 minutes, or until vegetables are soft.

6 Serve immediately or refrigerate up to 24 hours.

Savory
Soups&
❖ Salad

Spinach Soup

serving

SERVING SIZE: 1 RECIPE
COUNTS AS:

2 VEGETABLES

meals in minutes

✳ Ingredients

2 cups (500ml) very low-sodium chicken bouillon

1/4 teaspoon garlic powder

1 1/2 cup (375ml / 45g) fresh spinach, coarsely chopped

1/2 cup (250ml / 3g) fresh mushrooms, chopped

1 Tbsp lemon juice

1. In a medium saucepan combine chicken broth and garlic powder. Bring to a boil.

2. Stir in spinach and mushrooms, allowing spinach to wilt; return to boiling.

3. Reduce heat; cover and simmer for 2 minutes, or until vegetables are tender. Stir in lemon juice.

Chicken & Lemongrass Soup

servings

SERVING SIZE:
1 CUP (250ML)
COUNTS AS:

1/2 PROTEIN
1 VEGETABLE
1 DAIRY
1 FAT

✳ Ingredients

1 pound (448g) skinless chicken breast filets

4 stalks lemongrass, tender inner part only

2 green onions, finely sliced

finely grated zest and juice of 1 lime

1 Tbsp fish sauce

2-3 small fresh red or green chilies, deseeded

3 cups (750ml) low-sodium chicken broth

2 inch piece fresh ginger, peeled

1 Tbsp fresh coriander

1/2 tsp fennel seeds, lightly crushed

1 garlic clove

1 Tbsp oil

1/2 cup (125ml) light coconut milk

1 cup (250ml) evaporated skim milk

freshly ground pepper

1. Cut the chicken crossways into thin slices. Place in a non-metallic bowl.

2. Very finely slice one of the lemon grass stalks and scatter over the chicken with the onions.

3. Add the zest and fish sauce; mix together. Marinate chicken for 30-60 minutes.

4. Chop the remaining lemongrass and two chilies roughly and put in a pan with the stock, half the ginger, sliced and all the coriander stems (chop leaves and reserve).

5. Bring to the boil, then simmer covered for 30 minutes. Strain, reserving stock.

6. Gently fry the onion, fennel seeds, garlic and remaining ginger, finely chopped, in the oil in a large saucepan until onion is soft.

7. Add the strained stock and simmer for 10 minutes, then add the coconut milk and evaporated milk.

8. When the mixture comes back to a simmer, add the chicken with all its marinade and half the chopped coriander leaves.

9. Simmer gently for 6-7 minutes until chicken is cooked thoroughly.

10. Add the lime juice, seasoning to taste.

11. Sprinkle with the rest of the coriander and the third chili, finely sliced if desired.

31

Savory
Soups&
❖ Salads

Waldorf Salad

4 *servings*

- **SERVING SIZE:**
  1/4 OF RECIPE
- **COUNTS AS:**
  2 VEGETABLES
  1 FRUIT
  1 FAT

▶ *size according to plan*

☀ Ingredients

1/4 cup (60ml) lite mayonnaise

1/4 cup (60ml) plain nonfat yogurt

1 Tbsp artificial sweetener, or other sugar substitute

3 tart apples, peeled, cored and chopped

1 Tbsp lemon juice

1 cup (250ml / 92g) seedless grapes, sliced in half

2 celery stalks, chopped

3 green onions, sliced

1/4 cup (60ml / 29g) chopped walnuts, toasted

1 head of iceberg lettuce, quartered

1. In a small bowl, whisk together mayonnaise, yogurt and artificial sweetener. Set aside.

2. In a large bowl, toss apples with lemon juice. Add grapes, celery, onions and walnuts.

3. Add dressing to apple mixture; toss to coat. Cover and refrigerate for 1 hour.

4. To serve, arrange one quarter of lettuce in a shallow bowl or plate. Divide salad evenly among plates.

Spicy Shrimp Salad

4 *servings*

- **SERVING SIZE:**
  1/4 OF RECIPE
- **COUNTS AS:**
  1 PROTEIN
  2 VEGETABLES

▶ *size according to plan*

meals in minutes

☀ Ingredients

1 1/2 or 1 3/4 pounds (672 or 784g) small shrimp, peeled and deveined

1/4 cup (60ml / 60g) finely chopped celery

1/4 cup (60ml / 24g) finely chopped green onion

1/4 cup (60ml) country-style mustard

1 Tbsp fresh chopped parsley

1 Tbsp olive oil

1 Tbsp cider vinegar

2 tsp pepper sauce

8 cups salad greens (2 cups per salad)

1. Place shrimp and enough water to cover in a 2-quart saucepan over high heat and bring to boil.

2. Boil 2 minutes until shrimp are tender.

3. Drain well and set aside to cool.

4. Combine celery, green onions, mustard, parsley, olive oil, cider vinegar and pepper sauce in a bowl; toss in shrimp and mix.

5. To serve arrange on salad greens (2 cups) of choice.

Savory Soups & Salad

serving

SERVING SIZE: 1 RECIPE
COUNTS AS:
1/2 PROTEIN
2 VEGETABLES

e according to plan

meals in minutes

Sweet & Sour Cabbage

☀ Ingredients

1 egg

1/2 packet of artificial sweetener

1/4 cup (60ml) rice or red wine vinegar

2 Tbsp water

1/4 tsp lite salt

1/4 tsp dry mustard

1 cup (250ml / 70g) cabbage, shredded

1/2 green pepper, chopped

1 Beat egg until thick and lemon colored.

2 In a saucepan, heat artificial sweetener, vinegar, water, salt and dry mustard to boiling, stirring constantly.

3 Gradually stir at least half of the hot mixture into the egg, this is called tempering. Stir this; then back into the hot vinegar mixture.

4 Cook over low heat, stirring constantly, until slightly thickened.

5 Pour over cabbage and green pepper; toss to coat.

---

serving

SERVING SIZE: 1 RECIPE
COUNTS AS:
1 STARCH
3 VEGETABLES

e according to plan

Vegetable Pasta Salad

☀ Ingredients

1 cup (250ml / 130g) zucchini or yellow summer squash, sliced

1/2 medium green pepper, chopped

1 garlic clove, minced

1/3 cup (85ml / 57g) cooked pasta, such as macaroni

2 Tbsp white wine vinegar

1/4 tsp dried dill

1/8 tsp lite salt

freshly ground pepper

1 small tomato, chopped

1 In a large skillet, coated with nonfat cooking spray, sauté squash, green pepper and garlic over medium heat until crisp-tender.

2 Add macaroni, vinegar, dill, salt and pepper to vegetable mixture; toss to combine. Top with chopped tomato.

3 Refrigerate for 1 hour before serving.

Savory
Soups&
❖ Salads

Stir-Fried Chicken Salad

1 *serving*

- **SERVING SIZE: 1 RECIPE**
- **COUNTS AS:**
  - 1 PROTEIN
  - 3 VEGETABLES

▶ *size according to plan*

good source of fiber

❋ Ingredients

6 or 8oz (168 or 224g) raw chicken breast, size according to plan

3 Tbsp white wine vinegar

2 tsp Dijon mustard

1/2 packet artificial sweetener

1/4 tsp lite salt

1/8 tsp paprika

1/8 tsp freshly ground pepper

1 1/2 cups (375ml / 84g) fresh spinach

1 small tomato, chopped

1/4 medium carrot, shredded

nonfat cooking spray

1. Place chicken in a large plastic freezer bag.

2. In a small bowl, mix together vinegar, mustard, artificial sweetener, salt, paprika and pepper. Pour over chicken and close bag. Marinate chicken in refrigerator for 2-5 hours, turning bag frequently.

3. In a large bowl, combine spinach, tomato and carrot. Set aside.

4. Coat skillet or wok with nonfat cooking spray. Heat over medium flame.

5. Drain chicken, reserving marinade.

6. Stir fry chicken for 2-3 minutes or until no longer pink. Add marinade and heat until boiling.

7. Place spinach mixture on dinner plate. Pour hot chicken mixture over salad.

8. Serve immediately

Spaghetti Squash Salad

6 *servings*

- **SERVING SIZE:**
  1/6 OF RECIPE
- **COUNTS AS:**
  - 1 VEGETABLE
  - 1 STARCH
  - 1 FAT

▶ *size according to plan*

❋ Ingredients

3 pounds (1.3kg) spaghetti squash

1/4 cup (60ml) parsley, chopped

2 Tbsp olive oil

2 garlic cloves, minced

1/2 pound (224g) fresh mushrooms, sliced

1. With a knife, pierce the skin of the squash in several places, to allow steam to escape while cooking.

2. Place whole squash in the microwave and cook on high for 15 minutes, turning twice.

3. Remove from oven let stand for 10 minutes.

4. In a small bowl, mix parsley, olive oil and garlic.

5. Sauté mushrooms in a nonstick skillet coated with nonfat cooking spray.

6. Cut squash in half lengthwise and remove seeds with a spoon.

7. With a fork, gently pull spaghetti-like flesh away from the sides of the skin.

8. Combine squash with mushrooms. Toss to combine.

9. Pour oil mixture over; stir and serve.

Savory Soups & ❖ Salad

Mediterranean Tuna Salad

1 serving

SERVING SIZE: 1 RECIPE
COUNTS AS:
1 PROTEIN
2 VEGETABLES
1 FAT

ze according to plan

☀ Ingredients

6oz (168g) can of tuna, drained (choose low-sodium as available)

2 tsp lite mayonnaise

dash of lite salt

freshly ground pepper

1 Tbsp diced white onion

1 Tbsp diced red peppers

1 Tbsp shredded carrot

1 celery stalk, sliced finely

3 black olives, diced

1. Combine all ingredients, mixing well.
2. Cover and refrigerate at least 1 hour. Serve chilled.

Hot & Sour Salad

3 servings

SERVING SIZE:
1/2 CUP (125ML)
COUNTS AS:
1 VEGETABLE

ze according to plan

family fare

☀ Ingredients

3 cups (750ml / 210g) shredded bok choy

1/2 carrot, shredded

1 large red pepper, thinly sliced

5 green onions, sliced

1/4 cup (60ml / 18g) sliced mushrooms

1/2 tsp red pepper flakes

2 garlic cloves, sliced

1 Tbsp ginger, minced

1/2 tsp lite salt

1 tsp olive oil

1 packet artificial sweetener

2/3 cup (170ml) rice wine vinegar

1 tsp Dijon mustard

1. Combine bok choy, carrots, mushrooms, pepper and onion in large bowl.
2. Whisk together remaining ingredients in small bowl.
3. Pour vinegar mixture over vegetables.
4. Refrigerate 1-2 hours before serving.
5. Mix well before serving.

Savory
Soups&
❖ Salads

Crab Salad

1 *serving*

- **SERVING SIZE: 1 RECIPE**
- **COUNTS AS:**
  - 1 PROTEIN
  - 1 VEGETABLE

▶ *size according to plan*

☀ Ingredients

5 or 7oz (140 or 196g) raw crab meat; steamed, size as according to plan

1/2 tsp parsley

1/2 tsp chives

1 tsp fresh lemon juice

1/4 cucumber, peeled and diced

1 Toss together all ingredients in a medium bowl.

2 Cover and refrigerate at least 1 hour. Serve chilled.

Glazed Chicken & Avocado Salad

4 *servings*

- **SERVING SIZE: 1/4 OF RECIPE**
- **COUNTS AS:**
  - 1 PROTEIN
  - 3 VEGETABLES
  - 1 FRUIT
  - 1 FAT

▶ *size according to plan*

☀ Ingredients

1 cup (250ml / 48g) artificial sweetener

1/4 cup (60ml) water

1/2 cup (125ml) red wine

1 cup (250ml) fresh squeezed orange juice

1 tsp wasabi paste

1 1/2 or 2 pounds (672 or 896g) chicken breast, boneless and skinless, sliced into strips, size according to plan

1 large tomato, diced

1/4 cup (60ml / 40g) red onion, diced

2 Tbsp fresh cilantro

juice of 2 limes

1 avocado, peeled, pitted and diced

8 cups (2L / 240g) salad greens

hot sauce, to taste (optional)

nonfat cooking spray

1 Preheat oven to 400°F.

2 In a large Dutch oven, heat artificial sweetener and water together over medium high heat, stirring occasionally, until it turns to a deep amber color.

3 Remove from heat and slowly add the wine.

4 Return to heat and stir until all particles dissolve.

5 Add orange juice and wasabi paste; cook, stirring occasionally, until well combined.

6 Brush chicken strips with the glaze. Place on a baking sheet coated with nonfat cooking spray.

7 Bake until thoroughly cooked, about 20 minutes.

8 While the chicken is cooking, toss together the tomatoes, red onion, cilantro, lime juice, avocados and hot sauce (optional).

9 Arrange 2 cups (500ml) salad greens on 4 salad plates.

10 Top with 1/4 of the vegetable mixture and chicken strips; serve.

Savory
Soups&
❖ Salad

Rainbow Salad

servings

SERVING SIZE:
1 CUP (250ML)
COUNTS AS:
1 VEGETABLE

ze according to plan

good source of fiber

☀ Ingredients

1 pound (448g) fresh spinach

1/2 green pepper, diced

1/2 red pepper, diced

1/2 cup (125ml / 40g) fresh
  broccoli florets

1/2 red onion, diced

1 yellow summer squash, diced

10 cherry tomatoes

1 carrot, shredded

1/2 cup (125ml / 35g) fresh
  mushrooms, sliced

1 Place spinach in a large bowl.

2 Top with peppers, broccoli, onion, yellow summer
  squash, tomatoes, carrots and mushrooms.

3 Serve chilled with your choice of fat-free dressings.

Cheesy Taco Salad

serving

SERVING SIZE: 1 RECIPE
COUNTS AS:
1 PROTEIN
2 VEGETABLES
1 STARCH
1/2 DAIRY

ze according to plan

good source of fiber

☀ Ingredients

5 or 7oz (140 or 196g) fresh
  ground turkey breast; size
  according to plan

1/4 tsp garlic powder

1/4 tsp chili powder

1/4 tsp lite salt

1 cup (250ml / 30g) lettuce

1 small tomato

1oz (28g) reduced-fat
  cheddar cheese

1 bag L A Cheese Curls

2 Tbsp salsa

1 Cook turkey in medium sauté pan; add garlic powder,
  chili and salt to flavor.

2 Drain any excess oil or fat from turkey.

3 Assemble lettuce on plate.

4 Top lettuce with meat, tomatoes and cheese.

5 Top with L A Cheese Curls.

6 Garnish with salsa.

Savory
Soups&
✤ Salads

Garlic Tomato Salad

1 *serving*

- SERVING SIZE: 1 RECIPE
- COUNTS AS:
  1 VEGETABLES

▶ *size according to plan*

☀ Ingredients

1 medium tomato, cut into 1-inch slices

2 Tbsp fat-free Italian salad dressing

2 Tbsp red wine vinegar

1/8 tsp lite salt

dash red pepper sauce

2 large garlic cloves, finely chopped

1 cup (250ml / 56g) salad greens, torn into bite size pieces

1 Place tomato slices in glass dish.

2 Combine dressing, vinegar, salt, pepper sauce and garlic in covered container or jar and shake, vigorously, to mix.

3 Pour mixture over tomato slices.

4 Refrigerate for 1 hour before serving.

5 Serve on a bed of salad greens.

Cucumber & Shrimp Salad

1 *serving*

- SERVING SIZE: 1 RECIPE
- COUNTS AS:
  1 PROTEIN
  2 VEGETABLES

▶ *size according to plan*

☀ Ingredients

1/4 cup (60ml) vinegar

1/2 packet artificial sweetener

1 tsp low-sodium soy sauce

1/4 tsp lite salt

4 or 6oz (112 or 168g) cooked shrimp, size according to plan

1/4 medium cucumber, thinly sliced

1 cup (250ml / 56g) lettuce or salad greens torn in bite-size pieces

1/2 Tbsp sesame seeds

1 Mix vinegar, artificial sweetener, soy sauce and salt in a medium bowl.

2 Add shrimp and cucumbers; toss. Cover and refrigerate at least 1 hour.

3 Line salad plate with lettuce or salad greens.

4 Remove shrimp with slotted spoon; place on top of salad greens. Sprinkle with sesame seeds.

Savory
Soups&
✿ Salad

Fruited Chicken Salad

serving

SERVING SIZE: 1 RECIPE
COUNTS AS:
1 PROTEIN
1 VEGETABLE
1 FRUIT
1 FAT

ze according to plan

❋ Ingredients

5 or 7oz (140 or 196g) chicken, cooked and cut into bite-size pieces, size according to plan

1 Tbsp lite mayonnaise

1/2 Tbsp lemon juice

1 celery stalk, thinly sliced

15 green grapes, cut in half

dash lite salt

freshly ground pepper

1/8 tsp dried onion flakes

1 Combine all ingredients in a large bowl; toss to mix well.

2 Cover and refrigerate at least 1 hour. Serve chilled.

Oriental-Style Shrimp Salad

servings

family fare

SERVING SIZE:
1/4 OF RECIPE
COUNTS AS:
1 PROTEIN
1 STARCH
3 VEGETABLES

ze according to plan

❋ Ingredients

1-1 1/2 pounds (448 - 559g) large shrimp, peeled and deveined, size according to plan

1 garlic clove, minced

1 inch piece of ginger, peeled and minced

1/4 cup (60ml) low-sodium soy sauce, divided

6oz (168g) uncooked capellini/angel hair pasta

10oz (28g) baby spinach

1 cup (25ml / 200g) mung beans, cooked and drained

1/4 cup (60ml) mint leaves, firmly packed

5 medium scallions, chopped

2 baby carrots, shredded

juice from 1 lime

1 Toss shrimp with garlic, ginger and 2 Tbsp low-sodium soy sauce.

2 Cover; refrigerate and marinate for at least 30 minutes.

3 Meanwhile, cook pasta according to package directions.

4 Toss pasta with spinach, mung beans, mint, scallions and carrots.

5 Mix together lime juice and 2 Tbsp of low-sodium soy sauce and pour over the salad.

6 Allow to sit for 15 minutes while the shrimp is cooking.

7 Grill shrimp, or sauté, in a nonstick pan.

8 Allow shrimp to cool, and then toss with the salad.

Savory
Soups&
❖ Salads

Grilled Chicken Cobb Salad

4 *servings*

- **SERVING SIZE:**
  1/4 OF RECIPE
- **COUNTS AS:**
  1 PROTEIN
  2 VEGETABLES
  1 FAT

▶ *size according to plan*

✳ Ingredients

3 Tbsp lemon seasoning (see recipe on page 218)

12 or 16oz (336 or 448g) chicken breast, boneless and skinless, size according to plan

6 cups (1.5L / 180g) salad greens, of your choice, torn

2oz (56g) light cheese, shredded

2 large, hard-boiled eggs, sliced

1 large tomato, chopped

2 pieces low-sodium turkey bacon, cooked and drained, chopped

1 Preheat grill to medium high.

2 Put lemon seasoning on a plate. Coat chicken thoroughly in seasoning.

3 Cook on grill 5 minutes; turn and cook for another 5 minutes, or until juices run clear when a fork is inserted.

4 Remove from grill; cool and cut into chunks or strips. Set aside.

5 Onto each of four salad plates, arrange salad greens. Top greens with chicken, cheese, egg, chopped tomato and crumbled bacon. Drizzle with your favorite fat-free salad dressing.

Grape & Cabbage Salad

3 *servings*

- **SERVING SIZE:**
  1/3 OF RECIPE
- **COUNTS AS:**
  1 VEGETABLE
  1 FRUIT
  1 FAT

▶ *size according to plan*

✳ Ingredients

1 cup (250ml / 160g) green grapes

3 cups (750ml / 210g) cabbage, shredded

freshly ground pepper

1 Tbsp lemon juice, freshly squeeze

1/4 cup (60ml) lite mayonnaise

1 Combine grapes, cabbage, black pepper, lemon juice and mayonnaise in a bowl.

2 Mix well, tossing to coat.

3 Refrigerate, at least 30 minutes, or until ready to serve.

"The recipes from the L A Lite Cookbook take food items right from my menu plan!"

- Lynn K.

Savory
Soups &
❖ Salad

serving

SERVING SIZE: 1 RECIPE
COUNTS AS:
1 PROTEIN
2 VEGETABLES

ze according to plan

meals in minutes

Steak Caesar **Salad**

✳ Ingredients

4 or 6oz (112 or 168g) sirloin steak

1 cup (25ml / 30g) romaine lettuce

2 Tbsp fat-free Caesar salad dressing, divided

1 tsp parmesan cheese

2 green onions, chopped

nonfat cooking spray

1. Combine 1 Tbsp Caesar dressing, parmesan cheese and onions in medium bowl.

2. Cut beef into strips and place in bowl with marinade; toss to coat.

3. Coat skillet with nonfat cooking spray and heat over medium flame. Remove beef from marinade and place in skillet; discard marinade.

4. Sauté 5-6 minutes, or until beef is cooked to your liking.

5. Place lettuce on a serving plate. Top with beef and remaining dressing.

---

servings

SERVING SIZE:
1/4 OF RECIPE
COUNTS AS:
3 VEGETABLES

ze according to plan

family fare

Blackened Portabella **Salad**

✳ Ingredients

1/4 cup (60ml) red wine vinegar

1/4 cup (60ml) balsamic vinegar

1/4 cup (60ml) low-sodium tomato juice

2 tsp Dijon mustard

2 tsp stone ground mustard

1/4 tsp freshly ground pepper

4 whole portabella mushrooms

1 Tbsp Cajun seasoning (see recipe on page 215)

8 cups (2L / 240g) romaine lettuce

1 tomato

1/2 cup (125ml / 60g) red onion, thinly sliced

1. Combine the first 6 ingredients in a large zip-top plastic bag.

2. Add mushrooms to bag; seal. Marinate 10 minutes, turning occasionally.

3. Remove mushrooms from bag, reserving marinade.

4. Season mushrooms with Cajun spice.

5. Over medium-high heat, grill mushrooms for 2 minutes on each side, or until tender and browned.

6. Cool; cut diagonally into thin slices.

7. Arrange 2 cups romaine on each of 4 salad plates. Top with mushroom slices, 2 tomato wedges and onions.

8. Drizzle with the reserved marinade or use fat-free dressing of your choice.

Savory
Soups&
✤ Salads

Carrot Salad

 1 *serving*

- ■ SERVING SIZE: 1 RECIPE
- ■ COUNTS AS:
  - 1 VEGETABLES
  - 1 FRUIT

▶ *size according to plan*

 *good source of fiber*

✳ Ingredients

1/2 medium carrot, shredded

1 celery stalk, thinly sliced

1 tsp lemon zest

1 tsp lemon juice

1/2 tsp brown sugar artificial sweetener

2 Tbsp raisins

dash of ground ginger

1. Mix all ingredients together in small bowl.
2. Cover and chill for at least 1 hour before serving.

> "So many recipes in the cookbook I can choose something new every day."
> - *Amanda P.*

Chicken Broccoli Pasta Salad

 **6** *servings*

- ■ SERVING SIZE:
  1/6 OF RECIPE
- ■ COUNTS AS:
  - 1 PROTEIN
  - 2 VEGETABLES
  - 1 STARCH
  - 1 FAT

▶ *size according to plan*

✳ Ingredients

1/4 cup (60ml) lemon seasoning (see recipe on page 218), divided

8oz (224g) dry penne pasta (or pasta of choice)

2 1/4 or 3 pounds (1 or 1.3 kg) boneless chicken breast, cut into bite size pieces, size according to plan

2 Tbsp olive oil

2 cups (500ml / 160g) broccoli florets

3 Tbsp parmesan cheese

1/4 cup (60ml) very low-sodium chicken broth

1 cup (250ml / 150g) cherry tomatoes, halved

5 green onions, chopped

1. Add half of lemon seasoning to a large pot of boiling water; add pasta and cook according to package directions. Drain; set aside.
2. While pasta is cooking, heat 1 Tbsp olive oil in a large skillet. Sauté the chicken, about 6-8 minutes per side, over medium heat.
3. Add broth, broccoli, and lemon seasoning to the chicken; cover and cook for 3-5 minutes.
4. Toss pasta in a large bowl with remaining 1 Tbsp olive oil and parmesan cheese. Add chicken and broccoli and toss again.
5. Chill at least 1 hour.
6. Divide among 6 plates. Garnish with cherry tomatoes.

Savory Soups & Salad

Sweet Potato **Salad**

2 servings

SERVING SIZE:
1/2 CUP (125ML)
COUNTS AS:
1 STARCH
1 VEGETABLE

re according to plan

☀ Ingredients

6 sweet potatoes, boiled, peeled and cubed

1/2 cup (125ml / 7g) chopped red pepper

1/4 cup (60ml / 40g) chopped onion

1/2 tsp lite salt

1/4 tsp freshly ground pepper

1/3 cup (85ml) lite mayonnaise

1/4 tsp hot pepper sauce

1/2 tsp paprika

1 In large bowl, combine onion, pepper and potatoes.

2 Gently fold in remaining ingredients.

3 Chill 1-2 hours before serving.

"This cookbook is fantastic. It puts variety into my meals, and at the same time helps me stick to my meal plan."

- Karen D.

Asparagus **Salad**

serving

SERVING SIZE: 1 RECIPE
COUNTS AS:
1/2 PROTEIN
2 VEGETABLES
1/2 DAIRY

e according to plan

☀ Ingredients

4oz (125ml) nonfat plain yogurt

2 Tbsp fat-free French dressing

1/2 cup (125ml / 90g) cooked asparagus spears

1 hard cooked egg, sliced

1 cup (250ml / 56g) salad greens, torn in bite-size pieces

1 Mix nonfat yogurt and French dressing in a small bowl.

2 Cover and refrigerate at least 1 hour.

3 Arrange chilled asparagus on salad greens; top with egg slices.

4 Spoon dressing over top.

Savory
Soups&
✤Salads

Strawberry & Melon Salad

6 *servings*

- SERVING SIZE: 1 CUP (250ML)
- COUNTS AS:
  1 VEGETABLE
  1 FRUIT
  1 FAT

▶ *size according to plan*

※ Ingredients

1/4 cup (60ml) freshly squeezed orange juice

1 Tbsp olive oil

2 Tbsp water

10oz (280g) salad greens, of your choice

1 cup (250ml / 170g) honeydew, cubed

1 cup (250ml / 160g) cantaloupe, cubed

1 cup (250ml / 152g) watermelon, cubed

1 cup (250ml / 144g) strawberries, sliced

3 Tbsp sunflower seeds, unsalted

1. Mix juice, oil and water until blended.

2. Place salad greens, melon cubes and strawberry slices in a large bowl; toss.

3. Pour dressing over salad and sprinkle with sunflower seeds.

"The L A Lite Cookbook recipes are so easy to follow, my boyfriend has meals made and ready to eat when I get home from work."

- Rachel P.

Tomato Basil & Mozzarella Salad

meals in minutes

1 *serving*

- SERVING SIZE: 1 RECIPE
- COUNTS AS:
  1 VEGETABLE
  1 FAT
  1 DAIRY

▶ *size according to plan*

※ Ingredients

1 very ripe, small tomato

2oz (56g) light or reduced-fat mozzarella cheese, shredded or sliced

4 basil leaves, fresh

1 tsp olive oil

1 tsp balsamic vinegar

freshly ground pepper

1. Cut tomato into 4 thick slices.

2. Arrange slices on a salad plate. Top tomato slices with mozzarella.

3. Thinly slice basil; sprinkle over tomato and cheese.

4. Drizzle with oil and vinegar and a dash of freshly ground pepper.

Savory
Soups &
❖ Salad

7 Layer **Salad**

☀ Ingredients

1/2 head iceberg lettuce, chopped

1/2 cup (125ml / 60g) celery, chopped

1/4 cup (60ml / 24g) green onions, chopped

1/4 cup (60ml / 37g) green peppers, chopped

1/2 small (10oz / 280g) package frozen peas, thawed and drained

1/4 cup (60ml / 57g) lite mayonnaise

4 packets of artificial sweetener

4oz (112g) low-fat shredded cheddar cheese

1 In large salad bowl layer the lettuce, celery, onion, pepper and peas.

2 Spread mayo on top.

3 Sprinkle with artificial sweetener; then cheese.

4 Cover tightly and refrigerate at least 4 hours and up to 24 hours.

Citrus **Salad**

☀ Ingredients

1/4 cup (60ml) red wine vinegar

1 tsp Dijon mustard

1 tsp fennel seeds, crushed, toasted

1/3 cup (85ml) olive oil

freshly ground pepper

1 ruby red grapefruit, segmented

1 blood orange, segmented

1/2 head radicchio, torn into bite-size pieces

6 cups (1.5L / 180g) baby spinach leaves

3 leaves of endive, shredded

1 Combine vinegar, mustard and fennel seeds in a medium bowl.

2 Gradually whisk in oil.

3 Season with pepper.

4 Add in grapefruit segments and orange segments into the dressing and toss. Let stand about 15 minutes.

5 Toss radicchio, spinach and endive in a bowl.

6 Add fruit and dressing. Toss before serving.

45

Savory
Soups&
✤ Salads

Dilled Pasta Salad

 serving

- **SERVING SIZE: 1 RECIPE**
- **COUNTS AS:**
  - 1 STARCH
  - 1 FAT
  - 2 VEGETABLES

▶ *size according to plan*

☀ Ingredients

1/2 Tbsp snipped fresh dill or
  1/4 tsp dried dill

1/4 tsp lite salt

1/4 tsp dry mustard

freshly ground pepper

1 Tbsp lite mayonnaise

1/3 cup (85ml / 57g) cooked
  rotini pasta

1/4 cucumber, diced

1/4 medium carrot, shredded

2 green onions, diced

1 Mix together all ingredients in a large bowl.

2 Cover and refrigerate at least 2 hours before serving.

> "The L A Lite Cookbook recipes are so simple to make and so good to eat."
>
> *- Lynn K.*

Cucumber & Tomato Salad

 serving

- **SERVING SIZE: 1 RECIPE**
- **COUNTS AS:**
  - 3 VEGETABLES
  - 1/2 DAIRY

▶ *size according to plan*

☀ Ingredients

1/4 medium cucumber

5 green onions, thinly sliced

1 tomato, chopped

1/4 tsp lite salt

1/2 Tbsp snipped parsley

1/8 tsp ground cumin

freshly ground pepper

1 garlic clove, finely chopped

1/2 cup (125ml) nonfat plain
  yogurt

1 Cut cucumbers in half, lengthwise. Scoop seeds from cucumber with a spoon, then chop into bite-size pieces.

2 Mix cucumber, green onion and salt. Let stand 10 minutes.

3 Add tomatoes, parsley, cumin, pepper and garlic to cucumbers.

4 Cover and refrigerate 1 hour.

5 Just before serving, drain vegetables thoroughly in a colander or sieve. Add yogurt; mix well to combine.

Savory
Soups&
❖ Salad

Oriental Chicken Salad

SERVING SIZE: 1 RECIPE
COUNTS AS:
1 PROTEIN
3 VEGETABLES
1 FRUIT

e according to plan

☀ Ingredients

1 cup (250ml / 56g) lettuce, shredded

5 or 7oz (140 or 196g) chicken, cooked and cut into bite-size pieces, size according to plan

1/2 medium carrot, shredded

1/2 cup (125ml / 125g) mandarin oranges, drained

5 green onion with tops, sliced

1 Tbsp toasted sesame seeds

Ginger Dressing:

1/4 cup (60ml) white wine vinegar

1/2 to 1 packet artificial sweetener

2 tsp low-sodium soy sauce

1/4 tsp lite salt

freshly ground pepper

1/4 tsp ground ginger

1. Prepare dressing first. Combine vinegar, artificial sweetener, soy sauce, salt, pepper and ginger. Shake all ingredients in covered container or jar. Refrigerate.

2. Toss together lettuce, chicken, carrot, green onion and ginger dressing.

3. Place mixture on plate and top with oranges. Sprinkle with sesame seeds.

4. May also be served over brown rice for additional starch serving.

Tomato Pasta Salad

SERVING SIZE: 1 RECIPE
COUNTS AS:
1 STARCH
1 VEGETABLE

e according to plan

☀ Ingredients

1 small tomato, chopped

1 garlic clove, finely chopped

1 Tbsp snipped parsley

2 Tbsp fat-free Italian dressing

1/4 tsp dried basil leaves

1/3 cup (85ml / 57g) cooked pasta shells

1. Mix tomato, garlic, parsley, Italian dressing and basil.

2. Toss pasta shells with tomato mixture.

3. Cover and refrigerate at least 2 hours.

47

Savory
Soups&
✤ Salads

Cantaloupe with Chicken Salad

1 *serving*

- ■ SERVING SIZE: 1 RECIPE
- ■ COUNTS AS:
  - 1 PROTEIN
  - 1 VEGETABLE
  - 2 FRUIT
  - 1 FAT

▶ *size according to plan*

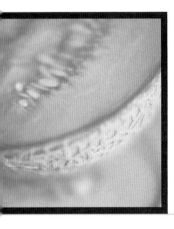

☀ Ingredients

5 or 7oz (140 or 196g) cooked chicken breast, cubed

1/4 cup (60ml / 36g) blueberries

10 grapes

1 celery stalk, sliced

1/8 cantaloupe, cubed

Dressing

1 Tbsp low-fat mayonnaise

1 Tbsp fat-free sour cream

1/4 tsp grated lemon peel

1 packet of sugar substitute

1. Mix together dressing and lemon pepper seasoning; blend and set aside.

2. Brush chicken with 1 Tbsp of dressing mixture.

3. Grill chicken until done.

4. Cool slightly and then cut chicken into strips.

5. Place romaine lettuce on a large dinner plate, top with mandarin oranges, mushrooms, onion and chicken. Drizzle dressing over the salad.

Spinach Tossed Salad

1 *serving*

- ■ SERVING SIZE: 1 RECIPE
- ■ COUNTS AS:
  - 1 STARCH
  - 3 VEGETABLES

▶ *size according to plan*

good source of fiber

☀ Ingredients

1 cup (250ml / 56g) spinach leaves

1/2 cup (125ml / 35g) mushrooms, sliced

1 cup (250ml / 45g) bean sprouts

3 melba toast, crumbled

2 green onions, thinly sliced

1. Tear spinach into small pieces. Toss all ingredients together.

2. Serve with freshly ground pepper and fat-free dressing of choice.

Savory
Soups&
❖ Salad

Coleslaw

☀ Ingredients

4oz (125ml) nonfat plain yogurt

1 Tbsp lite mayonnaise

1/2 packet artificial sweetener

1/4 tsp dry mustard

1/4 tsp lite salt

freshly ground pepper

1 cup (250ml / 70g) cabbage, shredded

1/2 medium carrot, finely shredded

dash of paprika or dried dill

1 Mix yogurt, mayonnaise, artificial sweetener, dry mustard, salt and pepper.

2 Toss with cabbage and carrot.

3 Sprinkle with paprika or dried dill.

Grilled Chicken Caesar **Salad**

☀ Ingredients

Chicken

6 or 8oz (168 or 224g) chicken breasts, boneless and skinless, size according to plan

2 Tbsp citrus rub (see recipe on page 224)

1 Tbsp olive oil

Dressing

2 Tbsp fresh lemon juice

1/2 tsp freshly ground pepper

1/4 cup (60ml) lite mayonnaise

1 Tbsp lemon seasoning (see recipe on page 218)

Salad

8 cups (2L / 240g) romaine lettuce, torn

1/4 cup (60ml) lite parmesan cheese, grated

1/2 cup (125ml) unseasoned fat-free croutons

1 Preheat grill or broiler to medium high.

2 Brush chicken on both sides with olive oil.

3 Season chicken with citrus rub, until well coated.

4 Grill for 5 minutes then turn and grill for 5 additional minutes or until juices run clear when pierced with a fork.

5 Remove from grill; cool and cut into strips; set aside.

6 For dressing, combine the lemon juice, mayonnaise, pepper and lemon seasoning; prepare while chicken is cooking.

7 For the salad, place 2 cups romaine on each of four salad plates. Divide chicken strips, evenly, among romaine; top with cheese, croutons and 2 Tbsp of dressing.

♣ Shrimp or steak may be substituted for the chicken in this recipe.

Savory
Soups&
♣ Salads

Grilled Asparagus, Tomato & Carrot Salad

 6 *servings*

■ SERVING SIZE: 1 CUP
■ COUNTS AS:
  3 VEGETABLES
  1 FAT

▶ *size according to plan*

family fare

☀ Ingredients

2 bunches asparagus

5 green onions

3 carrot, chopped into matchstick pieces

12 cherry tomatoes, halved

Marinade

1/4 cup (60ml) olive oil

1/4 cup (60ml) balsamic vinegar

freshly ground pepper

Vinaigrette

1/4 cup (60ml) olive oil

1/4 cup (60ml) vinegar

3 Tbsp fat-free sour cream

1 Tbsp chopped garlic

2 Tbsp finely chopped savory

1/2 tsp cumin

dash of low-sodium Worcestershire sauce

1 tsp lime juice

freshly ground pepper

1 Snap the bottom section off asparagus stalks at their natural break point.

2 Chop the remaining asparagus into thirds.

3 Remove bottoms from green onions and place in a large mixing bowl with the asparagus pieces.

4 Add the marinade ingredients to mixing bowl and toss well.

5 Grill vegetable mixture lightly over medium high heat for 2-3 minutes, so they still have crunch.

6 Remove from the grill to cool and chop green onions into small pieces.

7 In a separate salad bowl, mix all ingredients of vinaigrette and whisk vigorously.

8 Add grilled asparagus and green onions.

9 Add carrot pieces and cherry tomatoes.

10 Mix gently by hand, tossing to coat, cover and refrigerate until serving.

Shrimp Salad

 1 *serving*

■ SERVING SIZE: 1 RECIPE
■ COUNTS AS:
  1 PROTEIN
  1 VEGETABLE
  1 FAT

50

▶ *size according to plan*

☀ Ingredients

4 or 6oz (112 or 168g) cooked shrimp

1 Tbsp lite mayonnaise

1/2 Tbsp lemon juice

dash of lite salt

freshly ground pepper

1 celery stalk, finely sliced

1/2 tsp dried onion flakes

1 Combine all ingredients; mix well.

2 Cover and refrigerate at least 1 hour. Serve chilled.

Savory
Soups &
❖ Salad

serving

good source of fiber

Oriental Bean Salad

☀ Ingredients

1 Tbsp lime or lemon juice

1/2 Tbsp light soy sauce

1/2 Tbsp parsley

1/2 packet artificial sweetener

dash of garlic powder

dash of crushed red pepper

1/2 cup (125ml / 62g) cooked
   wax beans

1/2 cup (125ml / 62g) cooked
   green beans

1/2 cup (125ml / 42g) fresh
   bean sprouts

1/4 medium green pepper, cut
   into 1/2-inch pieces

1 tsp toasted sesame seeds

1 In a mixing bowl, stir together lime or lemon juice, soy sauce, parsley, artificial sweetener, garlic powder and crushed red pepper.

2 Add wax and green beans, bean sprouts and green pepper; toss to coat. Cover and refrigerate 1 hour.

3 Before serving, sprinkle with toasted sesame seeds.

Chicken Salad

serving

☀ Ingredients

5 or 7oz (140 or 196g) chicken,
   cooked and cut into bite-size
   pieces, size according to plan

1 Tbsp lite mayonnaise

1 tsp mustard

1 celery stalk, thinly sliced

freshly ground pepper

1/2 tsp parsley

1/2 tsp dried minced onion
   (optional)

1 Combine all ingredients. Cover and refrigerate, at least 1 hour.

2 Serve chilled.

Savory
Soups &
❖ Salads

Tuna Pasta Salad

1 *serving*

- **SERVING SIZE: 1 RECIPE**
- **COUNTS AS:**
  1 PROTEIN
  1 STARCH
  2 VEGETABLES

▶ *size according to plan*

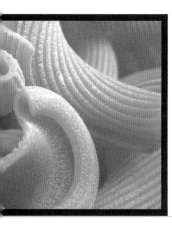

☀ Ingredients

6oz (168g) can of tuna,
  drained (choose low-sodium if
  available)

1 tomato, chopped

1/2 celery stalk, chopped

1 Tbsp white onion, chopped

1/4 medium carrot, diced

1 garlic clove, crushed

1/4 tsp dried onion flakes

1 Tbsp snipped parsley

1/4 tsp lite salt

1/4 tsp dried basil leaves

1/8 tsp dried oregano leaves

freshly ground pepper

2 Tbsp fat-free Italian dressing

1/3 cup (85ml / 57g) cooked
  pasta bows

1 Mix all ingredients, except pasta bows, in a large bowl.

2 Cover and refrigerate at least 1-2 hours.

3 Toss pasta with tuna mixture just before serving.

> "I love leftovers, so I double up the recipe."
>
> *- Kirsten D.*

good source of fiber

Strawberry Spinach Salad

4 *servings*

- **SERVING SIZE:
  1/4 OF RECIPE**
- **COUNTS AS:**
  1 FRUIT
  1/2 FAT

▶ *size according to plan*

☀ Ingredients

8oz (224g) spinach leaves

1 cup (250ml / 144g) fresh
  strawberries, sliced

1 kiwi, sliced

1 Tbsp slivered almonds

Dressing

2 Tbsp sugar-free raspberry
  preserves

1 Tbsp olive oil

1 Tbsp rice vinegar

1 Place salad ingredients in a large bowl.

2 For dressing, combine remaining ingredients in a small bowl; whisk vigorously.

3 Toss dressing with salad.

Savory
Soups &
♣ Salad

Fresh Vegetable Salad

servings

SERVING SIZE: 1 CUP (250ML)
COUNTS AS:
2 VEGETABLES

ze according to plan

☀ Ingredients

1 red bell pepper, sliced

1 yellow pepper, sliced

1 green pepper, sliced

1 medium red onion, thinly sliced

1 head of broccoli, cut into bite-size pieces

1 head of cauliflower, cut into bite-size pieces

1 small zucchini, thinly sliced

1 medium carrot, shredded

Dressing

2 Tbsp red wine vinegar

2 Tbsp fresh lemon juice

dash of white pepper

1/4 tsp dry mustard

1 Tbsp olive oil

fresh herbs, such as tarragon, basil, chives, dill, oregano, basil or mint (optional)

1 Combine all vegetable ingredients in a large salad bowl.

2 For dressing, whisk together vinegar, lemon juice, pepper and dry mustard.

3 Slowly stream olive oil into bowl, whisking continuously, to emulsify the dressing.

4 Stir in the herbs just before adding to the salad (optional).

"I still use this cookbook weekly even after completing and exceeding my goal. Thanks L A Weight Loss!"

- Michele G.

Sweet & Sour Dressing

servings

SERVING SIZE: 1 TBSP
COUNTS AS:
1 CONDIMENT

ze according to plan

☀ Ingredients

1 Tbsp lemon juice

1 Tbsp apple cider vinegar

1/3 cup (85ml) water

1 garlic clove, minced

1/4 tsp lite salt

freshly ground pepper

1/2 packet artificial sweetener

1 Combine all ingredients in a jar and shake to mix.

2 Store in the refrigerator for up to 1 week.

Savory
Soups&
❖ Salads

Lite **Vinaigrette**

8 *servings*

- **SERVING SIZE: 1 TBSP**
- **COUNTS AS:**
  1 CONDIMENT

▶ *size according to plan*

family fare

☀ Ingredients

1 packet artificial sweetener

1/4 tsp lite salt

2 garlic cloves, minced

1/8 tsp dry mustard

freshly ground pepper

1/4 cup (60ml) water

3 Tbsp wine vinegar or lemon juice

1 In a screw-top jar, combine artificial sweetener, salt, garlic, dry mustard and pepper.

2 Add water and vinegar.

3 Cover tightly with lid and shake until well blended. Let stand 3-4 minutes. Shake again.

4 Store in the refrigerator for up to 1 week.

Chicken Salad with **Orange Vinaigrette**

1 *serving*

- **SERVING SIZE: 1 RECIPE**
- **COUNTS AS:**
  1 PROTEIN
  2 VEGETABLES
  1 FRUIT

▶ *size according to plan*

☀ Ingredients

3 Tbsp fat-free red wine vinaigrette salad dressing

1 Tbsp lemon pepper seasoning blend

6 or 8oz (168 or 224g) chicken breast, boneless and skinless, size according to plan

1 cup (250ml / 30g) romaine lettuce, torn

1/2 cup (125ml / 112g) mandarin oranges

1 cup (250ml / 70g) fresh mushroom slices

1 Tbsp chopped onion

1 Mix together dressing and lemon pepper seasoning blend, set aside.

2 Brush chicken with 1 Tbsp of dressing mixture.

3 Grill chicken until done.

4 Cool slightly and then cut chicken into strips.

5 Place romaine lettuce on a large dinner plate, top with mandarin oranges, mushrooms, onion and chicken. Drizzle dressing over the salad.

54

Savory
Soups&
✲ Salad

Poppy Seed Vinaigrette

 servings

SERVING SIZE: 1 TBSP
COUNTS AS:
1 CONDIMENT

ze according to plan

☀ Ingredients

1/2 cup (125ml) cold water

1/2 cup (125ml) cider vinegar

1 tsp lemon juice

1/2 tsp lite salt

1/2 tsp freshly ground pepper

2 Tbsp poppy seeds

1 packet artificial sweetener

1 Combine all ingredients in a jar or container and shake well.

2 Store in the refrigerator for up to 1 week. Shake well before each use.

Yogurt-Dill Dressing

servings

SERVING SIZE: 1 TBSP
COUNTS AS:
1 CONDIMENT

ze according to plan

☀ Ingredients

8oz (250ml) plain, nonfat yogurt

3 green onions, chopped fine

1 tsp lemon juice

1/4 tsp dry mustard

1/4 tsp garlic powder

1/2 tsp dried dill weed

1 Mix all ingredients in a bowl; whisk thoroughly.

2 Store in the refrigerator for up to 1 week. Mix well before each use.

Savory
Soups&
❖ Salads

Appetite
✤ Delights

Appetizers are a family favorite! Appetizers can be a great combination with any soup or salad for a light meal, or be a perfect choice for entertaining. We have lightened up some old favorites to use for any eating occasion. We have also provided a number of dips that can be a great compliment to any vegetable snack. Enjoy!

Tortilla Roll-Up recipe can be found on page 60

Let's get the party started!

Appetizers are the main ingredients to any get together or special occasion. Keep in mind you don't want to fill up before the main course, so appetizers should be simple, tasty…and of course, light. Here are some tips to remember when preparing and serving appetizers for your own gathering, or bringing a special dish to a special occasion.

- Be sure not to offer excessive servings of appetizers. Appetizers are meant to tease the pallet, not to replace a full course meal.

- Using colorful garnish such as a sprig of parsley or a lemon and lime wedge give that extra added festive touch on any tray of appetizers.

- Try serving a medley of appetizers. Be sure that there is a little something for everyone – it doesn't need to be extravagant, perhaps roasted peppers for the veggie lovers and deviled eggs for those who are looking for a heartier snack.

- When preparing a veggie platter, try and incorporate some unusual and interesting vegetables such as fresh brussels sprouts and sugar snap peas. The platter will look more interesting and appealing.

- Spice up the dip by placing it in a brightly colored bowl. Get creative by hollowing out bread loaves, heads of cabbage or winter squash.

- Guests should be able to eat appetizers without utensils. Most partygoers are busy mingling and would rather not think about cutting their food.

- Keep the appetizer simple. Some guests may avoid food that looks messy to prevent the embarrassment of getting it all over their hands and faces.

TIP!

If an appetizer needs to be cooled before serving, use shallow containers and leave air space around the containers to promote rapid cooling of the food.

TIP!

When deciding how many appetizers to serve, estimate each guest will eat 5-6 pieces. If it's closer to mealtime, then assume they will eat 10-12 pieces. Younger guests tend to eat more and the older company will usually have less of an appetite.

Appetite
❖ Delight

Deviled Eggs

servings

SERVING SIZE: 2 OR 3 EGGS
COUNTS AS:
1 PROTEIN
1 FAT

ze according to plan

✳ Ingredients
- 6 eggs
- 2 Tbsp lite mayonnaise
- dash onion powder
- 1 tsp Dijon mustard
- 1/2 tsp paprika

1. Prepare hard cooked eggs.

2. Drain eggs and allow to cool. Cut eggs in half, lengthwise.

3. Remove egg yolks and mash them with a fork in a small mixing bowl.

4. Add mayonnaise, onion powder and dry mustard to egg yolks.

5. Spoon mixture into egg whites. Sprinkle with paprika. Chill before serving.

Creamed Crab & Veggie Dip

servings

good source of calcium

SERVING SIZE:
1/2 OF RECIPE
COUNTS AS:
1 PROTEIN
1/2 DAIRY
2 VEGETABLES
1 FAT

ze according to plan

✳ Ingredients
- 2oz (56g) part-skim ricotta cheese
- 4oz (125ml) skim milk
- 1 cup (125ml / 30g) fresh raw spinach
- 2 cups (500ml / 168g) fresh chopped artichoke hearts
- 3 green onions, chopped
- 1/4 red pepper, chopped
- 1/4 tsp garlic powder
- 2 garlic cloves, minced
- 1oz (28g) shredded reduced-fat cheese (recommend Monterey Jack or Mozzarella)
- 1 Tbsp low-fat mayonnaise
- 4 or 6oz (112g) fresh crabmeat, size according to plan
- 1/4 tsp hot sauce
- nonfat cooking spray

1. Spray casserole dish with nonfat cooking spray.

2. In small casserole dish, combine ricotta, mayonnaise and milk. Stir well and set aside.

3. Spray medium skillet with nonfat cooking spray. Add artichokes, onion, pepper, garlic powder and garlic. Sauté 2 minutes. Remove from heat.

4. Add spinach, hot sauce, vegetable mixture and crabmeat to cheese mixture.

5. Stir in 3/4 oz (21g) shredded cheese. Place in 350°F preheated oven.

6. Bake 15 minutes, stir mixture well and then top with remaining 1/4oz (7g) of cheese.

7. Bake 10-15 minutes, or until all cheese is melted and casserole is bubbly.

8. Serve over roasted veggies or as a dip for crackers and fresh veggies.

Appetite
❖ Delights

Tortilla Roll-Up Appetizer

10 *servings*

- SERVING SIZE: 4 PIECES
- COUNTS AS:
  1 VEGETABLE
  1 STARCH

▶ *size according to plan*

☀ Ingredients

2oz (56g) fat-free cream cheese, softened

2oz (56g) lite cream cheese, softened

5 green onions, sliced

1/4 cup (60ml) salsa

2oz (56g) lite or reduced-fat cheddar cheese, shredded

5- 8 inch whole wheat or spinach tortillas

1/4 cup (60ml) chopped black olives

1/2 cup (125ml / 36g) iceberg lettuce, shredded

1. In a medium bowl, with a hand-mixer, blend cream cheeses, until soft.

2. Add onion, salsa and cheese. Stir until well combined.

3. Divide cream cheese mixture among tortillas. Spread a thin layer on each.

4. Sprinkle each tortilla with black olives and lettuce.

5. Roll each tortilla and refrigerate about 4-6 hours before slicing.

6. Just before serving, slice each tortilla roll into 1-inch pieces.

---

5 Layer Dip

4 *servings*

- SERVING SIZE: 1 RECIPE
- COUNTS AS:
  1/2 PROTEIN
  1 VEGETABLE
  1 FAT
  1/2 DAIRY

▶ *size according to plan*

good source of fiber

☀ Ingredients

2 green onions, chopped

1 tsp oil

1/2 cup (125ml / 88g) cooked kidney beans

1/2 tomato, chopped

1oz (28g) reduced-fat cheddar cheese

2 Tbsp salsa

1 Tbsp fat-free sour cream

1. In medium bowl, combine 1 chopped green onion, oil and cooked beans.

2. With a fork, mash beans to form a paste.

3. Place bean paste in bottom of small bowl.

4. Top with chopped tomato.

5. Top tomato with cheese, and then follow with salsa.

6. Spread sour cream over cheese layer.

7. Sprinkle with remaining green onion.

Appetite
❖ Deligh

Eggplant Caponata

SERVING SIZE: 1/3 CUP (85ML)
COUNTS AS:
1 VEGETABLE

e according to plan

❊ Ingredients

1 Tbsp olive oil

1 medium eggplant, peeled and diced

2 garlic cloves

1/2 cup (125ml / 80g) red onion, chopped

1/2 cup (125ml / 74g) green bell pepper, chopped

1/4 cup (60ml) water

1/4 cup (60ml / 15g) fresh parsley, chopped

3-4 Tbsp black olives, pitted and chopped

2 Roma tomatoes, seeded and chopped

2 Tbsp red wine vinegar

1/4 tsp lite salt

1/8 tsp freshly ground pepper

1 Preheat oven to 350°F.

2 In a baking dish, combine olive oil, eggplant, garlic, onion and green pepper. Cover and bake in oven for 15 minutes.

3 Remove from oven; add water, parsley, black olives, tomatoes, vinegar, salt and pepper to baking dish. Stir to combine.

4 Return to oven and continue to bake 30 minutes, or until eggplant is soft.

5 Remove from oven and transfer to a bowl; cover and refrigerate at least 8 hours or overnight before serving.

Guacamole

servings

SERVING SIZE: 1/4 CUP (60ml)
COUNTS AS:
1 VEGETABLE
1 FAT

e according to plan

❊ Ingredients

2 avocados, diced

1/2 small onion, diced

1-2 garlic cloves, minced

1 Roma tomato, seeded and diced

juice of 1 lime

1/2 tsp lite salt

1 jalapeño, diced (optional)

1 In a large bowl, lightly mash avocado with a fork.

2 Next add remaining ingredients; toss to combine.

3 Chill 30 minutes before servings.

Appetite
❖ Delights

Roasted Garlic Spread

6 *servings*

- SERVING SIZE: 1/2 OF RECIPE
- COUNTS AS:
  - 1 CONDIMENT

▶ *size according to plan*

☀ Ingredients

1 head of garlic

1 tsp olive oil

1 Preheat oven to 450°F.

2 Trim 1/4-inch of top off the head of garlic. Place in the middle of a square piece of aluminum foil.

3 Drizzle with olive oil. Tightly form foil over the garlic bulb.

4 Roast in oven for approximately 1 hour.

5 Allow to cool at least 15 minutes before serving.

6 To use, squeeze cloves from bulb by applying pressure to the bottom, as if a tube of toothpaste.

7 With its creamy texture and sweet aroma, roasted garlic is great to use in place of butter on bread or bruschetta, as well as in dishes, such as pastas, vegetables, beef or poultry.

Balsamic Grilled Bruschetta

12 *servings*

- SERVING SIZE: 1 SLICE
- COUNTS AS:
  - 1 VEGETABLE
  - 1 STARCH

▶ *size according to plan*

☀ Ingredients

10 Roma tomatoes, seeded and diced

2-3 Tbsp fresh basil, chopped

2-3 garlic cloves, minced

2 Tbsp parmesan cheese, shredded

1 Tbsp olive oil

1 Tbsp balsamic vinegar

1/4 tsp lite salt

1/8 tsp freshly ground pepper

1 loaf French bread, cut into 12 slices

1 In a bowl, toss together tomatoes, basil, garlic, cheese, oil, vinegar, and salt and pepper.

2 Cover and refrigerate for 1-2 hours, to allow flavors to meld.

3 Meanwhile, grill bread until lightly browned.

4 Divide tomato mixture evenly among sliced bread before serving. If desired, garnish with extra basil and an extra drizzle of balsamic vinegar.

Appetite
❖ Delig

Tzatziki

servings

SERVING SIZE: 1/2 CUP (125ML)
COUNTS AS:

1 STARCH

e according to plan

☀ Ingredients

2 cups (500ml) plain nonfat
  yogurt

2 medium cucumbers, peeled
  and shredded

2-3 garlic cloves, minced

1-2 Tbsp lemon juice

1 Tbsp olive oil

2 Tbsp fresh mint, chopped

1/2 tsp lite salt

1/4 tsp freshly ground pepper

1　In a colander, squeeze any excess liquid out from
    cucumber; discard liquid.

2　In a bowl, combine all ingredients. Mix well.

3　Refrigerate, allowing flavors to combine, at least 2
    hours, before serving.

4　Great with fresh vegetables or pitas as a dip, or as a
    dressing for lamb or chicken.

Romaine Roll-up

serving

SERVING SIZE: 1 LETTUCE ROLL
COUNTS AS:

1 PROTEIN
1 VEGETABLE
1 FAT

e according to plan

☀ Ingredients

1 leaf romaine lettuce

filling of your choice, portion
  size as according to plan:

tuna

ground beef

fresh sliced chicken or turkey

1 Tbsp lite mayonnaise
  (optional)

1　Place lettuce sideways on a plate, gently press down to
    flatten lettuce. Spread with mayonnaise.

2　Place filling in center of lettuce leaf and roll up.

3　Use toothpick to hold in place.

4　Cut in half and serve.

Appetite
❖ Delights

Veggies with Tarragon Dip

7 *servings*

- **SERVING SIZE:**
  1 CUP (250ML) WITH 1 TBSP DIP
- **COUNTS AS:**
  2 VEGETABLES
  1 FAT

▶ *size according to plan*

☀ Ingredients

1 pound (448g) asparagus, trimmed

1 pound (448g) fresh green beans, trimmed

1/2 cup (125ml) lite mayonnaise

zest and juice of 1 lemon

1 small green onion, finely chopped

2 Tbsp chopped fresh tarragon

2 Tbsp chopped parsley leaves

1 Cook asparagus spears and green beans in 1-inch of boiling water, covered, for 3 or 4 minutes.

2 Drain and cool the vegetables and arrange them on a serving plate.

3 Combine remaining ingredients in a small bowl.

4 Place dip on side of serving plate.

Roasted Peppers

8 *servings*

- **SERVING SIZE: 1/2 PEPPER**
- **COUNTS AS:**
  1 VEGETABLE
  [IF USING OLIVE OIL TO STORE, COUNTS AS 1 VEGETABLE, 1 FAT]

▶ *size according to plan*

☀ Ingredients

4 large red or yellow bell peppers, halved

1 Preheat oven to 500°F.

2 Place clean peppers onto a baking sheet. Roast until skin begins to blister and turn black, approximately 30-45 minutes.

3 Remove peppers from oven and place in a paper or plastic bag for about 15-20 minutes, this will allow the skin to separate from the flesh using steam.

4 Once cool enough to touch, gently peel the skin from the flesh.

5 Store peppers in an air-tight container in the refrigerator; sprinkle with olive oil, balsamic vinegar and crushed garlic, if desired.

Appetite
❖ Delig

Spinach & Artichoke Dip

family fare

servings

SERVING SIZE:
/3 CUP (85ML)
COUNTS AS:
VEGETABLE
FAT

according to plan

※ Ingredients

1 cup (250ml /156g) frozen spinach, drained and thawed

1 cup (240ml / 180g) cooked sliced artichoke hearts

1/4 cup (60ml /4g) chopped white onions

1 tsp fat-free Italian salad dressing

1/2 tsp lite salt

freshly ground pepper

1 cup (250ml) lite sour cream

2 Tbsp dried onion

1 tsp garlic powder

1 Tbsp capers

3 Tbsp grated parmesan cheese

1 In large mixing bowl combine spinach, artichokes, onion and salad dressing. Sprinkle with salt and pepper.

2 Fold in sour cream and blend well. Add dried onion, garlic and capers. Mix in parmesan cheese. Chill for at least 1 hour.

Creamy Fruit Dip

servings

SERVING SIZE:
/2 CUP (125ML)
COUNTS AS:
1/2 DAIRY

according to plan

※ Ingredients

8oz (250ml) lite fruited yogurt, any flavor (such as strawberry or raspberry)

2 Tbsp fat-free whipped topping

1 Combine ingredients in a medium bowl and blend until smooth.

2 Cut up your fruit in bite sizes and dip.

"So many recipes to choose from, choose something new every day."

- Sharon T.

Appetite
♣ Delights

In House Steak House

Are you a meat and potatoes lover? Then you'll love our variety-packed In House Steak House recipes. From easy to elaborate, our savory beef dishes are hardy and satisfying. Whether you prefer to cozy up by the fire with a delicious cup of beef stew, or throw some marinated filets on the grill, we've got the recipes that will add that extra bit of zest to each mouthwatering bite. Plus you'll learn more ways to cook, prepare and store beef than you ever thought possible.

Stuffed Pepper recipe can be found on page 74

In House Steak House

Beef Kabobs

Beef Roast

Beef Dijon

Beef Teriyaki

London Broil

Italian-Style Beef

Beef & Broccoli

Sesame Beef

Meatloaf

Stuffed Pepper

Stuffed Cabbage

Salisbury Steak

Steak Fajitas

Herb-Crusted Steak

Beef Burgundy

Steak & Onions

Open-Faced Beef Sandwich

Italian-Style Burger

Meatball Sandwich

Mushroom & Swiss Burger

Beef Tenderloin with
   Mushroom Wine Sauce

Open-Face Burger with
   Mustard Sauce

Beef Stroganoff

Steak Burger

Savory Beef Stew

Cheesy Beef & Broccoli

Hot Beef Sandwich

Beef and Mushroom Kabobs

Hamburger

Philly Cheesesteak

BBQ Cheddar Burger

Cuts of Beef

Loin Cuts

- Porterhouse steak
- T-bone steak
- Strip steak
- Sirloin roast
- Tenderloin roast
- Tenderloin steak
- Sirloin steak

Round Cuts (Leg)

- Beef cutler
- Top Round steak
- Eye round steak
- Round cube steak
- Top round roast
- Eye round roast

Rib Cuts

- Boneless rib roast
- Boneless rib eye steak

Chuck/Shoulder Cuts

- Brisket
- Chuck eye steak

Round Cuts (Leg)

- Chuck roast
- Chuck steak
- Shoulder roast
- Shoulder steak
- Stew beef chunks

Flank

- Flank steak

Plate

- Short ribs
- Skirt steak

Basic cooking methods

- **Braising** — Cooking with a moist heat, which is great for less tender cuts of beef. Meat may be browned first to seal in juices and flavor, a small amount of liquid such as broth is then added to pan. Beef is then cooked at a low heat for a lengthy period of time. This works well for round, flank, plate and chuck cuts.

- **Oven Roasting** — Dry heat method. Best used for larger quantities of meat such as a loin or round roast. Meat cooked in the oven in an uncovered pan.

- **Grilling** — Preparing food on a grill over hot coals or other direct heat source. This method is great for cooking loin cuts and steaks.

- **Stir-Frying** — Quickly cooking food in a large pan or wok over very high heat. Food needs to be constantly stirred to prevent sticking. Good cooking method for sirloin steak strips.

- **Pan Searing** — Uses high heat to create a crust and seal in meat juices. Cooking is usually finished in the oven. Use this for loin, rib and round cuts.

TIP!

Beef is a great source of zinc, which helps keep your immune system working well.

Know what's best to buy

Sometimes it gets confusing to understand the labels of meat in the supermarket. Grades on the packages are determined mostly by marbling and age of the animal. There are three USDA grades that you should keep in mind when buying beef:

- **Prime** — Usually found in restaurants or specialty meat stores. Even though it holds one of the highest grades of meat it's often has the most marbling of the three grades. Often the most flavorful steak you can find.

- **Choice** — It is the most common grade in the supermarket. It's your next best choice under prime cut for flavor because it has less marbling.

- **Select** — his grade has the least fat of the three grades. It's leaner and often more tender.

Look for "loin" or "round" in any grade of meat for the leanest cuts, such as "sirloin" or "top round steak." When you want the freshest, most flavorful steak in the supermarket, look for meat that is bright red and any marbling should be creamy white.

TIP!

Beef is packed with protein that is essential for your body's tissues, muscles and organs. So for your active lifestyle, remember beef is a good source to keep your body strong.

Food Safety

- Keep raw beef away from cooked and ready to eat foods.

- Use a separate cutting board for beef.

- Never defrost beef at room temperature. Thaw overnight in the refrigerator; under cold running water; or in the microwave.

- Cook ground beef to an internal temperature of 160°F.

- Cook whole cuts of beef such as roasts and steaks to an internal temperature of 145°F (medium) to 160°F (well done).

Beef Roasting

- Preheat oven to 450°F.

- Season meat and place on roasting rack in roasting pan.

- Roast for 15 minutes at 450°F.

- Reduce heat to 350°F and cook:

- Tenderloin: 8-11 minutes per pound

- Sirloin, top rounds, rib roasts: 20-25 minutes per pound

- Check internal temperature to be sure meat is at desired doneness.

- Allow meat to rest 10-15 minutes before carving.

In House
❖ Steak
House

Beef Kabobs

1 *serving*

- **SERVING SIZE: 2-3 KABOBS**
- **COUNTS AS:**
  - 1 PROTEIN
  - 2 VEGETABLES
  - 1 FRUIT

▶ *size according to plan*

☀ Ingredients

juice from 1 orange

1 Tbsp brown sugar artificial sweetener

1/4 tsp ground ginger

4 or 6oz (112 or 168g) sirloin steak, cut into 1 inch pieces, size according to plan

1/4 medium green pepper cut into 1 inch squares

1 cup (250ml /113g) zucchini or yellow squash cut into 1-inch pieces

1/4 medium red onion, cut into 1-inch squares

1. Mix orange juice, brown sugar and ginger. Add beef and pepper; stir to coat meat. Cover and marinate for 1 hour in refrigerator. Drain reserve marinade.

2. On a skewer, alternate beef, pepper, zucchini or yellow squash and onion, leaving 1/4 inch between pieces. Place kabobs on broiler pan. Brush with marinade.

3. Broil 4 inches from heat about 8 minutes, or until desired doneness, turning and brushing kabobs with marinade while cooking.

Beef Roast

4 *servings*

family fare

- **SERVING SIZE: 3 OR 5OZ COOKED (84 OR140G)**
- **COUNTS AS:**
  - 1 PROTEIN
  - 2 VEGETABLES

▶ *size according to plan*

☀ Ingredients

1 pound (448g) eye round roast, size according to plan

1/2 cup (125ml) red wine

2 cups (500ml / 140g) fresh mushrooms, finely chopped

1/2 tsp dried dill weed

1/4 tsp lite salt

1/4 cup (60ml / 24g) green onions, thinly sliced

4oz (125ml) plain nonfat yogurt

dash white pepper

1 cup (250ml) low-sodium beef broth

2 Tbsp flour

1/2 cup (60ml) water

1. Trim any excess, visible fat from roast. Cut 2 pockets into sides of roast, making a 3-inch-deep cut. Place roast in large, zip-top plastic bag set in bowl or baking pan. Pour wine over roast. Close the bag. Marinate for 3-6 hours.

2. Combine mushrooms, water, dill weed and salt. Cook, uncovered, over medium heat until the liquid is evaporated. Stir in onion.

3. Remove roast from marinade. Place filling into pockets.

4. Bake in 325°F oven for 1-1 1/2 hours, or until meat temperature of 150°F.

5. For sauce, mix together yogurt, flour and pepper in a small saucepan. Stir in broth. Cook, until sauce thickened, over medium heat.

6. Slice roast between the 2 filled pockets. Place on dinner plate top with sauce.

In House
❧ Steak
House

Beef Dijon

SERVING SIZE: 1 ENTREE
COUNTS AS:
1 PROTEIN
3 VEGETABLES
1/2 DAIRY

e according to plan

✻ Ingredients

4 or 6oz (112 or 168g) beef flank steak, size according to plan

1 tsp freshly ground pepper

1 cup (250ml / 70g) fresh mushrooms, sliced

5 green onions, thinly sliced

1/4 cup (60ml) water

1/2 packet low-sodium beef bouillon

1/2 cup (125ml) nonfat plain yogurt

1 Tbsp flour

2 tsp Dijon mustard

1 cup (250ml / 134g) fresh asparagus spears

nonfat cooking spray

1. Rub pepper on both sides of the steak.

2. Broil steak, 3 inches from heat, for 6 minutes. Turn steak over and brown for 6-8 minutes more. Keep warm, allowing to rest 5-10 minutes before slicing.

3. Coat skillet with nonfat cooking spray. Combine mushrooms, green onion, water and beef bouillon; cook until mushrooms are tender.

4. Mix together yogurt, flour, and mustard. Stir into mushroom mixture. Cool and stir until thickened.

5. Cook asparagus by microwaving or steaming.

6. Slice steak, thinly, against the grain. Arrange steak slices and asparagus on dinner plate. Serve with sauce.

Beef Teriyaki

SERVING SIZE: 1 ENTREE
COUNTS AS:
1 PROTEIN

e according to plan

✻ Ingredients

4 or 6oz (112 or 168g) sirloin steak, cubed, size according to plan

2 Tbsp low-sodium soy sauce

2 Tbsp white wine

1/4 tsp ground ginger

1 packet artificial sweetener

1/2 tsp garlic powder

1. Place beef in a bowl.

2. Combine all other ingredients in a measuring cup or small bowl; pour over beef. Cover and refrigerate, at least 1 hour.

3. Remove beef from marinade; save marinade.

4. Brush meat with marinade and broil 4 inches from heat, about 5 minutes. Turn meat over; brush with marinade and broil another 5-6 minutes longer.

5. Another option is to serve the beef over brown rice; this would count as an additional 1 starch serving.

In House
✻ Steak
House

London Broil

1 *serving*

- **SERVING SIZE: I ENTREE**
- **COUNTS AS:**
  1 PROTEIN
  1 VEGETABLES

▸ *size according to plan*

☀ Ingredients

4 or 6oz (112 or 168g) flank
. steak, size according to plan

5 green onions, thinly sliced

1/4 tsp lite salt

1 tsp canola oil

1 tsp lemon juice

1/8 tsp freshly ground pepper

1 garlic clove, crushed

nonfat cooking spray

1 Score flank steak with a knife, diagonally, in a diamond pattern, about 1/8-inch deep.

2 Coat skillet with nonfat cooking spray. Sauté onion; set aside.

3 Combine salt, oil, lemon juice, pepper and garlic. Brush half of the mixture on one side of beef.

4 Broil 2-3 inches from heat until brown, about 5 minutes; turn meat over. Brush with remaining mixture and broil another 5-7 minutes.

5 Cut beef, against the grain, on a bias (an angle).

6 Serve with sautéed onions.

Italian-Style Beef

1 *serving*

- **SERVING SIZE: I ENTREE**
- **COUNTS AS:**
  1 PROTEIN
  3 VEGETABLES

▸ *size according to plan*

☀ Ingredients

4 or 6oz (112 or 168g) beef round
steak, size according to plan

1/2 cup (125ml / 35g) fresh
mushrooms, sliced

1/4 cup (60ml / 40g) white onion,
diced

1/2 green pepper, chopped

1/2 celery stalk, chopped

1 garlic clove, minced

1/2 tomato, diced

1/4 tsp dried basil, crushed

1/4 tsp dried oregano, crushed

1/8 tsp cayenne pepper

1 Tbsp grated parmesan cheese

nonfat cooking spray

1 Cut meat into 2-3 pieces. Coat skillet with nonfat cooking spray. Brown meat on all sides. Remove from skillet.

2 Combine mushrooms, onion, green pepper, celery and garlic in skillet; cook until vegetables are tender. Add tomatoes, basil, oregano and cayenne pepper.

3 Place meat back in skillet, top with vegetable mixture. Cover and simmer about 45-60 minutes, or until meat is tender, stirring occasionally.

4 Place meat on dinner plate, spoon vegetables over meat.

5 Top with grated parmesan cheese.

In House
❧ Steak
House

Beef & Broccoli

1 serving

SERVING SIZE: 1 ENTREE
COUNTS AS:
1 PROTEIN
2 VEGETABLES

ize according to plan

☀ Ingredients

4 or 6oz (112 or 168g) beef round steak, size according to plan

1 Tbsp low-sodium soy sauce

1 Tbsp vinegar

1 Tbsp brown sugar artificial sweetener

1 garlic clove, minced

1/8 tsp cayenne pepper

1/2 medium carrot, thinly sliced

1 cup (250ml / 70g) fresh broccoli florets

1 tsp cornstarch

1 Tbsp water

nonfat cooking spray

1. Partially freeze meat. Thinly slice meat across the grain into bite-size strips. Set aside.

2. In a bowl, stir together soy sauce, vinegar, artificial sweetener, garlic and cayenne pepper. Stir in meat. Cover and refrigerate for 10 minutes.

3. Coat skillet with nonfat cooking spray and heat over medium-high flame; add sauce mixture and meat. Cook until meat is no longer pink.

4. Add vegetables and cook until vegetables are tender.

5. Stir while cooking until thickened.

6. Stir together cornstarch and water; stir into skillet and cook until thickened.

7. May be served over brown rice for an additional starch exchange.

Sesame Beef

serving

SERVING SIZE: 1 ENTREE
COUNTS AS:
1 PROTEIN
1 FAT

ize according to plan

☀ Ingredients

4 or 6oz (112 or 168g) sirloin steak, size according to plan

1 packet artificial sweetener

1 tsp canola oil

1 Tbsp low-sodium soy sauce

1/8 tsp freshly ground pepper

2 green onions, finely chopped

1 garlic clove, crushed

1 Tbsp chopped green pepper

1 Tbsp sesame seeds

nonfat cooking spray

1. Cut beef into strips.

2. Mix artificial sweetener, oil, soy sauce, green pepper, freshly ground pepper, onions and garlic in non-metal bowl; stir in beef until well coated. Marinate for at least 30 minutes.

3. Drain beef from marinade. Coat skillet with nonfat cooking spray and in stir sesame seeds; cook until light brown. Remove from skillet.

4. Add beef to skillet and cook until browned. Sprinkle with sesame seeds and serve.

5. May be served over salad greens for additional vegetable exchanges.

In House
♣ Steak
House

Meatloaf

4 *servings*

- SERVING SIZE: 1/4 OF LOAF
- COUNTS AS:
  1 PROTEIN
  1 STARCH

▶ *size according to plan*

family fare

✳ Ingredients

1 pound (448g) lean ground sirloin

1/2 cup (125ml / 54g) breadcrumbs

1/4 cup (125ml) egg substitute

2 Tbsp dried onion

1 tsp low-sodium Worcestershire sauce

1/4 tsp lite salt

1/4 tsp freshly ground pepper

1 tsp garlic powder

3 Tbsp ketchup, divided

nonfat cooking spray

1 Mix together all ingredients, reserving 2 Tbsp of ketchup. Form into loaf.

2 Coat loaf pan with nonfat cooking spray. Place meatloaf in pan. Spoon remaining ketchup on top of loaf and spread evenly.

3 Bake at 350°F until desired doneness, or about 45 minutes. To be sure meat is fully cooked, insert thermometer and bake until internal temperature reaches 160°F.

Stuffed Pepper

2 *servings*

- SERVING SIZE: 2 PEPPER HALVES
- COUNTS AS:
  1 PROTEIN
  1 STARCH
  3 VEGETABLES
  1/2 DAIRY

▶ *size according to plan*

good source of calcium

✳ Ingredients

2 whole green peppers

8 or 12oz (224 or 336g) lean ground sirloin, size according to plan

1/4 cup (60ml / 40g) chopped white onion

2/3 cup (170ml / 106g) cooked brown rice

1/4 tsp lite salt

1 tsp garlic powder

1 small tomato, chopped

1/3 cup (85ml) lite tomato sauce

2oz (56g) reduced-fat mozzarella cheese, shredded

1/4 cup (60ml) water

nonfat cooking spray

1 Cut pepper in half and remove seeds. Cook peppers in boiling water for approximately 5 minutes, until just tender; drain and set aside.

2 Brown beef and onion in skillet that has been coated with nonfat cooking spray. Add rice, salt and garlic powder to skillet and heat through.

3 Stuff each pepper half with beef mixture. Coat baking pan with nonfat cooking spray. Place peppers in baking pan. Top with chopped tomato and tomato sauce. Add water to bottom of baking pan.

4 Cover and bake at 350°F for 30-45 minutes, or until peppers and tomatoes are tender.

5 Uncover; sprinkle with cheese. Place back in oven and bake until cheese is melted.

In House
❖ Steak
House

Stuffed Cabbage

☀ Ingredients

3-4 cabbage leaves

4 or 6oz (112 or 168g) lean ground sirloin, size according to plan

1/3 cup (85ml / 53g) cooked brown rice

1/4 cup (60ml) low-sodium beef broth

1/4 tsp lite salt

1/8 tsp freshly ground pepper

1 tsp garlic powder

1 Tbsp dried onion

1/2 tomato, chopped

2 Tbsp lite tomato sauce

1 Tbsp water

nonfat cooking spray

1 Steam cabbage leaves until tender.

2 Mix together beef, rice, broth, salt, pepper, garlic powder and onion. Divide meat mixture between the cabbage leaves. Roll and tuck in ends. Secure with a toothpick, if necessary.

3 Coat baking pan with nonfat cooking spray. Place cabbage rolls in baking pan.

4 In small bowl, combine chopped tomato, tomato sauce and water. Top rolls with tomato mixture.

5 Bake in 350°F oven for about 1 hour, or until beef has reached an internal temperature of 160°F.

Salisbury Steak

☀ Ingredients

4 or 6oz (112 or 168g) lean ground sirloin, size according to plan

1/4 cup (60ml / 27g) breadcrumbs

1/4 tsp lite salt

1/8 tsp freshly ground pepper

1 Tbsp dried onion

1 cup (250ml) low-sodium beef broth

1 cup (250ml / 70g) fresh mushrooms, sliced

1 Tbsp water

1 tsp cornstarch

nonfat cooking spray

1 Mix ground beef, breadcrumbs, salt, pepper and 1/4 cup (60ml) broth in a bowl; combine well. Form meat into oval patty.

2 Coat skillet with nonfat cooking spray. Heat skillet over medium flame. Cook patty in a skillet over medium heat, until brown on both sides.

3 Add onion, remaining broth and mushrooms. Heat to boiling; reduce heat and cover. Simmer until desired doneness.

4 Remove patty; keep warm. Again, heat mixture to boiling; mix in water and cornstarch and cook until thickened. Serve sauce over patty.

In House
❖ Steak
House

Steak Fajitas

good source of calcium

✳ Ingredients

4 or 6oz (112 or 168g) sirloin steak, size according to plan

1/4 cup (60ml) red wine vinegar

1 packet artificial sweetener

1/2 tsp oregano

1/2 tsp chili powder

1/4 tsp garlic powder

dash of freshly ground pepper

1/4 tsp lite salt

1/2 cup (125ml / 80g) raw white onions, sliced

1/2 green pepper, sliced

1oz (28g) reduced-fat cheddar or monterey jack cheese

3-4 large leaves of iceberg lettuce

1 Tbsp salsa

nonfat cooking spray

1 To make marinade, combine vinegar, artificial sweetener, oregano, chili powder, garlic powder, pepper and salt.

2 Cut beef in to strips and place into bowl with marinade. Refrigerate 30 minutes.

3 Coat large skillet with nonfat cooking spray and heat over high flame. Sauté green peppers and onions about 3-5 minutes, until they begin to soften.

4 Remove steak from marinade and place in skillet with vegetables. Cook 5-10 minutes, or until beef in cooked through.

5 Remove fajita mixture from skillet and place on plate. Use lettuce leaves as fajita wraps; top with cheese and salsa.

Herb-Crusted Steak

✳ Ingredients

4 or 6oz (112 or 168g) sirloin steak, size according to plan

small handful of mixed herbs to taste (such as thyme, rosemary, basil, sage, parsley)

2 garlic cloves, peeled

1 Tbsp green onion, finely chopped

1 slice (1oz / 28g) white country-loaf style bread

freshly ground pepper

nonfat cooking spray

1 Place the herbs, garlic, onion, bread and seasoning in a food processor and blend.

2 Coat skillet with nonfat cooking spray.

3 Sear the steak in a hot pan; top with herbed breadcrumb mixture.

4 Finish the steak in a preheated 375°F oven.

5 Cook for 8-10 minutes.

In House
❧ Steak
House

Beef Burgundy

serving

SERVING SIZE: 1 SERVING
COUNTS AS:
1 PROTEIN
2 VEGETABLES

ze according to plan

☀ Ingredients

4 or 6oz (112 or 168g) sirloin steak, size according to plan

1/4 cup (60ml) burgundy wine

1/4 cup (60ml) low-sodium beef broth

1/4 tsp garlic powder

1/4 tsp freshly ground pepper

1/4 tsp thyme

1/4 tsp lite salt

1/8 tsp oregano

1/4 tsp dried onion

1 cup (250ml / 70g) fresh mushroom slices

1/2 celery stalk, chopped

nonfat cooking spray

1. In a small bowl, combine garlic powder, pepper, salt, thyme, oregano and onion.
2. Rub seasoning blend into steak.
3. Coat medium skillet with nonfat cooking spray and heat over high flame.
4. Place beef on skillet, sear on each side, approximately 3 minutes, or until browned.
5. While beef is cooking, combine wine and broth in small bowl.
6. Once beef has been browned on all sides, pour wine mixture over beef. Add mushrooms and celery. Continue to cook until all liquid has evaporated. Serve hot.

Steak & Onions

servings

SERVING SIZE: 3 OR 5OZ (84-140G) COOKED; AND 1/4 CUP (60ML) SAUCE
COUNTS AS:
1 PROTEIN
1 VEGETABLE

ze according to plan

family fare

☀ Ingredients

2 pounds (900g) beef top round, cut into thin slices

freshly ground pepper, to taste

10 large olives, sliced

3 garlic cloves, peeled and chopped

1 cup (250ml) low-sodium beef broth, divided

1/3 cup (85ml) white vinegar

1 cup (250ml / 148g) green pepper, cut into strips

2 cups (500ml / 230g) Spanish yellow onion slices

nonfat cooking spray

1. Pound meat to tenderize. Season with freshly ground pepper.
2. Combine vinegar, 3/4 cup (200ml) of the broth. Add the olives and garlic; set aside.
3. Coat skillet with nonfat cooking spray, heat the remaining broth. Add green peppers and onions and sauté.
4. Remove peppers and onions with a slotted spoon and set aside.
5. Reheat skillet and sear beef on all sides.
6. Return peppers and onions to the skillet with the meat.
7. Pour the broth and vinegar mixture over the meat.
8. Cook, partially covered for 20 minutes, or until tender.

In House
✤ Steak
House

Open-Faced Beef Sandwich

4 *servings*

- **SERVING SIZE: 1/4 RECIPE**
- **COUNTS AS:**
  - 1 PROTEIN
  - 1 STARCH
  - 2 VEGETABLE

▶ *size according to plan*

family fare

☼ Ingredients

4 slices lite whole-wheat bread

1-1 1/2 pound (448 - 680g) round steak, size according to plan

2 tomato, diced

4 garlic cloves, minced

2 cups (500ml) low-sodium beef broth

1 tsp lite salt

1 Tbsp hot sauce

1 green pepper, diced

5 green onions, diced

water

nonfat cooking spray

1. Coat large saucepan with nonfat cooking spray. Heat over high heat.

2. Add onion, pepper, and garlic to skillet. Sauté 2 minutes.

3. Cut beef into cubes and add to skillet. Sprinkle with salt.

4. Sauté beef until brown.

5. Add tomato and hot sauce to beef mixture and cook 1-2 minutes.

6. Add beef broth the beef mixture and bring to a boil.

7. Reduce heat and cook 1-2 hours, stirring occasionally. More water may be added to cover meat while cooking; add 1/4 cup (60ml) of warm water at a time.

8. Meat is done when it can be shredded with a fork. Once beef is done, drain any remaining liquid. Place beef on place and shred.

9. Serve shredded beef over bread.

Italian-Style Burger

1 *serving*

- **SERVING SIZE: 1 BURGER**
- **COUNTS AS:**
  - 1 PROTEIN
  - 1 STARCH
  - 1/2 DAIRY

▶ *size according to plan*

good source of calcium

☼ Ingredients

4 or 6oz (112 or 168g) lean ground sirloin, size according to plan

1/3 cup (85ml / 36g) breadcrumbs

1/4 cup (60ml) low-sodium beef broth

1 Tbsp dried onion

1 Tbsp fresh parsley, snipped

1/8 tsp garlic powder

1/8 tsp freshly ground pepper

1 slice of tomato

1/8 tsp dried oregano, crushed

1oz (28g) reduced-fat mozzarella cheese, shredded

1. Mix together breadcrumbs, broth, onion, parsley, garlic powder and pepper. Add meat; mix well. Shape into patty.

2. Broil 3 inches from heat for 6 minutes. Turn and broil 6-8 minutes longer, or until meat is no longer pink.

3. Top patty with tomato slices. Sprinkle with oregano, then mozzarella cheese. Broil another 1-2 minutes more, or until cheese is melted.

In House
❧ Steak
House

Meatball Sandwich

servings

SERVING SIZE: 3 OR 5OZ
(84 OR 140G) COOKED WITH
1/2 CUP (125ML) SAUCE
COUNTS AS:
1 PROTEIN
1 VEGETABLES
1 STARCH
1/2 DAIRY

ze according to plan

family fare

☀ Ingredients

1 pound (448g) ground sirloin

1 tsp oregano

1 tsp basil

1 tsp lite salt

1 tsp freshly ground pepper

3 Tbsp chopped onion

5 garlic cloves, minced, divided

1 cup (250ml / 30g) chopped
fresh spinach

1 cup (250ml) lite tomato sauce

1/2 cup (125ml) hot water

1 tomato, seeded and diced

four 4-inch whole wheat pitas

4oz (112g) reduced-fat
mozzarella cheese

1 In medium bowl combine meat, oregano, basil, salt,
pepper, onion and half of the minced garlic. Mix well.

2 Form small balls with meat mixture.

3 Spray medium sauce pan with cooking spray. Sauté
remaining minced garlic. Gently add meatballs to
saucepan and sauté until brown.

4 Add spinach and sauté 1 minute.

5 Add tomato sauce, water, and tomato to pan.
Continue to simmer, until meatballs are cooked and
sauce reduces.

6 Use slotted spoon to remove meatballs and from sauce.
Place in pita and top with cheese.

Mushroom & Swiss Burger

serving

SERVING SIZE: 1 BURGER
COUNTS AS:
1 PROTEIN
1 DAIRY

ze according to plan

good source of calcium

☀ Ingredients

Hamburger Patty (see recipe on
page 84)

2oz (56g) reduced-fat Swiss cheese

1/4 cup (60ml / 18g) sliced
mushrooms

1/4 tsp garlic powder

1 green onion, sliced

nonfat cooking spray

1 Coat small skillet with nonfat cooking spray.

2 Place mushrooms, garlic powder and onion in skillet
and sauté until mushrooms are fully cooked.

3 Place mushrooms on top of burger.

4 Place cheese on burger and place on grill or under
broiler to melt cheese.

In House
❧ Steak
House

7 *servings*

- SERVING SIZE: 3 OR 5OZ (84-140G) COOKED AND 1/4 CUP (60ML) SAUCE
- COUNTS AS:
  1 PROTEIN
  1 STARCH
  1 VEGETABLE
  1 FAT

▶ *size according to plan*

family fare

Beef Tenderloin with Mushroom Wine Sauce

✳ Ingredients

1 1/2 pounds (672g) beef tenderloin

1/2 cup (125ml / 63g) flour

2 Tbsp olive oil

1 cup (250ml / 96g) chopped green onion

2 garlic cloves, chopped

2 celery stalks, chopped

2 cups (500ml / 140g) shitake mushrooms, chopped

2 Tbsp fresh thyme, chopped

1 bay leaf

1/2 tsp freshly ground pepper

1 1/2 cups (375ml) red wine

1 Tbsp low-sodium Worcestershire sauce

1 Tbsp balsamic vinegar

1. Preheat oven to 350°F.

2. Roll tenderloin, lightly, in flour. Sear all sides in a hot grill pan, and then remove to an ovenproof dish.

3. Place in oven for 15-20 minutes. Allow to rest 10-15 minutes; slice tenderloin thinly. Cover loosely with foil to keep warm.

4. In a pan, sauté the onion, garlic and celery in oil for about 2 minutes.

5. Add the mushrooms and continue to sauté for about 4-5 minutes.

6. Add all remaining ingredients and bring to a boil.

7. Reduce heat, cover and simmer about 20 minutes.

8. Remove bay leaf and serve over sliced beef tenderloin.

Open-Face Burger with Mustard Sauce

1 *serving*

- SERVING SIZE: 1 BURGER
- COUNTS AS:
  1 PROTEIN
  1 STARCH
  1 FAT

▶ *size according to plan*

✳ Ingredients

4 or 6oz (112 or 168g) lean ground sirloin, size according to plan

1/3 cup (85ml / 36g) breadcrumbs

1/4 cup (60ml) low-sodium beef broth

1 Tbsp dried onion

1 Tbsp fresh parsley, snipped

1/8 tsp lite salt

2 Tbsp fat-free sour cream

1 Tbsp lite mayonnaise

1 tsp Dijon mustard

1/8 tsp dried dill

1. Mix breadcrumbs, broth, onion, parsley and salt. Add meat and mix well. Shape into patty.

2. Broil patty 3 inches for 5 minutes. Turn and broil 5-7 minutes more, or until meat is no longer pink.

3. Stir together sour cream, mayonnaise, mustard and dill weed. Spoon sauce over burger.

4. Arrange on 1 leaf of lettuce.

In House
❧ Steak
House

Beef Stroganoff

family fare

servings

SERVING SIZE: 1 1/2 CUPS
(375ML)

COUNTS AS:
1 PROTEIN
1 STARCH
2 VEGETABLES
1 FAT

ze according to plan

☼ Ingredients

2 1/2 pounds (1.2kg) beef
tenderloin, thinly sliced

1 Tbsp olive oil

1 tsp freshly ground pepper

1 Tbsp butter

1 cup (250ml / 70g) mushrooms,
sliced

1/2 cup (125ml / 48g) chopped
green onion

1/4 cup (60ml) white wine

2 Tbsp tomato paste, no salt
added

2 tsp Dijon mustard

3 cups (750ml) low-sodium beef
broth

1 1/4 cups (310ml) fat-free
sour cream

1. In a large pot, heat oil over high heat.

2. Season beef with the pepper and sauté until browned.

3. Remove the beef from the pot and set aside, pour off
any excess fat from the pot.

4. Melt the butter in the pot and sauté the mushrooms
and onions.

5. Add the white wine and simmer until liquid is reduced
by half.

6. Stir in the tomato paste and mustard; cook for
2 minutes.

7. Add the broth and beef, bring to a boil.

8. Reduce the heat and simmer for 5 minutes.

9. Stir in the sour cream and adjust the seasoning
to taste.

Steak Burger

serving

SERVING SIZE: 1 BURGER
COUNTS AS:
1 PROTEIN
1 VEGETABLE

ze according to plan

☼ Ingredients

Hamburger Patty (see recipe
on page 84)

1/4 cup (60ml / 18g) sliced
mushrooms

1/4 tsp garlic powder

green onions, sliced

2 tsp steak sauce

nonfat cooking spray

1. Coat small skillet with nonfat cooking spray.

2. Place mushrooms, garlic powder, pepper and onion in
skillet; sauté until vegetables are fully cooked.

3. Place vegetables on top of burger.

4. Drizzle steak sauce over burger and vegetables.

In House
❖ Steak
House

4 *servings*

- **SERVING SIZE: 1 CUP (250ML)**
- **COUNTS AS:**
  1 PROTEIN
  1 STARCH
  1 VEGETABLE
  1 FAT

▶ *size according to plan*

family fare

Savory Beef Stew

☀ Ingredients

24oz (672g) beef top round, cut into 1-inch cubes

1 green pepper, seeded and chopped

4 sweet chili peppers, seeded and chopped

1 small onion, chopped

4 garlic cloves, chopped

6 fresh cilantro leaves, chopped

2 Tbsp vinegar

2 cups (500ml) low-sodium beef broth, divided

1 cup (250ml) hot water

1/2 tsp dried oregano, crushed

1/2 cup (125ml) lite tomato sauce

2 bay leaves

1/2 pound (224g) carrots, peeled and chopped

1/2 pound (224g) potatoes, peeled and cubed

1/4 pound (112g) green peas

12 olives, stuffed with pimientos

1 Tbsp capers

1 In a Dutch oven, heat 1 Tbsp of broth.

2 Add the beef and stir constantly, until meat begins to brown.

3 Add the next 11 ingredients (through bay leaves); mix and bring to a boil. Reduce heat to low, cover and cook for 1 hour.

4 Add carrots, to Dutch oven and stir.

5 Bring back to a boil, reduce heat to low, cover and cook until the meat is fork tender.

6 Add potatoes, peas, olives and capers.

7 Mix well, bring to a boil, then reduce heat to low. Cover and cook until vegetables are tender.

In House
❖ Steak
House

servings

SERVING SIZE: 1 SERVING
COUNTS AS:
1 PROTEIN
1 VEGETABLE
1/2 DAIRY

ze according to plan

good source of calcium

Cheesy Beef & Broccoli

☀ Ingredients

1-1 1/2 pound (448 - 680g) ground lean sirloin, size according to plan

1/2 cup (125ml / 80g) raw white onions

4 garlic cloves, minced

2 cup (500ml /140g) raw broccoli florets

2 Tbsp white flour

2 cups (500ml) skim milk

2 tsp Worcestershire sauce

4oz (112g) reduced-fat sharp cheddar cheese

nonfat cooking spray

1. Coat large skillet with nonfat cooking spray and heat over high flame.

2. Sauté onions and garlic 1-2 minutes, or until onions begin to soften.

3. Add beef and sauté until beef begins to brown.

4. Add broccoli and reduce heat to medium. Continue to cook until broccoli begins to soften.

5. Place broccoli mixture in middle of chicken and roll up chicken.

6. While broccoli and beef are cooking, whisk together flour, milk and Worcestershire sauce in small bowl.

7. Once broccoli is cooked, pour flour mixture over beef and bring to a simmer.

8. Slowly sprinkle cheese over beef mixture and mix well. Once cheese is melted, turn off heat and allow to sit for 3 minutes before serving. Serve hot.

---

servings

SERVING SIZE: 3 OR 5OZ
COOKED BEEF (84 OR 140G),
AND 1 SLICE OF LITE BREAD
COUNTS AS:
1 PROTEIN
1 VEGETABLE
1 FAT

ze according to plan

family fare

Hot Beef Sandwich

☀ Ingredients

1 pound (448g) beef round steak, size according to plan

1/4 tsp garlic powder

1/4 tsp freshly ground pepper

1/4 tsp lite salt

1 tomato, diced

3 Tbsp dried onion

1/2 medium carrot, chopped

2 Tbsp low-sodium Worcestershire sauce

2 Tbsp vinegar

2 Tbsp brown sugar artificial sweetener

2 tsp chili powder

1 tsp dried oregano, crushed

2 garlic cloves, minced

1 bay leaf

4 slices lite bread

nonfat cooking spray

1. Cut meat into 5-6 pieces. Sprinkle beef with garlic powder, pepper and salt.

2. Coat Dutch oven with nonfat cooking spray. Add beef and brown on both sides.

3. Add tomato, onion, carrot, Worcestershire sauce, vinegar, brown sugar, chili powder, oregano, garlic and bay leaf. Bring to boil; reduce heat.

4. Cover; simmer for 1 hour, or until meat is very tender.

5. Remove meat and shred with a fork. Remove bay leaf from sauce.

6. Return meat to sauce and heat through. Serve hot over bread.

In House
❖ Steak
House

Beef & Mushroom Kabobs

1 *serving*

- **SERVING SIZE: 1 RECIPE**
- **COUNTS AS:**
  1 PROTEIN
  2 VEGETABLES

▶ *size according to plan*

☀ Ingredients

4 or 6oz (112 or 168g) beef round steak, size according to plan

2 large slices white onion

1/2 green pepper

1 cup (250ml / 70g) fresh mushrooms

2 Tbsp balsamic vinegar

1/4 tsp lite salt

1/4 tsp freshly ground pepper

1/2 tsp onion powder

1/2 tsp garlic powder

1/4 tsp paprika

1/4 tsp thyme

kabob skewers

1. If using wooden skewers, soak in warm water.
2. Cut steak into cubes.
3. Slice onions and peppers into 1-inch chunks.
4. Place beef, onion, pepper and mushrooms on skewers, alternating meat and vegetables.
5. Brush the kabobs with balsamic vinegar, set remaining vinegar aside.
6. In a small bowl, combine salt, pepper, onion powder, garlic powder, paprika and thyme.
7. Sprinkle spice mixture over kabobs.
8. Place kabobs and grill over medium heat. Cook approximately 4-5 minutes and then turn them over and cook additional 4-5 minutes. Baste with remaining vinegar halfway through cooking.
9. Serve immediately.

Hamburger

4 *servings*

- **SERVING SIZE: 4 OR 6OZ (112 OR 168G) RAW HAMBURGER PATTY**
- **COUNTS AS:**
  1 PROTEIN

▶ *size according to plan*

☀ Ingredients

1 pound (448g) lean ground sirloin

3 Tbsp dried onion

1/4 tsp garlic powder

1 Tbsp water

1/2 tsp lite salt

1/2 tsp freshly ground pepper

1. Mix all ingredients together. Form into patties.
2. Broil 3 inches from heat until desired doneness.
3. Place any uncooked burgers in freezer bags, seal well and freeze up to 3 months.

In House
♣ Steak
House

Philly Cheesesteak

servings

SERVING SIZE: 1 SANDWICH
COUNTS AS:
1 PROTEIN
2 STARCHES
1/2 DAIRY
1 FAT

ze according to plan

☀ Ingredients

1-1 1/2 pound (448 - 680g) beef sirloin, size according to plan

nonfat cooking spray

1/2 tsp salt

1/2 tsp freshly ground pepper

1/2 tsp onion powder

1/2 tsp garlic powder

1/2 tsp dried basil

1 onion, sliced

1 green bell pepper, sliced

four 6-inch hoagie rolls, split

4oz (112g) lite mozzarella cheese, sliced

1. Combine seasonings in a small bowl; rub mixture into sirloin.
2. Wrap in plastic or wax paper. Partially freeze beef sirloin for about 30-60 minutes.
3. Remove from freezer and thinly slice sirloin.
4. Coat large skillet with nonfat cooking spray. Heat skillet over medium flame. Add onion and green pepper; sauté until soft and lightly browned. Remove from pan.
5. Coat skillet again with spray. Increase flame to high; add beef and cook about 5 minutes, or until desired level of doneness.
6. Divide meat and vegetables evenly among the 4 rolls; top with cheese. If desired, place in a warm oven or under a broiler to melt the cheese before serving.

BBQ Cheddar Burger

serving

SERVING SIZE: 1 BURGER
COUNTS AS:
1 PROTEIN
1/2 DAIRY
1 VEGETABLE

ze according to plan

☀ Ingredients

Hamburger Patty (see recipe on page 84)

1 Tbsp barbeque sauce

2 slices red onion

1 leaf lettuce

1 slice tomato

1oz (28g) reduced-fat cheddar cheese

1. Spread barbeque sauce over burger.
2. Top burger with cheese and place on grill or under broiler to melt cheese.
3. Once cheese is melted, top with onion, lettuce and tomato; serve immediately.

In House
❀ Steak
House

Sultry
Poultry

If chicken and turkey are on the tip of your taste buds than you'll be delighted with all the sultry poultry recipes inside. Hot dishes, wraps, chili, whatever suits your mood. You'll find a simple recipe for simply delicious dishes like Baked Chicken Parmesan, Garlic Chicken, Lemon Herb Roasted Turkey and Rolled Turkey Divan. Plus you'll learn all of the latest trends and healthiest methods for preparing, storing and cooking poultry.

Marinated Chicken Kabobs recipe can be found on page 94

Chicken Cooking Techniques

Cuts of chicken

- **Whole Fryer** — whole chicken with skin and bones. Recommended cooking methods include oven roasting and braising.

- **Cut up Fryer** — whole chicken that has been separated into parts. Still contains skin and bones. Recommended cooking methods include oven roasting, braising, and grilling.

- **Wings** — Usually still contain both skin and bones. They can be grilled, oven roasted or braised.

- **Thighs** — Dark meat cut from the leg. Can be found with bone-in or boneless. May still have skin attached. Tastes great grilled, oven roasted or braised.

- **Drumstick** — Dark meat cut from the leg. Usually contains both skin and bones. Recommended cooking methods include oven roasting, braising and grilling.

- **Leg Quarters** — Contains dark meat from both thigh and drumstick. Tastes great grilled, oven roasted or braised.

- **Split Breast** — White meat cut. Usually contains skin and bones. Recommended cooking methods include oven roasting, braising and grilling.

- **Boneless Skinless Breast** — White meat cut. Easy to use in recipes. They can be pan seared, oven roasted or stir-fried.

- **Tenders** — White meat slices of boneless breast meat. Convenient to use. Great in stir fries. Can also be pan seared.

- **Chicken Cutlet** — A thin cut of meat. Often pounded to increase tenderness. Best preparation method is pan searing.

TIP!

Rubbing fresh herbs such as basil, oregano or parsley on chicken before cooking is great way to add a burst of flavor, without adding any extra calories.

Basic cooking methods

- **Braising** — Cooking with a moist heat. Great for less tender cuts of chicken. Meat may be browned first to seal in juices and flavor, a small amount of liquid such as chicken broth is then added to pan. Chicken is then cooked at a low heat for a lengthy period of time. This method produces a very tender chicken.

- **Oven Roasting** — Dry heat method. Chicken will have a well-browned exterior and a moist interior. Best used for larger quantities of meat such as a whole chicken. Chicken is cooked in the oven in an uncovered pan.

- **Grilling** — Preparing food on a grill over hot coals or other direct heat source.

- **Stir-Frying** — Quickly cooking food in a large pan or wok over very high heat. Food needs to be constantly stirred to prevent sticking.

- **Pan-Searing** — Uses high heat to create a crust and seal in meat juices. Cooking is usually finished in the oven.

TIP!

When preparing chicken, be sure to cook or freeze chicken by the "use-by" date. However, chicken should remain fresh for 2-3 days after the "sell-by" date.

Food Safety

It's important to know the food safety rules when preparing dishes for yourself and your family. In today's busy world we often find ourselves throwing meals together without truly preparing in a way that is healthy and safe. Here is a quick "at a glance" safe cooking guide, when cooking poultry.

- Keep raw chicken away from cooked and ready to eat foods.

- Use a separate cutting board for raw chicken. Use plastic cutting boards for raw meats and poultry.

- Never defrost chicken at room temperature. Thaw overnight in the refrigerator; under cold running water; or in the microwave.

- Cook chicken to an internal temperature of 165°F.

Roasting Times

To roast chicken, use 375°F oven. Cook breast side up uncovered.

- *1½ to 2 pounds: 45-60 minutes*
- *2 to 2½ pounds: 60-90 minutes*
- *2½ to 3 pounds: 1½ hour – 1¾ hours*
- *3 to 4 pounds: 1¾ – 2¾ hours*
- *4 + pounds: at least 3 hours*

Chicken is done cooking when it reaches an internal temperature of 165°F.

Sultry ❀
Poultry

Cuts of Turkey

Whole Turkey

Whole or Half Bone-In Breast

▶ Medallions/Tenderloins

Turkey Breast Steaks

Turkey Breast Cutlets

Turkey Beast Chops

Ground Turkey

Ground Turkey Breast

Thighs — Boneless or Bone-In

Legs/Drumsticks

Wings

Basic Cooking Methods

■ **Grilling** — This method is to cook on a rack directly over hot coals or other direct heat source. Grilling works well for turkey breast, tenderloins, ground turkey, turkey burgers, thighs, legs and wings.

■ **Broil** — To cook directly under heat source, usually in the oven under the top broiling element. This works well for turkey breast, tenderloins, ground turkey and turkey burgers.

■ **Braising** — Cooking with a moist heat. Meat may be browned first to seal in juices and flavor, then a small amount of liquid such as broth is added to the pan. The meat is then cooked at a low heat for a lengthy period of time. This works well for turkey breast, legs and wings.

■ **Oven Roasting** — This is the process of cooking meat, uncovered, on a rack in a shallow pan in the oven without adding liquids. This works well for whole turkeys, turkey breast, tenderloins, thighs, legs and wings.

■ **Stir-Frying** — Quickly cooking food in a large pan or wok over high heat. Food needs to be moved constantly to prevent sticking and promote even cooking. This is a great method for cooking turkey breast and tenderloins.

■ **Pan-Searing** — This method uses high heat to create a crust and seal in meat juices; cooking is usually then finished in the oven. Use this method for cooking turkey breast, tenderloins, ground turkey or thighs.

TIP!

Cranberry sauce, made with fresh cranberries, as opposed to pre-made sauce, is a great light side for turkey. You can go as light on the sugar as you'd like and keep the sauce tart and lo-cal.

Roasting Turkey
Pre-heat oven to 325°F

■ Unstuffed

Weight	Roasting Time
8 to 12 pounds	2-3/4 hours to 3 hours
12 to 14 pounds	3 hours to 3-3/4 hours
14 to 18 pounds	3-3/4 hours to 4-1/4 hours
18 to 20 pounds	4-1/4 to 4-1/2 hours
20 to 24 pounds	4-1/2 hours to 5 hours
24 to 30 pounds	5 hours to 5-1/4 hours

■ Stuffed

8 to 12 pounds	3 hours to 3-1/2 hours
12 to 14 pounds	3-1/2 hours to 4 hours
14 to 18 pounds	4 hours to 4-1/4 hours
18 to 20 pounds	4-1/4 hours to 4-3/4 hours
20 to 24 pounds	4-3/4 hours to 5-1/4 hours
24 to 30 pounds	5-1/4 hours to 6-1/4 hours

❖TIP!

Sweet potatoes are a tasty compliment to any turkey dish. When preparing sweet potatoes be sure in substitute whole milk with nonfat or low-fat milk, and try using maple syrup in place of melted butter. Your taste buds will never know the difference, but your waistline will!

Food Safety
Keep raw turkey away from cooked and ready to eat foods. Never defrost turkey at room temperature. Thaw overnight in the refrigerator, allowing approximately 24 hours for each 5 pounds; under cold running water allowing 30 minutes for each pound; or in the microwave. Cook whole turkeys to an internal temperature of 180°F in the thigh or 170°F in the breast.

Easy Steps for Carving
As friends and guests look on in anticipation, you can carve that picture-perfect turkey like a pro! Just follow these simple steps and you'll be have a perfect plate of turkey in no time.

1. Cut band of skin holding drumsticks. Grasp end of drumstick. Place knife between drumstick/thigh and body of the turkey and cut through skin to joint. Remove entire leg by pulling out and back, using the point of the knife to disjoin it. Separate the thigh and drumstick at the joint.

2. Insert fork in upper wing to steady turkey. Make a long horizontal cut above wing joint through to body frame. Wing may be disjointed from body, if desired.

3. Slice straight down with an even stroke, beginning halfway up the breast. When knife reaches the cut above the wing joint, slice will fall free.

4. Continue to slice breast meat, starting the cut at a higher point each time.

Poof! You'll have a perfectly carved turkey that everyone will enjoy. Don't forget to save the wishbone!

Sultry ❖ Poultry

Adobo Chicken

1 *serving*

- SERVING SIZE: 1 RECIPE
- COUNTS AS:
  1 PROTEIN

▶ *size according to plan*

✷ Ingredients

6 or 8oz (168 or 224g)
boneless-skinless, chicken
breast, size according to plan

1-2 garlic cloves, crushed

2 Tbsp low-sodium soy sauce

3/4 cup (200ml) water

1/4 cup (60ml) distilled vinegar

1/8 tsp freshly ground pepper

1 bay leaf

nonfat cooking spray

1 Rinse chicken; pat dry. Set aside.

2 In a medium pot, mix garlic, soy sauce, water, vinegar, freshly ground pepper and bay leaf.

3 In a skillet coated with nonfat cooking spray, sear chicken over medium high heat, approximately 3-4 minutes.

4 Add chicken to marinade.

5 Simmer over low heat for 20-25 minutes, or until chicken is cooked through.

6 Remove chicken from pot. Continue to cook sauce until slightly thick or desired consistency.

Roast Chicken

family fare

4 *servings*

- SERVING SIZE: 1 PORTION
  COOKED CHICKEN BREAST
- COUNTS AS:
  1 PROTEIN

▶ *size according to plan*

✷ Ingredients

whole chicken, skin removed

lite salt

freshly ground pepper, to taste

1 tsp dried thyme

1 tsp dried rosemary, crushed

nonfat cooking spray

1 Preheat oven to 350°F.

2 Rinse chicken, inside and out; pat dry.

3 Combine salt, freshly ground pepper, thyme and rosemary.

4 Rub chicken with herb mixture.

5 Place chicken in a roasting pan, with rack, coated with nonfat cooking spray. Place chicken on rack, breast side up.

6 Cook in 350°F oven and cook until done, or approximately 180°F, as measured by a meat thermometer when placed in the thigh.

7 Use the following roasting times:

- 3-4 pound (1.3-1.8kg) whole chicken for 1 1/4-1 1/2 hours.

- 5-7 pound (2.2-3.1kg) whole chicken for 2-2 1/4 hours.

- 6 or 8oz (168 or 224kg) bone-in breast halves for 30-40 minutes.

Sultry ❖
Poultry

serving

SERVING SIZE: 1 RECIPE
COUNTS AS:
1 PROTEIN
2 VEGETABLES

e according to plan

meals in minutes

Chicken Marsala

✳ Ingredients

6 or 8oz (168 or 224g) boneless-skinless, chicken breast, size according to plan

1 cup (250ml / 70g) fresh mushrooms

5 green onion, sliced

2 Tbsp water

1/8 tsp lite salt

1/4 cup (60ml) dry Marsala or cooking sherry

nonfat cooking spray

1 With meat mallet, pound chicken to 1/4-inch thickness.

2 Coat skillet with nonfat cooking spray. Preheat over medium heat. Add chicken to pan and cook until tender and no longer pink.

3 Remove chicken from pan and keep warm.

4 Add mushrooms, green onion, water and salt to skillet. Cook mushrooms until tender and most the liquid has evaporated. Add Marsala or cooking sherry to skillet. Heat through.

5 Top chicken with vegetables before serving.

Curried Stuffed Chicken Breast

serving

SERVING SIZE: 1 RECIPE
COUNTS AS:
1 PROTEIN
1 STARCH
2 VEGETABLES
1 FRUIT

e according to plan

✳ Ingredients

6 or 8oz (168 or 224g) boneless-skinless, chicken breast, size according to plan

1/2 medium carrot, shredded

5 green onions, sliced

1/2 tsp curry powder

1 slice lite bread, toasted and cubed

2 Tbsp raisins

1 Tbsp water

1/8 tsp lite salt

1/8 tsp paprika

1 In a small saucepan combine, 1 Tbsp water, carrot, green onion and curry powder. Cook until vegetables are tender.

2 Remove pan from heat; add bread cubes and raisins. Toss ingredients together to combine.

3 With meat mallet, pound chicken to 1/4-inch thickness. Sprinkle chicken with salt. Place chicken in a baking dish.

4 Place stuffing on one half of chicken breast; fold breast in half. Sprinkle with paprika. If needed, secure with a toothpick.

5 Bake in a 350°F oven for 20 minutes, or until chicken is no longer pink and juices run clear.

Sultry ❖ Poultry

Marinated Chicken Kabobs

1 *serving*

- **SERVING SIZE: 2-3 KABOBS**
- **COUNTS AS:**
  1 PROTEIN
  2 VEGETABLES

▶ *size according to plan*

☼ Ingredients

6 or 8oz (168 or 224g) boneless-skinless, chicken breast, size according to plan, cut into 1-inch cubes

2 Tbsp lemon juice

2 Tbsp water

1/2 tsp dried tarragon, crushed

1/8 tsp lite salt

1 clove garlic, minced

1 cup (250ml / 120g) zucchini, cut into 1-inch pieces

1/2 medium green pepper, cut into 1-inch pieces

1. For the marinade, combine lemon juice, water, tarragon, salt and garlic in a non-metal bowl. Add chicken cubes and toss to combine.

2. Place bowl in refrigerator and marinate for approximately 20 minutes.

3. Drain chicken; reserve marinade.

4. On skewers alternate chicken, zucchini and green pepper. Place on broiler pan.

5. Broil 4-5 inches from heat about 8-10 minutes or until chicken is tender and no longer pink. Brush chicken with marinade throughout cooking.

Italian-Style Chicken Tenders

2 *servings*

family fare

- **SERVING SIZE: 5 OR 7OZ (140 OR 196G) COOKED**
- **COUNTS AS:**
  1 PROTEIN
  1 STARCH

▶ *size according to plan*

☼ Ingredients

1 pound (448g) boneless chicken tenders

1 cup (250ml / 108g) breadcrumbs (see recipe on pg 154)

1/2 cup (125ml) egg substitute

1/2 tsp hot sauce (optional)

1 Tbsp water

nonfat cooking spray

1. In a small bowl, combine egg substitute, water and hot sauce.

2. Coat cooking sheet with nonfat cooking spray; preheat oven to 375°F.

3. Sprinkle 1/2 of the breadcrumbs on to a plate.

4. Drip each chicken tender in the egg mixture and then into breadcrumbs. Place on baking sheet.

5. Once all tenders have been breaded, coat them with nonfat cooking spray.

6. Bake at 375°F for approximately 10 minutes.

7. Remove from oven and turn over, coat again with cooking spray.

8. Place back in the oven and bake additional 10 minutes, or until crispy.

9. Serve over salad or with your favorite dipping sauce.

Sultry ✿
Poultry

Caraway Chicken

☀ Ingredients

6 or 8oz (168 or 224g) boneless-skinless, chicken breast, size according to plan

1/2 cup (125ml) low-sodium chicken broth

5 green onion, thinly sliced

1/2 tsp caraway seed, slightly crushed

freshly ground pepper

1/2 cup (125ml) skim milk

1 1/2 tsp cornstarch

nonfat cooking spray

1 Coat skillet with nonfat cooking spray. Add chicken and cook 10 minutes, turning to brown evenly.

2 Add broth, green onion, caraway seed and pepper. Bring to a boil; reduce heat.

3 Cover and simmer for 20-30 minutes or till chicken is no longer pink. Remove chicken from skillet; keep warm.

4 Stir milk and cornstarch together; add to skillet.

5 Stir while cooking until thickened.

6 Top chicken with sauce before serving.

7 Serving suggestion: serve over 1/3 cup (85ml / 12.5g) cooked noodles or 1/3 cup (85ml / 65g) cooked rice, count as 1 Starch.

Oven Fried Chicken

☀ Ingredients

6 or 8oz (168 or 224g) boneless-skinless, chicken breast, size according to plan

1/2 cup (125ml / 54g) breadcrumbs (see recipe on page 154)

1 Tbsp snipped fresh parsley

1/2 cup (125ml) nonfat plain yogurt

1 garlic clove, minced

2 tsp white wine or water

dash cayenne pepper

1 Combine breadcrumbs and parsley in a shallow bowl; set aside.

2 In a separate shallow bowl, combine yogurt, garlic, wine and red pepper.

3 Dip chicken into yogurt mixture, then coat with breadcrumbs.

4 Bake at 350°F in oven for 30-45 minutes, or until chicken is no longer pink and juices run clear.

Sultry ❧ Poultry

Indian-Style Chicken

1 *serving*

- **SERVING SIZE: 1 CHICKEN BREAST WITH RICE AND VEGETABLES**
- **COUNTS AS:**
  1 PROTEIN
  2 STARCHES
  2 VEGETABLES
  1 DAIRY

▶ *size according to plan*

☀ Ingredients

6 or 8oz (168 or 224g) boneless-skinless, chicken breast, size according to plan

2 garlic cloves, minced

1/3 cup (85ml / 65g) cooked brown rice

1 cup (250ml) plain nonfat yogurt

2 Tbsp flour

1 tsp ground cumin

1/4 tsp ground ginger

1 medium green pepper, chopped

1 small tomato, seeded and chopped

nonfat cooking spray

1 Coat skillet with nonfat cooking spray. Sauté onion and garlic. Stir in cooked rice.

2 Coat casserole dish with nonfat cooking spray. Spread rice mixture on bottom of casserole. Place chicken on top of rice.

3 In a bowl, mix together yogurt, flour, cumin and ginger. Stir in chopped green pepper. Spoon over chicken.

4 Cover and bake in a 350°F oven for 30-40 minutes, or until chicken is cooked through and no longer pink.

5 Add tomatoes before serving.

Orange Chicken with Carrots

1 *serving*

- **SERVING SIZE: 1 CHICKEN BREAST WITH VEGETABLES AND SAUCE**
- **COUNTS AS:**
  1 PROTEIN
  2 VEGETABLES
  1 FRUIT

▶ *size according to plan*

☀ Ingredients

6 or 8oz (168 or 224g) boneless-skinless, chicken breast, size according to plan

juice from 1 orange

1/4 tsp ground ginger

1/4 medium carrot, shredded

3 green onions, thinly sliced

2 Tbsp sherry

2 tsp cornstarch

1/2 cup (125ml) low-sodium chicken broth

1 In a bowl, mix together orange juice, sherry, cornstarch, broth and ginger. Set aside.

2 In a casserole, combine carrot and green onion. Arrange chicken on top of vegetables.

3 Pour orange juice mixture over chicken and vegetables.

4 Cover and bake in a 350°F oven for 30-40 minutes, or until chicken is cooked through.

Sultry ❧
Poultr

Vegetable Chicken Bake

serving

SERVING SIZE: 1 CHICKEN
BREAST WITH VEGETABLES
WITH SAUCE.
COUNTS AS:
1 PROTEIN
1 STARCH
2 VEGETABLES
1/2 DAIRY

ze according to plan

☀ Ingredients

6 or 8oz (168 or 224g) boneless-skinless, chicken breast, size according to plan, cut into cubes

1/2 cup (125ml) low-sodium chicken broth

1/2 cup (125ml / 55g) fresh green beans, cut into bite-size pieces

1/4 medium carrot, thinly sliced

1 large celery stalk, thinly sliced

1/4 tsp poultry seasoning

1/8 tsp lite salt

freshly ground pepper

2 Tbsp cornstarch

1/2 cup (125ml) skim milk

2 Tbsp white wine

1/3 cup (85ml / 36g) breadcrumbs (see recipe on page 154)

nonfat cooking spray

1 Coat skillet with nonfat cooking spray and sauté chicken until cooked through. Set aside.

2 In a saucepan, combine broth, green beans, carrot, celery, poultry seasoning, salt and pepper.

3 Bring to a boil; reduce heat. Cover and simmer for 5 minutes.

4 In a small bowl, mix cornstarch and milk.

5 Add milk to vegetable mixture. Cook until thickened.

6 Stir cooked chicken and wine into vegetable mixture.

7 Pour into a casserole. Sprinkle with breadcrumbs.

8 Bake, uncovered, in a 350°F oven for 15-20 minutes, or until heated through and bubbling.

Soy-Glazed Chicken

serving

SERVING SIZE: 1 CHICKEN
BREAST
COUNTS AS:
1 PROTEIN

ze according to plan

☀ Ingredients

6 or 8oz (168 or 224g) boneless-skinless, chicken breast, size according to plan

1/4 cup (60ml) white vinegar

2 Tbsp brown sugar artificial sweetener

2 Tbsp low-sodium soy sauce

2 garlic cloves, minced

1/4 tsp ground ginger

1/4 tsp onion powder

1 For marinade, mix together vinegar, brown sugar, soy sauce, garlic, ginger and onion powder. Add chicken and marinate in refrigerator for at least 20 minutes, but no longer than 24 hours.

2 Remove chicken and save marinade. Arrange chicken in baking dish and pour marinade over the chicken.

3 Bake, uncovered, at 350°F for 20 minutes, or until chicken is cooked through.

Sultry ❖ Poultry

Lemon Chicken

1 *serving*

- SERVING SIZE: 1 SERVING
- COUNTS AS:
  1 PROTEIN
  2 FRUITS

▶ *size according to plan*

☀ Ingredients

6 or 8oz (168 or 224g) boneless-skinless chicken breast

2 lemons

1/4 cup (60ml) low-sodium broth

2 tsp flour

1 packet artificial sweetener

1/4 tsp lite salt

1/4 tsp freshly ground pepper

1/4 tsp dried oregano

2 Tbsp dry white wine

1 garlic clove, minced

nonfat cooking spray

1. Slice lemons in half. Juice 3 of the lemon halves, set aside.

2. Zest the 3 lemon halves (that have been juiced already). You will need 1-2 tsp lemon zest, depending on taste.

3. Use a meat mallet to pound out chicken until approximately 1/4-inch thick.

4. Sprinkle chicken with salt, pepper, oregano and flour.

5. Coat large skillet with nonfat cooking spray.

6. Place chicken in pan, cook 1-2 minutes on each side on high heat.

7. Turn down heat to medium; add white wine, sweetener, lemon juice, garlic and broth.

8. Cook approx 5-10 minutes or until liquid reduces and forms thin syrup.

9. Add lemon zest and serve over rice or roasted vegetables.

10. Slice remaining lemon half and use as garnish. You may squeeze juice over chicken for additional lemon flavor.

Chicken Nuggets

1 *serving*

- SERVING SIZE: 1 CHICKEN BREAST, OR APPROXIMATELY 8 CHICKEN NUGGETS
- COUNTS AS:
  1 PROTEIN
  1 STARCH
  1/2 DAIRY

▶ *size according to plan*

☀ Ingredients

6 or 8oz (168 or 224g) boneless-skinless, chicken breast, size according to plan, cut into bite-size pieces

1/2 cup (125ml) nonfat buttermilk

1/2 cup (125ml / 54g) breadcrumbs (see recipe on page 154)

dash of lite salt

freshly ground pepper

1. Place chicken and buttermilk in a bowl and refrigerate for 20-30 minutes, allowing to marinade. Drain chicken and set aside.

2. Combine breadcrumbs and seasonings in a plastic, zip-top bag.

3. Add chicken to breadcrumbs and shake bag to coat chicken.

4. Bake in a 350°F oven for 20-30 minutes, or until cooked through.

Sultry ❀
Poultry

Sweet & Sour Chicken

1 *serving*

SERVING SIZE: RECIPE
COUNTS AS:
1 PROTEIN
2 VEGETABLE
1 FRUIT

ze according to plan

meals in minutes

☀ Ingredients

6 or 8oz (168 or 224g) boneless-skinless, chicken breast, size according to plan

3 green onions, thinly sliced

1/4 medium green pepper, cut into 1-inch pieces

2 Tbsp red wine vinegar

1 Tbsp cornstarch

3/4 cup (200ml / 147g) fresh pineapple, cut into 1-inch pieces

2 Tbsp brown sugar artificial sweetener

2 Tbsp ketchup

1/2 tomato, seeded and diced

1/2 cup (125ml) low-sodium chicken broth

1. Cut chicken into strips or 1-inch pieces.

2. Coat skillet or wok with nonfat cooking spray. Add onion and green pepper; stir-fry over medium heat until vegetables are crisp-tender. Remove and set aside.

3. Coat skillet or wok, again, with nonfat cooking spray. Add chicken pieces and stir-fry over medium heat until chicken is cooked through.

4. Mix vinegar, cornstarch, chicken broth, brown sugar and ketchup together.

5. Add sauce to skillet, or wok, with chicken. Cook, stirring constantly, until sauce thickens.

6. Return onion and green pepper to skillet or wok. Stir in pineapple chunks. Cover and cook 2 minutes, or until heated through. Stir in tomato just before serving.

Herbed Chicken Breast

1 *serving*

SERVING SIZE: 1 CHICKEN BREAST
COUNTS AS:
1 PROTEIN

ze according to plan

meals in minutes

☀ Ingredients

6 or 8oz (168 or 224g) boneless-skinless, chicken breast, size according to plan

1 Tbsp dried minced onion

1 clove garlic, crushed

1 Tbsp water

1/2 tsp dried thyme

1/4 tsp lite salt

freshly ground pepper

1/4 tsp dried rosemary

1/8 tsp rubbed sage

1/8 tsp dried marjoram

dash of hot sauce (optional)

nonfat cooking spray

1. In a bowl, combine minced onion, garlic, water, thyme, salt, pepper, rosemary, sage, marjoram and hot sauce.

2. Dip chicken in sauce, coating all sides.

3. Coat baking pan with nonfat cooking spray. Place chicken in pan.

4. Bake at 350°F oven for 20 minutes, or until chicken is cooked through.

Sultry Poultry

1 *serving*

- SERVING SIZE: 1 SERVING
- COUNTS AS:
  - 1/2 PROTEIN
  - 1 STARCH
  - 1 VEGETABLE
  - 1/2 DAIRY

▶ *size according to plan*

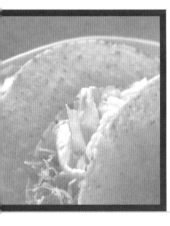

meals in minutes

Greek Chicken Pita

☼ Ingredients

3 or 4oz (84 or 112g) raw boneless-skinless chicken breast, size according to plan

4 inch whole wheat pita

1oz (28g) reduced-fat or lite feta cheese

2 tsp lemon juice

dash of oregano

1/4 tsp salt

freshly ground pepper

1 tsp fat-free Italian dressing

1/8 cucumber, sliced

1/2 tomato, diced

nonfat cooking spray

1 Cut chicken into cubes. With a fork, pierce each piece of chicken to tenderize.

2 In a medium bowl, combine lemon juice, dressing, salt, pepper and oregano. Add chicken to marinade and coat well.

3 Coat skillet with nonfat cooking spray and head over medium heat. Add chicken and cook approximately 5 minutes, or until chicken is no longer pink when cut.

4 Place chicken in pita and top with cheese, tomato and cucumber.

Creamy Chicken Casserole

1 *serving*

- SERVING SIZE: 1 SERVING
- COUNTS AS:
  - 1 PROTEIN
  - 1 STARCH
  - 1 VEGETABLE
  - 1 LA LITE

▶ *size according to plan*

☼ Ingredients

6 or 8oz (168 or 224g) boneless-skinless chicken breast; size according to plan

1 packet L A Lite Cream of Chicken soup mix

1 cup (250ml / 70g) raw white mushrooms, sliced

8oz (250ml) boiling water

2 green onions, sliced

1 garlic clove, minced

1/3 cup (85ml / 55g) cooked brown rice

nonfat cooking spray

1 Dice chicken breasts.

2 Coat medium skillet with nonfat cooking spray. Sauté mushrooms, onion and garlic 2-3 minutes over high heat. Set aside.

3 In a small casserole or baking dish, combine boiling water and L A Lite soup mix. Whisk together until smooth.

4 Add chicken, mushroom mixture and rice and mix well.

5 Cover casserole and place in 375°F preheated oven. Bake 15 minutes. Remove cover and bake additional 5-10 minutes, or until chicken is cooked through. Serve hot.

Sultry ✿
Poultry

Almond Chicken

servings

SERVING SIZE: 1/4 OF RECIPE
COUNTS AS:
1 PROTEIN
3 VEGETABLES
1 FAT

ze according to plan

family fare

☀ Ingredients

2 Tbsp almonds, chopped

24 or 32oz (670 or 900g) boneless-skinless chicken breast, size according to plan

3 celery stalks, diced

1 carrot, diced

1 cup (250ml / 120g) raw white onion, diced

2 cups (500ml / 68g) raw bean sprouts

2 cups (500ml) low-sodium broth

1 tsp ground ginger

1 Tbsp low-sodium soy sauce

4 garlic cloves, minced

nonfat cooking spray

1. Dice chicken into small cubes, set aside.

2. Spray large skillet with cooking spray. Add onion and cook 1-2 minutes; add carrots and celery and sauté over high heat 1-2 minutes.

3. Add chicken, garlic and ginger to pan and sauté over medium high heat, until chicken is no longer pink.

4. Add broth, bean sprouts and soy sauce and bring to boil.

5. Reduce heat and simmer.

6. Once liquid has evaporated and chicken is cooked through, add chopped almonds. Serve immediately.

BBQ Chicken Skewers

servings

SERVING SIZE:
1/4 OF RECIPE
COUNTS AS:
1 PROTEIN
1 VEGETABLE

ze according to plan

family fare

☀ Ingredients

24 or 32oz (670 or 900g) boneless-skinless chicken breast

1/4 cup (60ml) BBQ sauce

1-2 Tbsp hot sauce

2 Tbsp water

2 green peppers

4 packets brown sugar artificial sweetener

kabob skewers

1. Cut chicken into cubes.

2. In a small bowl, combine hot sauce, water, sugar substitute and half of the BBQ sauce.

3. Toss chicken in marinade to coat.

4. Cut green pepper in to 1-inch squares.

5. Alternate chicken and pepper on skewers; grill or cook in 400°F preheated oven.

6. While cooking, brush remaining BBQ sauce over skewers.

7. Cook approx 10-15 minutes, or until chicken is no longer pink.

Sultry ✤
Poultry

Cheese & Apple-Stuffed Chicken

1 *serving*

- **SERVING SIZE: 1 ROLLED CHICKEN BREAST AND SLICED APPLES**
- **COUNTS AS:**
  1 PROTEIN
  1 VEGETABLE
  1 FRUIT
  1/2 DAIRY

▶ *size according to plan*

☀ Ingredients

6 or 8oz (168 or 224g) boneless-skinless, chicken breast, size according to plan

1 small apple, divided

1oz (28g) reduced-fat mozzarella or cheddar cheese, shredded

5 green onions, sliced

1/4 cup (60ml) low-sodium chicken broth

1 tsp cornstarch

1 tsp water

1. With meat mallet pound chicken to 1/4-inch thickness.

2. Chop one half of the apple and set aside. Slice the other half.

3. Top chicken with chopped apple and cheese.

4. Roll-up chicken, folding in sides. Secure with toothpicks or string.

5. Arrange apple slices and green onion in a baking dish. Top with chicken.

6. Mix 1 teaspoon cold water and cornstarch; pour over rolled chicken breast and sliced apple.

7. Bake at 350°F for 20 minutes or until chicken is cooked through.

Chicken Caesar Wrap

1 *serving*

- **SERVING SIZE: 1 WRAP**
- **COUNTS AS:**
  1 PROTEIN
  2 STARCHES
  1 VEGETABLE

▶ *size according to plan*

☀ Ingredients

6 or 8oz (168 or 224g) boneless-skinless chicken breast, size according to plan

6-inch whole wheat flour tortilla

2 Tbsp fat-free Caesar dressing

1 tsp lemon juice

1/2 cup (125ml) romaine lettuce

1/4 small tomato, diced

2 green onions, diced

1/4 tsp freshly ground pepper

nonfat cooking spray

1. In a small bowl, combine 1 Tbsp Caesar dressing, pepper and lemon juice.

2. Cut chicken in to 1-inch cubes and place in dressing marinade. Allow to marinade 1 hour to overnight.

3. Remove chicken from marinade and place on baking sheet that has been coated with nonfat cooking spray.

4. Bake in 350°F preheated oven for 15 minutes, or until chicken is cooked through.

5. Cool chicken 5 minutes.

6. To make wrap, place chicken, lettuce, tomato and onion in middle of tortilla. Drizzle with remaining dressing. Roll up all ingredients.

Sultry ❖ Poultry

Chicken & Greenbean Casserole

serving

SERVING SIZE: 1 CASSEROLE
COUNTS AS:
1 PROTEIN
2 VEGETABLES
1/2 DAIRY
1 LA LITE

ze according to plan

☀ Ingredients

6 or 8oz (168 or 224g) boneless-skinless chicken breast, size according to plan

1 cup (250ml / 110g) fresh cut green beans

1/2 cup (125ml / 35g) fresh chopped mushrooms

3 green onions

1/4 tsp freshly ground pepper

1/4 tsp garlic powder

1 packet L A Lite Cream of Mushroom soup

3/4 cup (200ml) boiling water

1/2 cup (125ml) skim milk

1 Coat small casserole dish with nonfat cooking spray.

2 Use meat mallet to pound out chicken until approximately 1/4 inch thick.

3 Sprinkle chicken with pepper and garlic powder.

4 Combine boiling water and soup mix in casserole dish, mix well.

5 Add chopped mushrooms, cut green beans, chicken and milk to casserole dish.

6 Cover and place in preheated 375°F oven for 20 minutes.

7 Uncover and bake additional 10-15 minutes, or until chicken is no longer pink. Serve hot.

Chicken Cheesesteak

serving

SERVING SIZE: 1 SERVING
COUNTS AS:
1 PROTEIN
1 STARCH
1 VEGETABLE
1/2 DAIRY

ze according to plan

meals in minutes

☀ Ingredients

6 or 8oz (168 or 224g) ground white meat chicken breast, size according to plan

1oz (28g) reduced-fat provolone or mozzarella cheese

1/4 cup (125ml / 40g) raw white onions

1 Tbsp green pepper, chopped

1/4 tsp lite salt

1/4 tsp onion powder

4 inch whole wheat pita

nonfat cooking spray

1 Coat medium skillet with nonfat cooking spray.

2 Place onion and pepper in skillet and sauté over high heat 1 minute.

3 Add chicken, sprinkle with salt and onion powder.

4 Stir fry the chicken and vegetables until chicken is fully cooked.

5 Turn off heat, push all of the chicken to one side of skillet.

6 Place cheese over chicken meat and cover loosely with foil to melt.

7 Place chicken and cheese in pita. Serve hot.

Sultry ✿ Poultry

Buffalo Chicken Tenders

3 *servings*

- **SERVING SIZE: 5 OR 7OZ (140 OR 196G) COOKED**
- **COUNTS AS:**
  1 PROTEIN
  1 FAT

▶ *size according to plan*

family fare

☀ Ingredients

1-1 1/2 pound (448 - 680g) boneless chicken tenders

3 Tbsp lite margarine

1-2 Tbsp hot sauce

1/4 tsp garlic powder

1/8 tsp lemon juice

nonfat cooking spray

1 Melt margarine in small sauce pan.

2 Whisk in hot sauce, lemon juice and garlic powder.

3 Place chicken tenders on baking sheet that has been coated with nonfat cooking spray.

4 Drizzle hot sauce mixture over chicken. Toss chicken to coat well.

5 Bake at 375°F approx 15-20 minutes, or until chicken is cooked through.

6 Serve warm over salad with celery sticks and fat-free blue cheese dressing, if desired.

Spinach & Feta Stuffed Chicken

1 *serving*

- **SERVING SIZE: 1 SERVING**
- **COUNTS AS:**
  1 PROTEIN
  1/2 DAIRY

▶ *size according to plan*

good source of calcium

☀ Ingredients

6 or 8oz (168 or 224g) boneless-skinless chicken breast, size according to plan

1/4 cup (60ml / 7.5g) frozen chopped spinach, thawed and drained well

2 garlic cloves, minced

1oz (28g) reduced-fat feta cheese

1/4 tsp freshly ground pepper

nonfat cooking spray

1 Use meat mallet to pound chicken breast until 1/4-inch thick.

2 In small bowl combine spinach, feta and half of the garlic. Mix well.

3 Place chicken on piece of aluminum foil that has been coated with cooking spray. Sprinkle chicken with pepper.

4 Place spinach mixture in middle of chicken and roll up chicken.

5 Top chicken with remaining minced garlic.

6 Roll chicken in foil to help keep it together, place in refrigerator for 1 hour to set.

7 Preheat oven to 375°F.

8 Place chicken in the foil on baking sheet and bake 20 minutes.

9 Cut open top of foil and place back in oven for 5 minutes, to brown top of chicken and garlic.

10 Serve hot with your favorite roasted veggies.

Sultry ❖ Poultry

Broccoli & Cheddar Stuffed Chicken

serving

SERVING SIZE: 1 SERVING
COUNTS AS:
1 PROTEIN
1 VEGETABLE
1/2 DAIRY

ze according to plan

☀ Ingredients

6 or 8oz (168 or 224g) boneless-skinless chicken breast, size according to plan

1/4 cup (60ml / 46g) frozen chopped broccoli, thawed and drained well

1 Tbsp chopped red pepper

2 garlic cloves, minced

1oz (28g) reduced-fat cheddar cheese

1/4 tsp freshly ground pepper

nonfat cooking spray

1. Use meat mallet to pound chicken breast until 1/4-inch thick.

2. In a small bowl, combine broccoli, red pepper, cheddar and half of the garlic. Mix well.

3. Place chicken on piece of aluminum foil that has been coated with cooking spray.

4. Sprinkle chicken with pepper.

5. Place broccoli mixture in middle of chicken and roll up chicken.

6. Top chicken with remaining clove of minced garlic.

7. Roll chicken in foil to help keep it together, place in fridge for 1 hour to set.

8. Pre-heat oven to 375°F.

9. Place chicken inside the foil on baking sheet and bake 20 minutes.

10. Cut a slit in the top of foil packet and place back in oven for 5 minutes, to brown top of chicken and garlic.

11. Serve hot with your favorite roasted veggies.

Garlic Chicken

serving

meals in minutes

SERVING SIZE: 1 SERVING
COUNTS AS:
1 PROTEIN
1 VEGETABLE
1 FAT

ze according to plan

☀ Ingredients

6 or 8oz (168 or 224g) boneless chicken tenders

4 garlic cloves, slices

1/2 cup (125ml / 35g) fresh mushrooms, sliced

2 green onions, sliced

1 tsp olive oil

1/4 tsp garlic powder

1/4 tsp lemon juice

1 Tbsp dry white wine

1/2 tsp Italian herb blend (see recipe on pg 224)

nonfat cooking spray

1. With a fork, pierce each chicken tender to tenderize.

2. Sprinkle chicken with Italian herb blend.

3. Coat large skillet with nonfat cooking spray.

4. Place chicken, garlic, mushrooms, and onions in skillet; sauté 5 minutes or until chicken is cooked through.

5. Add lemon juice, garlic powder, and wine.

6. Continue to sauté chicken additional 5-10 minutes, or until chicken is no longer white inside.

7. Serve hot over rice or roasted veggies.

Sultry ✿
Poultry

4 *servings*

- SERVING SIZE: 1 SLICE
- COUNTS AS:
  - 1 PROTEIN
  - 1 STARCH

▶ *size according to plan*

family fare

Vegetable Chicken Loaf

☀ Ingredients

1-1 1/2 pound (448 - 680g) ground white meat chicken breast

1/4 cup (60ml / 30g) zucchini, finely chopped

1/4 cup (60ml / 18g) mushrooms, finely chopped

1/4 cup (60ml / 40g) chopped white onions

1/4 cup (60ml / 37g) green peppers, chopped

1/4 cup (60ml / 30g) chopped carrot

1/4 cup (60ml / 15g) parsley, chopped

1 Tbsp fresh basil, chopped

1 tsp garlic powder

1 tsp fresh thyme, chopped

1/4 cup (60ml) egg substitute

1/3 cup (85ml / 36g) breadcrumbs (see recipe on pg 154)

nonfat cooking spray

1 In a large mixing bowl, combine all ingredients. Mix well.

2 Coat loaf pan with nonfat cooking spray.

3 Spread meat mixture in to loaf pan.

4 Preheat oven to 375°F.

5 Bake 35-45 minutes, or until internal temperature is 165°F.

6 Remove from oven and cool 10 minutes before slicing.

---

1 *serving*

- SERVING SIZE: 1 WRAP
- COUNTS AS:
  - 1 PROTEIN
  - 1 STARCH
  - 1 FAT

▶ *size according to plan*

meals in minutes

Chicken & Avocado Wraps

☀ Ingredients

5 or 7oz (140 or 196g) plain, cooked chicken, size according to plan

2 Tbsp salsa

1/8 ripe avocado, peeled, pitted and chopped

1 Tbsp red onion, diced

1 1/2 tsp pepper sauce (optional)

1/2 whole wheat flour tortilla

1 In a bowl combine, chicken, salsa, avocado, red onion and pepper sauce.

2 Place chicken salad on tortilla and roll.

Sultry ❖
Poultry

White Chicken Chili

serving

SERVING SIZE: 1/2 RECIPE
COUNTS AS:
1 PROTEIN
1 STARCH
1 VEGETABLE

ze according to plan

family fare

☀ Ingredients

12 or 16oz (336 or 448g) ground white meat chicken breast

5 green onions, chopped

1/2 white onion, chopped

2 small tomatoes, chopped

1 cup (250ml / 70g) fresh mushroom slices

1/2 cup (125ml) dried cooked white beans

2 1/2 cups (625ml) low-sodium chicken broth

3 garlic cloves, minced

1-2 tsp chili powder, to taste

1/4 tsp lite salt

1/4 tsp ground cumin

1 tsp cilantro

dash of hot sauce

nonfat cooking spray

1. Coat large saucepan with nonfat cooking spray.

2. Add green and white onions and mushrooms to pan; sauté 2 minutes.

3. Add chicken, tomato, garlic, chili powder, salt, cilantro and cumin to pot. Cook until chicken is browned.

4. Add broth and beans. Bring to a boil, cover and reduce heat.

5. Simmer 30 minutes, or until reaches desired consistency. You may add a dash of hot sauce to reach your desired taste.

Sesame Chicken

serving

SERVING SIZE: 2-3 SKEWERS
COUNTS AS:
1 PROTEIN
1 FAT

ze according to plan

☀ Ingredients

6 or 8oz (168 or 224g) boneless-skinless, chicken breast, size according to plan, cut into strips

2 Tbsp low-sodium teriyaki sauce

1 Tbsp water

1 garlic clove, minced

1/8 tsp ground ginger

1 Tbsp sesame seeds, toasted

1. For marinade, combine teriyaki sauce, water, garlic and ginger.

2. Stir in chicken. Let marinate for 20 minutes.

3. Thread chicken, accordion-style, onto skewers.

4. Place on broiler pan. Broil 4-5 inches from heat for 3 minutes.

5. Turn over and broil another 3-4 minutes or until chicken is no longer pink.

6. Sprinkle with toasted sesame seeds.

Sultry ✤ Poultry

Curry Chicken

4 *servings*

- **SERVING SIZE: 1/4 RECIPE**
- **COUNTS AS:**
  - 1 PROTEIN
  - 1 STARCH
  - 2 VEGETABLES
  - 1 FAT

▶ *size according to plan*

family fare

☀ Ingredients

24 or 32oz (670 or 900g) boneless-skinless, chicken breast, size according to plan

1 lime, juiced

1/2 cup (125ml / 63g) flour

freshly ground pepper

2 Tbsp butter

5 green onions, chopped

1 Tbsp curry powder

garlic powder to taste

1 cup (250ml) low-sodium beef broth

1 small can low-sodium stewed tomatoes

2 Tbsp plain nonfat yogurt

1. Marinade chicken in lime juice, refrigerated, for approximately 20 minutes.
2. Season flour with pepper.
3. Lightly coat each piece of chicken in flour, shaking to remove excess.
4. In a nonstick skillet, sauté chopped onions in 1 Tbsp butter until golden. Remove and set aside.
5. Sauté chicken in remaining butter until brown.
6. Add sautéed onions, curry powder, garlic powder, consommé and stewed tomatoes to pan. Bring to a boil.
7. Cover and simmer on medium-low heat for 30 minutes, or until chicken is done. Season to taste.
8. Remove chicken from pan and stir yogurt into sauce.
9. Place chicken back in sauce.
10. Serve with rice if desired.

Honey Mustard Glazed Chicken

8 *servings*

- **SERVING SIZE: 5 OR 7OZ (140 OR 196G) COOKED**
- **COUNTS AS:**
  - 1 PROTEIN
  - 1 VEGETABLE

▶ *size according to plan*

family fare

☀ Ingredients

3-3 1/2 pounds (1.3-1.6kg) boneless skinless chicken breast

2 lemons

1/3 cup (85ml) chipotle pepper sauce

1/4 cup (60ml) honey mustard, fat-free or lite

1 packet artificial sweetener

1. Remove the rind from one of the lemons and chop finely.
2. Juice the lemons and marinate the chicken in the lemon juice and half of the chipotle pepper sauce.
3. In a glass bowl or zip-top bag, marinate for at least 1 hour or up to 2 hours.
4. Remove chicken from marinade; discard the marinade.
5. Make the glaze from remaining chipotle pepper sauce, artificial sweetener, honey mustard and lemon zest.
6. Grill over medium high heat, about 8 minutes per side, brushing with glaze towards the end of cooking.

Sultry ❖ Poultry

Jerk Chicken

servings

SERVING SIZE: 5 OR 7OZ (140 OR 196G) COOKED CHICKEN

COUNTS AS:

1 PROTEIN
2 VEGETABLES
1 FAT

e according to plan

☀ Ingredients

5 green onion, chopped

4 garlic cloves, chopped

4 fresh Scotch bonnet or Habanero chilies, seeded and chopped

2 Tbsp fresh lime juice

2 Tbsp fresh lemon juice

3 Tbsp olive oil

2 Tbsp low-sodium soy sauce

1 Tbsp brown sugar

1 Tbsp fresh thyme leaves

2 tsp ground allspice

2 tsp freshly ground pepper

3/4 tsp freshly grated nutmeg

1/2 tsp cinnamon

4 boneless-skinless, chicken breasts, each 6 or 8oz (168 or 224g), size according to plan

1 Place onion and garlic into a blender. Add chilies.

2 Squeeze in fresh lime juice, lemon juice, soy sauce, olive oil, brown sugar, thyme, allspice, pepper, nutmeg and cinnamon. Blend until marinade is smooth.

3 Using 2 separate zip-top plastic bags, pour in marinade, dividing evenly among the bags.

4 Divide the chicken between the bags and seal, pressing out any excess air.

5 Place bags into a shallow pan and into the refrigerator and marinate for 24 hours. Turn bags occasionally to evenly coat chicken with marinade.

6 Let chicken stand at room temperature for 10 minutes before cooking.

7 Preheat grill to medium temperature. Grill and cook chicken until browned on all sides. Then, lower the heat and cover until chicken is cooked through.

Chicken with Broccoli & Ziti

servings

SERVING SIZE: 5 OR 7OZ (140 OR 196G) COOKED

COUNTS AS:

1 PROTEIN
1 STARCH
2 VEGETABLES
1 FAT
1/2 DAIRY

ze according to plan

☀ Ingredients

6 or 8oz (168 or 224g) boneless-skinless, chicken breast, cubed, size according to plan

garlic powder

1/3 cup (85ml / 53g) cooked pasta

1 cup (250ml / 184g) cooked broccoli

1 tsp olive oil

1oz (28g) part-skim shredded mozzarella

nonfat cooking spray

1 Coat skillet with nonfat cooking spray. Season chicken with garlic powder.

2 Sauté chicken until cooked through.

3 Once chicken has been cooked, add broccoli and pasta.

4 Toss with oil and top with cheese, before serving.

Sultry ❖ Poultry

Chicken Normandy

1 *serving*

■ SERVING SIZE: 1/4 RECIPE
■ COUNTS AS:
  1 PROTEIN
  1 FRUIT
  1 DAIRY

▶ *size according to plan*

family fare

※ Ingredients

4 boneless-skinless, chicken breasts, 6 or 8oz each (168 or 224g), size according to plan

freshly ground pepper

2 medium granny smith apples, sliced

5 green onions and tops, sliced

2/3 cup (175ml) unsweetened apple juice

2 tsp low-sodium chicken bouillon crystals

1 1/2 tsp dried sage leaves

2/3 cup (175ml) fat-free half & half

2 tsp flour

1/4 cup (60ml) artificial sweetener

nonfat cooking spray

1 Coat large skillet with nonfat cooking spray; heat over medium-high flame. Sauté chicken breast until brown, 3-5 minutes on each side.

2 Season to taste with pepper.

3 Add apples, onions, apple juice, bouillon and sage to skillet; heat to boiling.

4 Reduce heat and simmer, covered, until chicken is tender, 10-12 minutes. Remove chicken and apples to serving platter. Cover loosely to keep warm.

5 Continue simmering juice mixture until reduced and almost completely evaporated.

6 Combine half & half and artificial sweetener in glass measuring cup; pour into skillet.

7 Heat to boiling; boil, stirring constantly, until thickened, about 1 minute.

8 Pour over chicken and apples.

Chicken Patties

3 *servings*

■ SERVING SIZE: 1 PATTY
■ COUNTS AS:
  1 PROTEIN
  1 STARCH

▶ *size according to plan*

※ Ingredients

1-1 1/2 pound (448 - 680g) ground white meat chicken breast

1 granny smith apple, chopped

5 green onions, chopped

1/3 cup (85ml / 36g) breadcrumbs (see recipe on pg 154)

1 tsp mint, chopped

2 Tbsp thyme, chopped

freshly ground pepper

1 Combine all the ingredients in large mixing bowl. Form into 3 patties.

2 For best results and taste place them in the refrigerator for about 30 minutes.

3 Cook in a skillet, heated over a medium flame, 5 minutes per side.

Sultry ❖ Poultry

Baked Chicken Parmesan

servings

family fare

SERVING SIZE: 1 CHICKEN BREAST
COUNTS AS:
1 PROTEIN
1 VEGETABLE
1/2 DAIRY

ze according to plan

☼ Ingredients

- 1 1/2 or 2 pounds (672 or 896g) boneless-skinless, chicken breast, size according to plan
- 1/4 cup (60ml) egg substitute
- 1/2 cup (125ml / 54g) breadcrumbs (see recipe on pg 154)
- 1 1/2 cups (375ml) lite tomato sauce
- 2oz (56g) part-skim mozzarella cheese, shredded
- 1/4 tsp basil
- 1/4 tsp garlic powder
- 1/4 tsp oregano

1. Rinse chicken breast and dip into the egg substitute.
2. Mix in another bowl the breadcrumbs, basil, oregano and garlic powder. Place next to egg substitute. Dip chicken from egg substitute into breadcrumbs and coat well.
3. Pour 1/2 cup tomato sauce on the bottom of a baking pan.
4. Place breaded chicken breast in pan.
5. Using the remaining sauce, cover each chicken breasts.
6. Evenly sprinkle the shredded cheese over each chicken breast.
7. Cover pan with aluminum foil.
8. Bake in preheated oven 375°F for 20 minutes.
9. Remove foil and continue baking for 10-15 minutes longer to allow cheese to melt and chicken is cooked through.
10. Serve with pasta or your favorite vegetable.

Lemon-Herb Marinated Chicken

serving

SERVING SIZE: 1 SERVING
COUNTS AS:
1 PROTEIN
1 FAT

ze according to plan

☼ Ingredients

- 1 Tbsp canola oil
- 1 Tbsp lemon juice
- 1/2 tsp rosemary
- 1/2 tsp lite salt
- 1/4 tsp freshly ground pepper
- 6 or 8oz (168 or 224g) boneless-skinless chicken, size according to plan

1. Mix oil, lemon juice, rosemary, pepper and salt.
2. Pour over chicken.
3. Allow to sit 30 minutes.
4. Remove from marinade.
5. Grill or broil.
6. Serve hot, garnish with fresh lemon slices.

Sultry ❖ Poultry

Ginger Chicken & Apricots

 8 *servings*

- **SERVING SIZE: 5 OR 7OZ (140 OR 196G) COOKED, AND 1/4 CUP (60ML) SAUCE**
- **COUNTS AS:**
  - 1 PROTEIN
  - 1 VEGETABLE
  - 1 FRUIT

▶ *size according to plan*

family fare

☀ Ingredients

- 3-3 1/2 pounds (1.3kg) boneless-skinless, chicken breast
- 1 tsp ground ginger
- 1 1/2 cups (375ml) dried apricots
- 1 1/2 cup (375ml) boiling water
- 1 Tbsp olive oil
- 1 Tbsp butter
- 5 green onions, finely chopped
- 1 1/2 tsp artificial sweetener
- 2 Tbsp finely grated ginger
- 1 cinnamon stick roughly separated
- 8 green cardamom pod, lightly crushed
- 1/4 tsp ground cloves
- 1/4 tsp freshly ground pepper
- 1 1/2 cups (375ml) low-sodium tomato juice
- 1/3 cup (85ml) finely chopped fresh coriander

1. Place chicken breast in a bowl; sprinkle ginger over chicken, rubbing well to coat pieces evenly.
2. Cover and refrigerate for 1-12 hours.
3. Meanwhile cover apricots with boiling water; let stand for 30 minutes.
4. In a large, deep skillet, heat oil over medium-high flame. Brown chicken on all sides; transfer to a plate.
5. Drain off any fat; reduce heat to medium.
6. Melt butter; stir in onion, artificial sweetener, ginger, cinnamon stick, cardamom, cloves and pepper. Cook, stirring often until tender and golden, about 8 minutes.
7. Stir in tomatoes, tomato juice, and apricots with their soaking water.
8. Bring to boil over high heat, stirring up brown bits; boil for 5 minutes or until tomatoes melt into the liquid.
9. Add the coriander.
10. Return chicken to pan and reduce heat to medium-low; cover and simmer, turning chicken once, until juices run clear when chicken is pierced, about 20 minutes.

Chicken Sun-dried Tomato Pesto

 4 *servings*

- **SERVING SIZE: 1 RECIPE**
- **COUNTS AS:**
  - 1 PROTEIN
  - 1 FAT
  - 2 VEGETABLES

▶ *size according to plan*

☀ Ingredients

- 4 skinless, boneless chicken breast halves, 6 or 8oz each, size according to plan
- freshly ground pepper
- 2 tsp olive oil
- 1 (14.5oz) can diced tomatoes with green peppers and onions
- 1/4 cup sun-dried tomato pesto
- 1 (14oz) can artichoke hearts in water, drained and quartered

1. Season both sides of chicken breasts with salt and pepper.
2. Heat oil in a large skillet over medium-high heat.
3. Place chicken in skillet; cook, turning once to brown each side. Remove chicken from pan, and set aside.
4. Pour tomatoes into pan; cook for 1 minute, stirring constantly.
5. Stir in pesto and artichokes, and return chicken to pan. Cover, and reduce heat to medium.
6. Simmer for 5-10 minutes, or until chicken is cooked through.

 Sultry ❈ Poultry

Turkey Kielbasa

SERVING SIZE: 1/6 OF RECIPE
COUNTS AS:
1 PROTEIN
1 STARCH
1 VEGETABLE

e according to plan

☀ Ingredients

1 bottle (12 oz) dark beer or ale

2 Tbsp Dijon-style mustard

1/2 tsp caraway seeds

6 cup coarsely shredded cabbage

1-1 1/2 lb turkey kielbasa or smoked turkey sausage (low-sodium), cut on the diagonal into 2-inch pieces

1 Granny Smith apple (or Braeburn or Winesap), cut into 1/4-inch wedges

1 can (16 oz) sweet potatoes, drained, cut into 1-1/2-inch cubes

1 In a large deep skillet over high heat, combine beer, mustard and caraway seeds. Bring to boil.

2 Add cabbage, reduce heat to medium-low and cover. Simmer 5 to 8 minutes or until cabbage is crisp-tender.

3 Add turkey kielbasa, apple and sweet potatoes.

4 Increase heat to high and bring mixture to boil.

5 Reduce heat to medium-low, cover and simmer 3 to 5 minutes or until apple is crisp-tender and all ingredients are hot.

Turkey Waldorf Sandwich

SERVING SIZE: 1 RECIPE
COUNTS AS:
1 PROTEIN
1 STARCH

e according to plan

☀ Ingredients

1 1/2 or 3oz cooked turkey breast, cubed, size according to plan

1/8 cup diced celery

1/4 small tart red apple, cored and cut into small cubes

1/2 Tbsp walnuts, chopped

1/4 Tbsp reduced-calorie mayonnaise

1/4 Tbsp nonfat yogurt, plain or vanilla

pinch of freshly grated nutmeg

pinch of ground cinnamon

1 lettuce leaf, washed, cleaned and crisp

2 slices reduced-calorie raisin bread

1 In medium bowl combine turkey, celery, apple, walnuts, mayonnaise, yogurt, nutmeg and cinnamon. Blend well.

2 Cover and refrigerate at least 1 hour to allow flavors to blend.

3 To serve, arrange a lettuce leaf on a bread slice. Spoon turkey mixture over lettuce leaf and top with another slice of bread.

Sultry ✣
Poultry

Lemon-Herb Roasted Turkey

 10 *servings*

■ SERVING SIZE: 4 OR 6OZ (112 OR 168G) COOKED SKINLESS TURKEY

■ COUNTS AS:
  1 PROTEIN

▸ *size according to plan*

Can make 10-20 servings (depending on size of turkey)

family fare

☀ Ingredients

1 12-14 pound (5-6kg) fresh or frozen turkey, thawed

nonfat cooking spray

1/3 cup (85ml / 11g) chopped fresh sage

1/3 cup (85ml / 9g) chopped fresh rosemary

1/3 cup (85ml / 20g) chopped fresh parsley

1 Tbsp lemon zest

3 Tbsp olive oil

1/2 cup (125ml) low-sodium chicken broth

1 tsp lite salt

3 Tbsp lemon juice

2 Tbsp honey, divided

2 lemons, quartered

1 Preheat oven to 325°F.

2 To prepare turkey, remove and discard giblets; rinse turkey inside and out with cold water, and pat dry.

3 Trim away any excess fat from the body. Starting around the neck, use your fingertips to loosen the skin of the bird from the flesh. Tuck wings under the body of the bird.

4 Place turkey on a broiler pan (or roasting pan with rack) coated with cooking spray. Combine sage, parsley, rosemary, lemon zest, olive oil and salt in a small bowl. Rub the herb mixture under the skin of the bird and along the cavity. Combine broth, lemon juice and honey; pour half of mixture over the turkey. Stuff cavity of bird with lemon pieces.

5 Insert an oven-safe meat thermometer into the meaty part of the thigh, making sure not to touch the bone. Roast in oven for approximately 3 hours or until thermometer registers 180°F.

6 Halfway through roasting pour remaining lemon juice mixture over turkey. Remove bird from oven, cover loosely with foil and let stand 15-20 minutes, before carving.

Turkey Meatballs

4 *servings*

■ SERVING SIZE: 4 or 6 MEATBALLS

■ COUNTS AS:
  1 PROTEIN
  1 VEGETABLE

▸ *size according to plan*

family fare

☀ Ingredients

1 pound (448g) raw ground turkey breast

1/4 cup (60ml / 27g) breadcrumbs (see recipe on page 154)

2 Tbsp egg substitute

2 tsp low-sodium Worcestershire sauce

1 cup low-sodium chicken broth

3 green onions, sliced

2 tsp garlic powder

1 In a bowl, combine breadcrumbs, garlic powder, onions and Worcestershire sauce. Add turkey and egg; mix well to combine all ingredients. Shape into 16 meatballs.

2 Coat baking dish with nonfat cooking spray. Arrange meatballs in a baking dish. Pour broth over meatballs. Bake in 350°F oven until no longer pink. Drain off any excess fat.

3 Serve meatballs over pasta for an additional starch serving.

Sultry Poultry

Rolled Turkey Divan

☀ Ingredients

5 or 7oz (140 or 196g) turkey breast tenderloin, size according to plan

1/2 cup (125ml) low-sodium chicken broth

1 cup (50ml / 70g) fresh mushrooms, sliced

1/2 cup (125ml) skim milk

2 Tbsp dry sherry

1/8 tsp ground nutmeg

dash of cayenne pepper

8 broccoli spears, cooked and drained

1 Tbsp cornstarch

1 Tbsp cold water

1 Tbsp parmesan cheese

nonfat cooking spray

1 Cut turkey into 2-4 equal portions. Place piece of turkey between 2 pieces of wax paper or plastic wrap. Working from center to the edges, pound the turkey lightly with a meat mallet until the tenderloin is 1/4 inch thick. Repeat with remaining turkey.

2 For sauce, whisk together chicken broth, milk, sherry, nutmeg, red pepper, cold water and cornstarch in a bowl; set aside.

3 Coat large skillet with nonfat cooking spray. Sauté mushrooms over medium heat until tender. Add to sauce mixture.

4 Divide broccoli among turkey slices, placing spears cross-wise near one end of each slice.

5 Spoon about 1 Tbsp of the sauce over each portion of broccoli. Roll turkey over broccoli and sauce. Secure with a toothpick, if necessary.

6 Coat baking dish with nonfat cooking spray. Arrange turkey rolls, seam side down, in baking dish. Pour remaining sauce over turkey rolls. Sprinkle with Parmesan cheese.

7 Bake, uncovered, in a 350°F oven for 30 minutes, or until turkey is no longer pink.

Turkey with Barbeque Sauce

☀ Ingredients

5 or 7oz (140 or 196g) fresh turkey breast tenderloin, size according to plan

2 Tbsp barbeque sauce

1 Tbsp water

1/2 packet artificial sweetener

1/2 tsp lemon juice

dash of garlic powder

1/8 tsp dried thyme, crushed

1 Place turkey breast in baking pan.

2 Combine barbeque sauce, water, lemon juice, artificial sweetener, garlic powder and thyme. Pour mixture over turkey. In a 350°F oven bake turkey approximately 20 minutes or until cooked through.

Sultry ❖ Poultry

Spinach Stuffed Turkey

4 *servings*

■ SERVING SIZE: 1/4 OF RECIPE
■ COUNTS AS:
  1 PROTEIN
  1 VEGETABLE
  1/2 DAIRY

▶ *size according to plan*

☀ Ingredients

2 garlic cloves, minced

1/2 cup (125ml / 80g) chopped onions

1 cup (250ml / 70g) button mushrooms, sliced

1 bag (10oz / 280g) baby spinach leaves

4oz (112g) reduced-fat shredded cheddar cheese

1-1 1/2 pound (448g) turkey breast cutlets size according to plan

dash of lite salt

freshly ground pepper

2 tsp butter

1 Tbsp flour

1/2 cup (125ml) low-sodium chicken broth

nonfat cooking spray

1 Coat skillet with nonfat. Heat over medium heat. Add garlic and onions; sauté 1-2 minutes, until tender.

2 Add mushrooms, tossing with other ingredients to combine; cook until mushrooms soften.

3 Next, add spinach and 1/2 cup (125ml) broth to pan; toss ingredients together to allow spinach to wilt and cook down. Remove from heat and allow to cool to room temperature.

4 Rinse off turkey cutlets and pat dry. Season with salt and pepper.

5 Divide spinach mixture evenly among turkey cutlets, forming a mound in the center of each cutlet. Sprinkle half of cheese over turkey. Gently roll turkey over spinach, securing with butcher's string or toothpicks, as needed.

6 Transfer stuffed turkey breasts to an oven safe skillet or sauté pan that has been sprayed with cooking spray.

7 Bake in a 350°F oven for approximately 15 minutes. Top with remaining cheese and cook until all cheese is melted.

Turkey á la King

1 *serving*

■ SERVING SIZE: 1 LOIN
■ COUNTS AS:
  1 PROTEIN
  2 VEGETABLES
  1 LA LITE

▶ *size according to plan*

meals in minutes

☀ Ingredients

5 or 7oz (140 or 196g) fresh turkey tenderloins, size according to plan

1/4 cup (60ml / 40g) frozen peas, thawed

1/2 cup (125ml / 35g) fresh mushrooms, sliced

1 green onion, sliced

1 packet L A Lite Cream of Mushroom soup mix

3/4 cup (200ml) boiling water

nonfat cooking spray

1 Chop turkey into 1-inch pieces.

2 Spray medium skillet with cooking spray.

3 Add onion, mushrooms, and turkey to skillet. Sauté 5 minutes.

4 Add peas and turn heat to low flame, continue to sauté until turkey is cooked through.

5 While turkey is cooking, combine boiling water and soup mix. Whisk together with a fork until smooth to make a gravy.

6 Turn off heat and pour gravy over turkey, stir to combine.

7 Serve over rice or vegetables.

Sultry ❋
Poultry

Mama Lou's Raspberry Turkey Delite

meals in minutes

1 serving

SERVING SIZE: 1 RECIPE
COUNTS AS:
1 PROTEIN
3 VEGETABLES
1 FRUIT (optional)

size according to plan

☀ Ingredients

1 cup (250ml / 70g) fresh mushroom slices

1/2 medium green pepper

5 green onions

5 or 7oz (140 or 196g) fresh ground turkey breast, size according to plan

3oz (90ml) white zinfandel wine (optional)

1 Tbsp fat-free raspberry vinaigrette

nonfat cooking spray

1. Coat pan with nonfat cooking spray.
2. Sauté mushrooms, green peppers and whole green onions; set aside.
3. Form turkey into patty.
4. Place turkey patty in skillet and brown on each side.
5. Return vegetables to pan.
6. Pour wine into pan, simmer another 5 minutes, or until turkey is cooked through.
7. Serve hot, drizzle with raspberry vinaigrette, before serving.

Sloppy Joe

family fare

1 servings

SERVING SIZE: 1/4 OF RECIPE
COUNTS AS:
1 PROTEIN
1 STARCH
1 VEGETABLE

size according to plan

☀ Ingredients

1-1 1/2 pound (448g) ground turkey breast, size according to plan

1/2 cup (125ml / 80g) diced white onion

1/2 cup (125ml / 74g) diced green pepper

2 small tomatoes, diced

2 Tbsp ketchup

1/2 tsp garlic powder

1/4 tsp paprika

2 tsp vinegar

1 packet artificial sweetener

1 tsp Worcestershire sauce

dash of hot sauce

dash of oregano

dash of red pepper flakes

4 slices lite bread

nonfat cooking spray

1. Coat Dutch oven with nonfat cooking spray. Brown ground turkey, onions and peppers. Add remaining ingredients.
2. Cook over low heat 10-15 minutes.
3. Serve over diet bread.

"So many recipes to choose from, something new every day."

- Morgan D.

Sultry ✿ Poultry

Vegetable Stuffed Turkey Roll

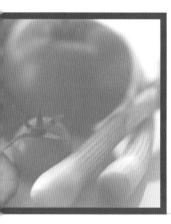

1 *serving*

- SERVING SIZE: 1 ENTRÉE
- COUNTS AS:
  1 PROTEIN
  1 STARCH
  2 VEGETABLES

▶ *size according to plan*

good source of fiber

☀ Ingredients

5 or 7oz (140 or 196g) turkey breast tenderloin

1/2 cup (125ml / 35g) mushrooms, sliced

1/4 medium carrot, shredded

1 rib celery, thinly sliced

2 Tbsp diced white onions

1/2 tsp dried thyme, crushed

1/2 tsp dried sage

1/4 tsp lite salt

freshly ground pepper

1 slice whole wheat lite bread, toasted and cubed

1-2 Tbsp water

nonfat cooking spray

1. Rinse turkey; pat dry. Place between 2 pieces of clear plastic wrap or wax paper. With a meat mallet, pound turkey to 1/2 inch thickness.

2. Coat skillet with nonfat cooking spray. Add mushrooms, carrot, celery, onion, thyme, sage, salt and pepper; cook over medium heat until tender.

3. Add bread cubes and toss lightly to mix. Stir in enough of water to moisten. Spoon stuffing over pounded turkey.

4. Roll turkey over stuffing, tucking ends under; secure with string or a toothpick. Place on a rack in a shallow baking pan.

5. Bake in a 350°F oven, covered loosely with foil, for 20-30 minutes. Remove foil. Bake 5-10 minutes more. Remove string. Let stand 10 minutes before slicing.

Open Faced Turkey Sandwich

1 *serving*

- SERVING SIZE: 1 SANDWICH
- COUNTS AS:
  1 PROTEIN
  1 STARCH
  1 VEGETABLE
  1 LA LITE

▶ *size according to plan*

☀ Ingredients

5 or 7oz (140 or 196g) fresh turkey tenderloins, size according to plan

1/4 tsp artificial flavoring

1/4 tsp freshly ground pepper

1/4 tsp onion powder

1/4 tsp garlic powder

1 slice whole wheat lite bread

1 packet L A Lite Cream of Chicken soup mix

3/4 cup (200ml) boiling water

1/2 cup (125ml / 63g) green beans, cooked

1. Coat large baking sheet with nonfat cooking spray.

2. Place turkey on sheet, sprinkle with onion, pepper, salt and garlic.

3. Place in preheated 375°F oven. Bake approximately 25 minutes, or until turkey is cooked through.

4. While turkey is cooking, combine boiling water and soup mix. Whisk together with a fork until smooth to make a gravy.

5. Remove turkey from oven and place on top of bread. Serve green beans on the side.

6. Top turkey and green beans with gravy.

Sultry ❖
Poultry

Turkey Chili

family fare

servings

SERVING SIZE: SERVING IS 1 1/2 CUPS (375ML)
COUNTS AS:
1 PROTEIN
3 VEGETABLES

ze according to plan

☼ Ingredients

1-1 1/2 pounds (448g) ground turkey breast, size according to plan

2 garlic cloves

1 1/2 cup (375ml) water

1 cup (250ml) low-sodium chicken broth

6 tomatoes, seeded and chopped

1/2 cup (125ml / 80g) raw white onions, chopped

1/2 cup (125ml / 128g) canned kidney beans, drained and rinsed

1/2 Tbsp chili powder

1/2 tsp cumin

1/2 tsp paprika

1/2 tsp lite salt

1/2 tsp freshly ground pepper

nonfat cooking spray

1. Heat a large sauce pan over medium flame, coated with nonfat cooking spray.
2. Add garlic and cook until golden brown.
3. Add turkey breast; drizzle with water. Brown turkey in pot.
4. Once turkey is brown, add in chopped vegetables, beans and spices.
5. Simmer over medium-low heat for 45 minutes.

"The chili recipe is my favorite...so tasty. Thought I would never be able to eat it again but L A Weight Loss proved me wrong."

- Gina H.

Basic Turkey Burger

serving

SERVING SIZE: 1 BURGER
COUNTS AS:
1 PROTEIN

ze according to plan

☼ Ingredients

5 or 7oz (140 or 196g) fresh ground turkey breast, size according to plan

freshly ground pepper

dash of onion powder

1/8 tsp sage

nonfat cooking spray

1. Combine turkey and spices.
2. Shape into a patty.
3. Coat skillet with nonfat cooking spray. Brown both sides of the patty; turn down heat to low and finish cooking until juices run clear.
4. This burger is also great on the grill!

119

Sultry ❖ Poultry

Pineapple-Sauced Duck Breast

6 *servings*

family fare

- SERVING SIZE: 2 OR 4OZ (56 OR 84G) COOKED DUCK WITH 2-3 TBSP SAUCE
- COUNTS AS:
  - 1 PROTEIN
  - 1 VEGETABLE
  - 1 FRUIT

▶ *size according to plan*

☀ Ingredients

2 cups (500ml) canned, crushed pineapple, with juice

1/4 cup (60ml) water

2oz (56g) dried cherries

1-2 packets artificial sweetener

2 Tbsp red onion, minced

2 Tbsp red bell pepper, diced

1 Tbsp minced fresh ginger

1-2 garlic cloves, minced

1/2 jalapeño, seeded and minced

12 or 20oz (336 or 560g) duck breast, skinned, size according to plan

1/2 tsp lite salt

1/2 tsp freshly ground pepper

2 green onions, sliced

2 Tbsp cilantro, chopped

nonfat cooking spray

1 In a small saucepan, combine pineapple in juice and next eight ingredients. Bring to a boil over medium-high heat; reduce heat. Simmer, uncovered, approximately 10-15 minutes, until slightly thickened and syrupy. Remove from heat and cool to room temperature.

2 Rinse duck breast and pat dry. Season with salt and pepper. Coat skillet with nonfat cooking spray; heat over medium flame.

3 Cook duck in skillet, about 4-6 minutes per side, or until cooked through. Remove from pan and let stand about 5 minutes, to allow juices to redistribute throughout the meat. Slice each breast into strips, or as desired.

4 Just before serving, add green onions and cilantro to pineapple sauce; stir to combine. Spoon sauce over duck slices.

California Turkey Burger

1 *serving*

- SERVING SIZE: 1 BURGER
- COUNTS AS:
  - 1 PROTEIN
  - 1 VEGETABLE
  - 1 FAT

▶ *size according to plan*

☀ Ingredients

cooked (see Basic Turkey Burger recipe on page 119)

2 Tbsp mashed avocado

1 Tbsp chopped green pepper

1 leaf lettuce

2 slices onion

1/8 cucumber, sliced

1 Spread avocado over turkey burger.

2 Sprinkle with chopped pepper.

3 Top with lettuce, cucumber and onion.

Sultry ❖
Poultry

Turkey - Broccoli Bake

SERVING SIZE: 1 RECIPE
COUNTS AS:
1 PROTEIN
1 STARCH
1 VEGETABLE
1 FAT
1/2 DAIRY

ze according to plan

good source of fiber

※ Ingredients

5 or 7oz (140 or 196g) fresh turkey tenderloins, size according to plan

1 cup (250ml / 184g) frozen chopped broccoli, thawed and drained

1 Tbsp margarine, melted

1 tsp garlic powder

1oz (28gm) reduced-fat shredded cheddar cheese

3 Melba toasts

nonfat cooking spray

1 Coat small casserole dish with nonfat cooking spray.

2 Chop turkey into 1-inch pieces.

3 Combine turkey, melted margarine, and broccoli in casserole dish and sprinkle with garlic powder.

4 Place in preheated 375°F oven and bake 25-30 minutes, or until turkey is just opaque.

5 While turkey is baking, crumble Melba toasts in to small bowl. Add cheese to Melba mixture and toss well to combine.

6 Remove turkey from oven, sprinkle Melba mixture over casserole.

7 Place back in oven and bake another 10-15 minutes, or until turkey is cooked through and cheese has melted.

8 Serve immediately.

Turkey Melt

SERVING SIZE: 1 SANDWICH
COUNTS AS:
1 PROTEIN
1 STARCH
1/2 DAIRY

ze according to plan

good source of calcium

※ Ingredients

2 slices light bread

1 Tbsp Dijon mustard

4 or 6oz (112 or 168g) cooked turkey breast, size according to plan, sliced

1 slice tomato

1oz (28g) reduced-fat swiss cheese

nonfat cooking spray

1 Spread mustard over bread.

2 Place turkey, tomato, and cheese on one piece of bread. Top with other slice.

3 Coat small skillet with nonfat cooking spray.

4 Place sandwich in skillet over medium heat, cook 2 minutes, or until cheese begins to melt.

5 Flip sandwich over and cook on second side until cheese melted.

6 Serve immediately.

Sultry ❖
Poultry

Roast Turkey with Cider

8 *servings approx 8-10*

■ SERVING SIZE: 4 OR 6OZ (112 OR 168G) COOKED TURKEY BREAST, SKIN REMOVED, 2 TBSP GRAVY, AND 1/4 CUP (60ML) OF STUFFING

■ COUNTS AS:
1 PROTEIN
1 STARCH
1 VEGETABLE

▶ *size according to plan*

☀ Ingredients

12 pound (5.4kg) oven-ready turkey

freshly ground pepper

5 yellow onions, cut into wedges

4 garlic cloves

1 1/2 cups (375ml) dry cider

1 Tbsp softened tub margarine

1 Tbsp flour

3 Tbsp fat-free half & half

Stuffing

1 Tbsp olive oil

10 green onions, chopped

2 garlic cloves, crushed

1 cooking apple, peeled, cored and chopped

1/2 cup (125ml / 54g) fresh breadcrumbs (see recipe on pg 154)

3oz (84g) dried prunes, chopped

2 Tbsp freshly chopped mint

1/4 cup (60ml) egg substitute

1 Preheat the oven to 375°F.

2 Rinse turkey inside and out; pat dry. Season the body cavity with pepper.

3 To make stuffing, heat olive oil in a pan over medium flame. Sauté the onion and garlic for 5 minutes or until softened.

4 Stir in the apple. Remove from the heat and add remaining stuffing ingredients, with seasoning to taste. Mix well to form a stiff consistency.

5 Stuff the neck cavity with prepared stuffing then fold the neck flap over and secure with skewers or trussing needle and twine.

6 Place the onion wedges and whole garlic cloves in the body cavity.

7 Weigh the turkey and calculate the cooking time allowing 18 minutes per pound (448g).

8 Place breast side down in the roasting pan; pour 1/2 cup (125ml) of the cider on top of the turkey. Place in the oven and roast for the calculated cooking time.

9 Twenty minutes before the end of the cooking time, turn the turkey over, pour over 1/2 cup (125ml) of the cider and continue to cook, loosely covered with aluminum foil.

10 Cook the turkey to an internal temperature of 180°F.

11 Remove from the oven, place turkey on a serving plate, loosely cover with aluminum foil and stand for 20 minutes before carving.

Gravy

1 Strain 1 cup (250ml) of the juices from the roasting pan into a saucepan and stir in the remaining cider, bring to a boil.

2 Cream the margarine with the flour, then gradually whisk into the cider mixture.

3 Cook for 2 minutes, adjust seasoning and stir in the fat-free half & half.

4 Heat gently for 1 minute; serve with the cooked turkey.

Sultry ✿ Poultry

servings

SERVING SIZE: 2 OR 4OZ
(56 OR 84G) COOKED DUCK
WITH 2-3 TBSP SAUCE
COUNTS AS:
1 PROTEIN
1 FRUIT

ze according to plan

family fare

Raspberry Glazed Duck

☀ Ingredients

12 or 20oz (336 or 560g) duck breast, skinned, size according to plan

1 tsp lite salt

2 tsp cinnamon

1/4 tsp ground ginger

2 packets artificial sweetener

1 Tbsp sugar

1/2 cup (125ml) red wine

3 Tbsp sugar-free raspberry jam

1/2 cup (125ml / 62g) fresh raspberries

nonfat cooking spray

1 Preheat broiler.

2 Coat large skillet with nonfat cooking spray and heat over medium-high flame.

3 Cook one side of duck breast until browned, about 5-10 minutes.

4 Meanwhile, while duck is cooking combine artificial sweetener, sugar, salt, ginger and cinnamon in small bowl.

5 Turn breasts over and cook other side until browned.

6 Remove duck from skillet. Sprinkle one side of duck with cinnamon mixture then set aside.

7 Combine red wine and jam in skillet and heat over medium heat, bring up to a low simmer and cook for 3 minutes. Add raspberries and cook 1 minute. Remove sauce from heat.

8 Place duck breasts in broiler pan and broil for about 2 minutes, or until cinnamon mixture begins to brown.

9 Remove duck from broiler and allow to rest 2-3 minutes. Slice thinly and top with sauce.

serving

SERVING SIZE: 1 BURGER
COUNTS AS:
1 PROTEIN
1 VEGETABLE
1/2 DAIRY

ze according to plan

good source of calcium

Spanish-Style Turkey Burger

☀ Ingredients

cooked "Basic Turkey Burger" (see recipe on page 119)

1/4 cup (60ml / 24g) chopped onions

1/4 cup (60ml / 37g) green peppers, chopped

1/2 tsp hot sauce

1 Tbsp salsa

1oz (28g) reduced-fat cheddar cheese

nonfat cooking spray

1 Spray small skillet with cooking spray.

2 Sauté onion, pepper and hot sauce, until vegetables are cooked.

3 Spread salsa over cooked turkey burger.

4 Top burger with vegetable mixture.

5 Place cheese over burger and melt under broiler.

6 Serve hot.

123

Sultry ✤
Poultry

Sassy Sides

A diverse collection of starches and side dishes can make the difference between a bland meal and a gourmet meal. You'll find plenty of ways in this section, to spruce up favorite sides such as potatoes, rice and mixed vegetables. Spicy Broccoli, Herbed Eggplant and Pineapple Stuffing are amongst the many fabulous recipes inside!

Stuffed Summer Squash recipe can be found on page 148

Storage Tips

- Root vegetables such as squashes and potatoes should be stored in a cool, well ventilated place at 50-60°F.

- Corn and peas should be stored in a ventilated container.

- Store dry ingredients such as rice and flours in a dry, cool storage area and in airtight containers once original packaging is opened.

Potatoes

- **Russet potatoes** — Also known as the Idaho potato, the russet is long and slightly rounded. The skin is brown and rough and has many eyes. These are best for baked potatoes and French fries because of their low moisture content and high starch content.

- **Round red potatoes** — These are also called boiling potatoes. They have a waxy flesh with less starch and more moisture than the russet, making them a good choice for boiling. These are also good for roasting, frying and mashing.

- **Yukon gold potatoes** — These have a golden skin and the flesh ranges from buttery yellow to golden brown. These boiling potatoes have a moist texture. Yukon gold potatoes are great for making mashed potatoes.

- **New potatoes** — These are young potatoes of any variety. Because they are younger than most potatoes, they have not converted all of their sugar into starch. This gives them a crisp and waxy texture and a very thin skin. They are small enough to be cooked whole; new potatoes can be oven roasted or boiled. New potatoes are also popular when making potato salad because they retain their shape better than an older potato.

- **Sweet potatoes** — This large edible root is not actually a potato; the texture is often moister than a regular potato and the flavor is sweeter. There are many varieties of sweet potatoes, each with their own distinctive flavor.

- **Yams** — Yams are not the same as a sweet potato, although canned sweet potatoes are commonly referred to as yams. They are similar in size and shape to sweet potatoes, but have more natural sugars and higher moisture content. Yams can be substituted for sweet potatoes in most recipes.

❖TIPS!

Steam vegetables in steaming rack or basket over 1-inch boiling water. Depending on size of vegetables, steam for 2 minutes or longer. Vegetables are best when they are still slightly crunchy.

Sassy
❖Sides

Rice

- **Arborio rice** — This is an Italian grown grain with a high starch content. The grains are shorter and fatter than other types of short-grain rice. It is typically used in risotto due to its increased starch content, which provides a creamy texture.

- **Basmati rice** — Basmati is a long-grained rice with a very fine texture. It has a nut-like flavor and aroma because it is aged to decrease the moisture content. It is often found in Indian and Middle Eastern markets and cooking.

- **Brown rice** — This rice refers to the entire grain of rice with only the inedible husk removed. The bran coating gives it a light brown color, nutty flavor and chewy texture, and provides a higher fiber content than white rice. Brown rice takes longer to cook than white rice, although some quick cooking brown rices have recently become available in the market.

- **Long-grain rice** — This rice has a length that is four to five times that of its width. Both white and brown rice come in long-grain varieties. When cooked, long-grain rice produces a light product that separate easily.

- **Medium-grain rice** — This rice is shorter and moister than long-grain and not as starchy as short-grain. Medium-grain rice is fluffy immediately after cooking, but clumps once it cools.

- **Short-grain rice** — This rice has a fat, almost round grain. The grains have high starch content and, when cooked, it is moist and sticky. This variety is sometimes called glutinous rice (although it is gluten free) and is often seen in Asian cooking.

- **White rice** — This variety has had the husk, bran and germ removed. It is lower in fiber than brown rice, which still has the bran and germ.

Vegetables

Fresh vegetables provide the diet with a variety of vitamins and minerals; they are low in fat and provide fiber. Many vegetables also contain antioxidants, which may protect against certain types of cancers and other disease. Portion sizes are, unless noted, 1/2 cup cooked or 1 cup raw. Water loss during cooking is due to heat breaking down the cell membranes, leaving a more concentrated food item; this is why cooked vegetables have a smaller portion size than raw vegetables.

Basic Cooking Methods

- **Steaming** — Cooking vegetables over boiling water. Steaming is a preferred cooking method for vegetables as it will help retain the vegetables flavor and color. Steaming also helps vegetables to retain many nutrients that may be lost when vegetables are boiled.

- **Sautéing** — Cooking vegetables quickly in a small amount of fat in a skillet over direct heat. This works well for fast cooking vegetables such as spinach and other greens.

- **Boiling** — Cooking in boiling water or other liquid.

- **Grilling** — Cooking over hot coals or other direct heat source. This works best for larger chunks of vegetables such as eggplant, zucchini, onions and sweet peppers.

- **Blanching** — To place vegetables into boiling water briefly, then place in cold water to stop the cooking process; this method is used to set color and flavor while keeping vegetables crisp.

- **Roasting** — This is a dry heat method most often done in the oven in an uncovered pan; vegetables are cooked at extremely high temperatures to develop the natural sweetness and flavors.

Sassy
❖ Sides

Cabbage with Apples

- SERVING SIZE: 1 RECIPE
- COUNTS AS:
  2 VEGETABLES
  1 FRUIT

▶ *size according to plan*

good source of fiber

☀ Ingredients

1 cup (250ml / 70g) cabbage, shredded

5 green onions, thinly sliced

1/4 cup (60ml) water

1 Tbsp lemon juice

1/4 cup (60ml) low-sodium chicken broth

1/4 tsp caraway seeds

1 small apple, cored and cut into bite-size pieces

1. In a saucepan, combine cabbage, onion, water, lemon juice, broth and caraway seeds.

2. Bring mixture to boiling; reduce heat. Cover and simmer for 7-8 minutes, or until cabbage is nearly tender.

3. Stir in apple. Cook for 2-3 minutes more, or until apple is tender.

Garlic & Pepper Stir-Fry

2 *servings*

- SERVING SIZE: 1/2 OF RECIPE
- COUNTS AS:
  3 VEGETABLES

▶ *size according to plan*

☀ Ingredients

2 garlic cloves, minced

1/2 medium carrot, sliced

1/2 medium green pepper, sliced

1/2 medium red pepper, sliced

1/2 medium yellow or orange pepper, sliced

5 green onions, sliced

1 cup (250ml / 70g) fresh mushrooms, sliced

1 tsp garlic powder (optional)

nonfat cooking spray

1. Preheat a wok or skillet over medium flame; coat with nonfat cooking spray. Add garlic and stir-fry for 1 minute.

2. Add carrot slices and stir-fry for 2 minutes. Add pepper strips and onion stir-fry for another 2 minutes.

3. Add mushrooms and garlic powder; stir-fry about 2 minutes more or until vegetables are crisp-tender.

> "I never really cooked until I bought the L A Weight Loss cookbook—now I love getting creative in the kitchen."
>
> *- B. Garvett*

Sassy
❖ Sides

Breaded Zucchini **Sticks**

2 servings

**SERVING SIZE: 1/2 OF RECIPE
COUNTS AS:**
1 STARCH
1 VEGETABLE

...ze according to plan

✳ Ingredients

2 cups (500ml / 226g) zucchini, cut
  into sticks

2/3 cup (175ml / 72g) breadcrumbs
  (see recipe on page 154)

dash of lite salt

freshly ground pepper

dash of seasoning blend

nonfat cooking spray

1 Combine breadcrumbs, pepper, salt and seasoning
   blend in small bowl.

2 Rinse off zucchini sticks in water and shake off excess
   water.

3 Roll in crumbs and place on a cookie sheet coated
   with nonfat cooking spray.

4 Bake at 375°F for 20 minutes, until lightly browned.

Twice Baked **Potatoes**

3 servings

**SERVING SIZE: 1/2 POTATO
COUNTS AS:**
1 STARCH
1 FAT
1/2 DAIRY

...ze according to plan

family fare

✳ Ingredients

4 small potatoes, baked

4oz (112g) shredded reduced-fat
  cheddar cheese

2 Tbsp skim milk

2 Tbsp low-fat sour cream

2 tsp garlic powder

1 Tbsp chives, diced

1 Preheat oven to 325°F.

2 Slice a small hole on the top of each baked potato.

3 Using a spoon, remove the flesh of the potato and
   place into a medium mixing bowl.

4 Add milk, sour cream, garlic and chives to potato
   mixture.

5 Stir until well blended and smooth.

6 Add cheese and combine.

7 Spoon potato mixture back into the potato skins.

8 Place stuffed potatoes on a baking sheet that has been
   coated with nonfat cooking spray.

9 Bake 12-15 minutes, or until top of potato filling starts
   to brown.

Sassy
❖ Sides

Pineapple Stuffing

4 *servings*

- **SERVING SIZE: 1/4 PAN**
- **COUNTS AS:**
  - 1 STARCH
  - 1 FRUIT
  - 1 FAT

▶ *size according to plan*

family fare

☀ Ingredients

4 slices of lite bread

2 cups (500ml / 390g) canned, crushed pineapple, drained

1/4 cup (60ml) egg substitute

1/2 tsp cinnamon

1/4 tsp ginger

1/4 cup (60ml) lite margarine

nonfat cooking spray

1. Preheat oven to 350°F.
2. Dice bread in to 1-inch cubes.
3. In medium bowl, mix bread and pineapple.
4. Add egg to moisten bread.
5. Mix in cinnamon and ginger.
6. Melt margarine in small microwave-safe bowl.
7. Pour half of the melted margarine over bread mixture and mix well.
8. Coat 8-inch square baking pan with nonfat cooking spray.
9. Spread bread mixture evenly in the pan.
10. Pour remaining margarine over stuffing.
11. Bake 15 minutes; center of the dish will be firm when done.

Spaghetti Squash Parmesan

1 *serving*

- **SERVING SIZE: 1 RECIPE**
- **COUNTS AS:**
  - 1 STARCH
  - 1 VEGETABLE

▶ *size according to plan*

☀ Ingredients

1/2 cup (125ml / 78g) cooked spaghetti squash

2 Tbsp lite tomato sauce

1 Tbsp parmesan cheese

1. Place squash on microwave safe plate.
2. Top with sauce and cheese.
3. Heat 1-2 minutes until sauce is hot.
4. Serve hot.

"I'm eating healthier, feeling energized and loving it!"

- Paula R.

Sassy
❖ Sides

Garlic **Grits**

3 *servings*

SERVING SIZE:
1/3 CUP (85ML) COOKED
COUNTS AS:
1 STARCH

ze according to plan

☀ Ingredients

3 1/2 cups (625ml) water

1/2 cup (125ml) skim milk

1/2 tsp lite salt

1 cup (250ml / 156g) quick
   cooking grits (not instant!)

1 tsp garlic powder

2 cloves roasted garlic, chopped

2 Tbsp lite margarine

1/4 cup (60ml) water

1 Combine water, milk, and salt in medium pot.
   Bring to a boil.

2 Stir in grits slowly. Bring back to a boil, stirring for
   1 minute.

3 Reduce heat to low. Add garlic powder, stir.

4 Cook, stirring occasionally, about 5-10 minutes.

5 Grits should have a thick, yet creamy texture.

6 More water may need to be added during cooking if
   grits appear too thick; try adding 1/4 cup (60ml) of
   water at a time.

7 Stir in margarine and roasted garlic just before serving.

Turnip **Casserole**

4 *servings*

SERVING SIZE:
1/2 CUP (125ML)
COUNTS AS:
1 VEGETABLE
1 FAT
1/2 DAIRY

ze according to plan

good source of fiber

☀ Ingredients

2 cups raw turnips

1 Tbsp lite margarine

1 tsp flour

1/4 cup (60ml) skim milk

1 tsp fat-free cream cheese

nonfat cooking spray

1 Preheat oven to 350°F.

2 Peel and chop turnips; boil in water until tender.
   Drain and set aside.

3 Coat small casserole dish with nonfat cooking spray.

4 In small saucepan, combine margarine, flour and skim
   milk. Cook, stirring constantly, until smooth, over
   medium heat.

5 Place turnips in casserole dish.

6 Put pieces of fat-free cream cheese over turnips.

7 Pour sauce over casserole.

8 Bake at 350°F for about 30-35 minutes or until
   browned.

Sassy
❖ Sides

Whole Wheat Rigatoni

3 *servings*

■ SERVING SIZE:
2/3 CUP (170ML)
■ COUNTS AS:
1 VEGETABLE
1 STARCH
1 FAT

▶ *size according to plan*

good source of fiber

☀ Ingredients

1 Tbsp lite margarine

2 garlic cloves, minced

1 cup (250ml / 56g) raw spinach

1/2 cup (125ml / 90g) cooked sliced artichoke hearts

1 cup (250ml /140g) cooked whole wheat rigatoni

1 Tbsp fat-free Italian dressing

2 Tbsp pine nuts

1 Tbsp parmesan cheese

1 Melt margarine in small saucepan. Add garlic and spinach; stir over low heat until spinach is wilted down.

2 Add artichokes, pasta and dressing. Mix well.

3 Sprinkle with pine nuts and cheese. Serve immediately.

Croutons

2 *servings*

■ SERVING SIZE: 1/2 OF RECIPE
■ COUNTS AS:
1 STARCH

▶ *size according to plan*

☀ Ingredients

2 slices lite bread

nonfat cooking spray

garlic powder, to taste

1/4 tsp lite salt

onion powder to taste

oregano to taste

1 Dice bread into 1-inch cubes.

2 Coat baking sheet with nonfat cooking spray. Place bread cubes on sheet.

3 Next, coat the bread cubes with cooking spray. Sprinkle with garlic powder, onion powder, oregano and salt.

4 Bake in 375°F oven for 6-8 minutes, or until bread is lightly browned and crisp.

Sassy
❖ Sides

Curried Rice

1 serving

SERVING SIZE: 1/3 CUP (85ML)
COUNTS AS:
1 STARCH
1 FAT

ze according to plan

☀ Ingredients

1 tsp dried minced onion

1/2 tsp curry powder

freshly ground pepper

1/3 cup (85ml / 53g) cooked
brown or white rice

1 Tbsp slivered almonds, chopped

2 pimiento-stuffed olives or ripe
olives, chopped (optional)

nonfat cooking spray

1. Coat small saucepan with nonfat cooking spray; add onion and sauté until soft.

2. Add curry powder and pepper; cook, stirring, for 30 seconds.

3. Stir in hot rice and almonds. Sprinkle with olives, if desired.

Noodles with Mushrooms

1 serving

SERVING SIZE: 1 RECIPE
COUNTS AS:
1 STARCH
1 VEGETABLE
1/2 DAIRY

ze according to plan

☀ Ingredients

1/3 cup (85ml / 46g) cooked
egg noodles

1 cup (250ml / 70g) fresh
mushrooms, sliced

1 Tbsp flour

1 Tbsp lemon juice

1 tsp lemon zest

1/2 cup (125ml) skim milk

1 Tbsp parsley, chopped

nonfat cooking spray

1. Coat skillet with nonfat cooking spray; add mushrooms and sauté until tender.

2. Stir in flour, lemon juice and lemon zest.

3. Gradually add milk. Heat to boiling, stirring constantly.

4. Cook approximately 5 minutes until slightly thickened.

5. Stir in noodles and parsley.

Sassy
❖ Sides

Cornbread

 12 *servings*

- **SERVING SIZE: 1/12th OF BREAD**
- **COUNTS AS:**
  - 1 STARCH
  - 1 FAT

▸ *size according to plan*

☀ Ingredients

1 cup (250ml / 122g) cornmeal

1/2 cup (125ml / 62g) all-purpose flour

2 tsp baking powder

2 tsp sugar

1 cup (250ml) skim milk

1/4 cup (60ml) egg substitute

3 Tbsp canola oil

nonfat cooking spray

1. Preheat oven to 425°F.
2. Coat 8-inch baking dish with nonfat cooking spray.
3. In medium bowl, combine cornmeal, flour, baking powder and sugar.
4. In separate bowl, combine milk, egg substitute and oil.
5. Add wet ingredients to dry ingredients, stirring, until just moistened.
6. Pour batter into prepared dish. Allow to rest 5 minutes before baking.
7. Bake about 15 minutes, or until lightly browned, and when a tooth pick is inserted into center comes out clean.
8. Cut into squares.

Zucchini-Tomato Bake

1 *serving*

- **SERVING SIZE: 1 RECIPE**
- **COUNTS AS:**
  - 2 VEGETABLES
  - 1/2 DAIRY

▸ *size according to plan*

☀ Ingredients

2 cups (500ml / 226g) zucchini, sliced

1/4 tsp lite salt

1 tsp Italian seasoning

1 small tomato, sliced

1 Tbsp water

1oz (28g) part-skim mozzarella cheese

nonfat cooking spray

1. Coat baking dish with nonfat cooking spray. Place zucchini slices in baking dish.
2. Sprinkle with salt and Italian seasoning.
3. Place tomato slices on top of zucchini. Sprinkle with water.
4. Cover and bake in 350°F oven for 10-15 minutes, or until tender.
5. Remove from oven and sprinkle with cheese. Bake uncovered 5-10 minutes, or until cheese is melted.

Sassy ❖ Sides

Ratatouille

servings

SERVING SIZE: 1/2 OF RECIPE
COUNTS AS:
2 VEGETABLES
1 FAT

ze according to plan

☀ Ingredients

1 cup (250ml / 82g) diced eggplant

1 cup (250ml / 113g) sliced zucchini

1/2 medium green pepper, chopped

1 small tomato

2 Tbsp lite margarine

1/4 tsp lite salt

1/4 tsp freshly ground pepper

1 garlic clove, crushed

1. Melt margarine in a large skillet.
2. Add garlic and sauté until tender.
3. Add remaining ingredients.
4. Cover and cook over medium heat, stirring occasionally, about 5 minutes.

Pickles

servings

SERVING SIZE: 1/2 CUCUMBER
COUNTS AS:
2 VEGETABLES

ze according to plan

☀ Ingredients

2 medium cucumbers, sliced or quartered

1/2 cup (125ml) water

1/2 cup (125ml) vinegar

1/4 tsp dill

dash garlic powder

1. Combine cucumbers, water and vinegar in a sealable container.
2. Add dill and garlic powder. Toss to coat.
3. Let stand at least 2 hours before serving.

"My husband uses the cookbook more than I do. He actually started losing weight without even trying."

- Rosie M.

Sassy
♣ Sides

Stir-Fried Oriental Style Vegetables

2 *servings*

- SERVING SIZE: 1/2 OF RECIPE
- COUNTS AS:
  2 VEGETABLES

▶ *size according to plan*

☀ Ingredients

1 Tbsp brown sugar artificial sweetener

1 Tbsp reduced-sodium soy sauce

1 Tbsp vinegar

1 tsp grated fresh ginger

2 green onions, sliced

1 tsp garlic powder

1/2 cup (125ml / 35g) fresh mushrooms, sliced

1 cup (250ml / 70g) cabbage, shredded

1/2 medium green pepper, sliced

1/2 medium red pepper, sliced

1/2 cup (125ml / 16g) fresh bean sprouts

nonfat cooking spray

1. To make sauce, stir together artificial sweetener, soy sauce and vinegar. Set aside.

2. Coat a wok or skillet with nonfat cooking spray. Preheat skillet over medium-high flame. Stir-fry ginger for 30 seconds.

3. Add onions and garlic powder and stir fry for 1 minute. Add cabbage and stir-fry for 2 minutes. Add peppers and bean sprouts; stir-fry for another minute, or until vegetables are crisp-tender.

4. Pour sauce over vegetables and toss to coat all vegetables.

Cauliflower with Cheese

1 *serving*

- SERVING SIZE:
  1/2 CUP COOKED
- COUNTS AS:
  1 VEGETABLE
  1 DAIRY

▶ *size according to plan*

good source of calcium

☀ Ingredients

1 cup (250ml / 100g) raw cauliflower florets

1/4 cup (60ml) water

1oz (28g) low-fat cheddar cheese, shredded

1/2 cup (125ml) skim milk

1 drop red pepper sauce, if desired

1. Place cauliflower in a microwave safe dish. Pour water over cauliflower. Heat on high for 3-5 minutes or until tender. Drain and set aside.

2. In saucepan, heat remaining ingredients over medium heat, stirring frequently, until cheese is melted and mixture is smooth.

3. Pour over cauliflower before serving.

Sassy
❖ Sides

Sherried Mushrooms

serving

SERVING SIZE: 1 RECIPE
COUNTS AS:
2 VEGETABLES

ze according to plan

✳ Ingredients

1 cup (250ml / 70g) fresh whole
  mushrooms

1 green onion, chopped

1/4 cup (60ml) low-sodium broth

pinch dried tarragon, crushed

1 Tbsp dry sherry

1 tsp cornstarch

1. Gently clean mushrooms with a damp paper towel or soft brush.

2. In a medium skillet, combine mushrooms, onion, broth and tarragon. Bring to boil; reduce heat and cover. Simmer for 10-12 minutes, or until mushrooms are just tender.

3. In a small bowl, whisk together sherry and cornstarch until smooth; stir into skillet.

4. Cook, stirring, until slightly thickened and bubbly. Continue to cook another 2 minutes before serving.

Zucchini & Peppers

serving

SERVING SIZE: 1 RECIPE
COUNTS AS:
3 VEGETABLES
1 FAT

ze according to plan

✳ Ingredients

1 cup (250ml / 113g) zucchini,
  sliced

1/2 medium green pepper,
  chopped

1 garlic clove, crushed

1/4 tsp lite salt

1/8 tsp freshly ground pepper

1 tomato, cut into wedges

1 Tbsp lite margarine

nonfat cooking spray

1. Coat large skillet with nonfat cooking spray. Add zucchini, pepper, garlic, salt and pepper.

2. Cover and cook over medium heat, stirring occasionally, until vegetables are crisp-tender, about 5 minutes.

3. Add tomato. Cover again and cook over low heat just until tomato is heated through, about 3 minutes. Add margarine and heat until melted.

Sassy
❖ Sides

Stewed Tomatoes

4 *servings*

- SERVING SIZE: 1/4 OF RECIPE
- COUNTS AS:
  1 VEGETABLE

▶ *size according to plan*

✳ Ingredients

4 tomatoes, chopped

5 green onions, finely chopped

1/2 medium green pepper, chopped

1 packet artificial sweetener

1/2 tsp lite salt

freshly ground pepper

1 tsp garlic powder

1/4 tsp oregano

1. Combine all ingredients in medium saucepan.

2. Cover and heat to boiling; reduce heat.

3. Simmer, uncovered, 10-15 minutes.

Corn O'Brien

2 *servings*

- SERVING SIZE: 1/2 OF RECIPE
- COUNTS AS:
  1 STARCH
  1 VEGETABLE

▶ *size according to plan*

✳ Ingredients

1 cup (250ml / 164g) frozen, whole kernel corn

1 large celery stalk, diced

1/4 tsp crushed red pepper

1/2 medium green pepper, diced

nonfat cooking spray

1. Cook corn by steaming or microwaving.

2. Coat skillet with nonfat cooking spray. Add celery, crushed red pepper and green pepper; sauté until tender.

3. Add corn. Cook over low heat, stirring occasionally, until corn is heated through.

Sassy
❖ Sides

Classic Mashed Potatoes

servings

SERVING SIZE: 1/2 CUP (12ML)
COUNTS AS:
1 STARCH

ze according to plan

☀ Ingredients

3 small potatoes, cooked

1/4 cup (60ml) milk

2 Tbsp lite margarine,
melted

1/2 tsp lite salt

1/2 tsp garlic powder

freshly ground pepper

1 Remove skin from potatoes.

2 Chop potatoes into a large dice and place in large mixing bowl.

3 Add milk, melted margarine, salt, garlic powder and pepper.
For creamy potatoes: Mix using electric mixer 1-2 minutes.
For chunky potatoes: Use a masher to soften potatoes, mix well until all ingredients are combined.

Peas & Mushrooms

servings

SERVING SIZE:
1/2 OF RECIPE
COUNTS AS:
1 STARCH
1 VEGETABLE

ze according to plan

good source of fiber

☀ Ingredients

1 cup (250ml / 70g) mushrooms,
sliced

2 green onions, chopped

1/4 tsp lite soup

1/2 tsp garlic powder

1/8 tsp freshly ground pepper

1 cup (250ml / 144g) frozen peas,
thawed

nonfat cooking spray

1 Coat skillet with nonfat cooking spray and heat over medium flame. Add mushrooms, onions, garlic powder, salt and pepper. Sauté until mushrooms are tender.

2 Add peas to skillet and heat through.

3 Heat well.

4 Season with hot pepper sauce (optional).

"With 'No-Fuss' foods, I'm eating healthier and liking it!"

- Paula R.

Sassy
❖Sides

Garlic n' Herb Pita Chips

2 *servings*

- SERVING SIZE: 8 CHIPS EACH
- COUNTS AS:
  1 STARCH

▸ *size according to plan*

meals in minutes

✹ Ingredients

6-inch whole wheat pita

nonfat cooking spray

1 tsp garlic powder

1/4 tsp lite salt

oregano or thyme, sprinkle to taste

1 Cut pita in to 8 small pieces; separate layers into 16 wedges.

2 Preheat oven to 375°F.

3 Spray cookie sheet, place pitas on sheet.

4 Spray pieces with nonfat cooking spray.

5 Sprinkle with garlic powder, salt and herbs, as desired.

6 Bake for 5 minutes, or until lightly browned.

7 Serve with dip or salsa.

Grilled Corn on the Cob

6 *servings*

- SERVING SIZE: 1 EAR
- COUNTS AS:
  1 STARCH

▸ *size according to plan*

family fare

✹ Ingredients

6 ears of corn

6 tsp lite margarine

lite salt to taste

freshly ground pepper

1 Peel corn, remove silk, wash well and pat dry.

2 Preheat grill to medium.

3 Place each piece of corn on individual piece of aluminum foil.

4 Spread 1 tsp of softened lite margarine over each piece of corn.

5 Sprinkle lightly with salt and pepper.

6 Wrap each piece of corn tightly in aluminum foil.

7 Place on grill; cook approximately 25 minutes, turning occasionally until corn is tender.

Sassy
❖ Sides

Italian-Style Beans

good source of fiber

☀ Ingredients

1 cup (250ml / 110g) fresh green beans

2 Tbsp fat-free Italian dressing

1/2 tomato, chopped

1 Tbsp grated parmesan cheese

1 Place green beans, dressing and tomato in small saucepan.

2 Cook, uncovered, over low heat until heated through.

3 Remove from heat. Sprinkle with parmesan cheese just before serving.

Broccoli with Cheese

good source of calcium

☀ Ingredients

1 cup (250ml / 70g) raw broccoli florets

1/4 cup (60ml) water

1oz (28g) low-fat cheddar cheese, shredded

1/2 cup (125ml) skim milk

1 drop red pepper sauce, if desired

1 Place broccoli in microwave safe dish. Pour water over broccoli. Heat on high for 3-5 minutes or until tender. Drain and set aside.

2 In saucepan, heat remaining ingredients over medium heat, stirring frequently, until cheese is melted and mixture is smooth.

3 Pour over broccoli. Serve immediately.

Sassy
❖ Sides

Creamy Cucumbers

2 *servings*

- **SERVING SIZE:**
  1/2 OF RECIPE
- **COUNTS AS:**
  3 VEGETABLES
  1/2 DAIRY

▸ *size according to plan*

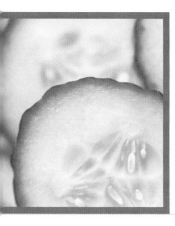

good source of calcium

☀ Ingredients

6 slices low-sodium turkey bacon

1 cup (250ml / 160g) onions, chopped

1 pound (448g) potato, thin-skinned, cut into 1/2-inch cubes

2 1/2 cups (625ml) low-sodium chicken broth

3 Tbsp flour

2 1/2 cups (625ml) skim milk

1/2 tsp freshly ground pepper

1/4 cup (60ml / 15g) chopped fresh parsley sprigs

nonfat cooking spray

1 In a small saucepan coated with nonfat cooking spray, add shrimp, onion, pepper and garlic. Sauté until seafood is cooked.

2 Add soup mix, milk and half & half; stir until smooth.

3 Heat well.

4 Season with hot pepper sauce (optional).

Spanish Rice

4 *servings*

- **SERVING SIZE:**
  1/2 CUP (125ML)
- **COUNTS AS:**
  1 STARCH
  1 VEGETABLE
  1/2 DAIRY

▸ *size according to plan*

family fare

☀ Ingredients

1 1/3 cup (330ml) water

1/2 medium green pepper, diced

1/2 cup (125ml / 80g) white or yellow onion, diced

1/2 celery stalk, diced

1/4 tsp of lite salt

2 small tomatoes, chopped

2/3 cup (170ml / 126g) raw brown or white rice

1/4 tsp chili powder

freshly ground pepper

dash of hot sauce

1 In a medium saucepan, combine water, green pepper, onion, celery and salt. Bring to a boil. Then reduce heat and cover. Simmer for 5 minutes.

2 Stir in tomatoes, rice, chili powder, pepper and hot sauce. Return to boil. Reduce heat to low; cover and simmer approximately 20 minutes, or until liquid is absorbed.

"This is a fantastic side dish with a turkey burger. Better than instant rice."

- Michele G.

Sassy
❖ Sides

Balsamic-Glazed Vegetables

servings

SERVING SIZE:
1/2 CUP (125ML) COOKED
COUNTS AS:
2 VEGETABLES

e according to plan

☀ Ingredients

1 1/2 pounds (672g) of your choice baby carrots, yellow squash, broccoli, cauliflower, zucchini

1/2 cup (125ml) water

1/2 cup (125ml) balsamic vinegar

1 tsp garlic or onion powder

1 Tbsp butter

freshly ground pepper

chopped parsley leaves, for garnish

1 Place vegetables in a pan with water, garlic or onion powder and vinegar.

2 Bring to a boil and cover. Reduce heat to medium and cook 10 minutes. Remove lid and raise heat back up.

3 Allow the water to boil away and the vinegar to reduce and glaze the vegetables, about 5 minutes.

4 When the vegetables are glazed, to a rich brown color add the butter to the pan.

5 Turn vegetables to coat lightly with butter.

6 Season with black pepper. Garnish with parsley.

Creamed Spinach

good source of fiber

servings

SERVING SIZE:
1/2 CUP (125ML)
COUNTS AS:
1 VEGETABLE
1 FAT

e according to plan

☀ Ingredients

2 pounds (896g) fresh baby spinach

2 Tbsp lite margarine

2 tsp flour

3/4 cup (200ml) skim milk

1/4 tsp freshly ground pepper

dash of nutmeg

1 Cut and discard tough stems from spinach. Rinse and lightly pat dry.

2 Bring 2 quarts (2L) water to boil.

3 Add the spinach, bringing back to a boil and cook exactly 3 minutes.

4 Drain in colander; press spinach with hands to remove any excess moisture.

5 Chop spinach fine.

6 Melt margarine in a saucepan, add flour and cook, stirring until a light golden brown.

7 Slowly add milk, stirring with a wire whisk, until mixture thickens.

8 Add spinach, pepper and nutmeg; toss together and serve.

Sassy
Sides

Ginger Carrots

■ SERVING SIZE: 1/2 CUP (125ML)
■ COUNTS AS:
  1 VEGETABLE

▶ *size according to plan*

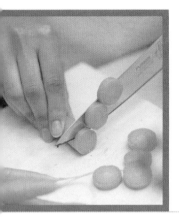

☀ Ingredients

1 pound (448g) carrot, peeled, sliced on an angle

1 Tbsp lite margarine

2 Tbsp artificial sweetener

2 Tbsp fresh squeezed orange juice

2 Tbsp grated ginger

1 In a pot of water, bring carrots to a boil and cook for approximately 5 minutes, or until fork tender. Drain.

2 In a sauté pan, over low heat, add margarine and artificial sweetener.

3 Stir for approximately 2 minutes, or until artificial sweetener begins to brown.

4 Add orange juice, ginger and carrots.

5 Simmer for approximately 5 minutes, or until liquid slightly thickens.

6 Serve immediately.

Lemon Green Beans

4 *servings*

good source of fiber

■ SERVING SIZE:
  1/2 CUP (125ML)
■ COUNTS AS:
  2 VEGETABLES

▶ *size according to plan*

☀ Ingredients

1 pound (448g) fresh green beans, cleaned and trimmed

1/4 cup (60ml / 37g) green or yellow peppers, chopped

2 Tbsp fresh dill

1 fresh green onion, sliced, thinly

1 tsp fresh garlic, ground

2 tsp olive oil

2 Tbsp lemon juice

freshly ground pepper

1 Place beans in 4 quarts (4L) of boiling water.

2 Cook green beans for 4-5 minutes in boiling water.

3 Drain beans and run cold water over them to stop cooking process.

4 Place green beans in a bowl; add the peppers, dill, onion, garlic, olive oil and lemon juice.

5 Toss together until coated and serve.

Sassy
❖ Sides

Spicy Broccoli

✳ Ingredients

2 cups (500ml / 140g) raw broccoli florets

2 tsp oil

1 tsp crushed red pepper flakes

4 garlic cloves, chopped

1 Simmer broccoli, covered, in 1-inch of water for 5-7 minutes, until tender. Drain broccoli and return skillet to heat.

2 Heat skillet over high flame.

3 Add oil, crushed pepper and garlic.

4 Add broccoli to spiced oil and toss to combine.

5 Serve immediately.

Green Beans with Mushrooms

servings

SERVING SIZE: 1/2 CUP (125ML)
COUNTS AS:
2 VEGETABLES

e according to plan

✳ Ingredients

1 1/4 pounds (560g) green beans, trimmed and halved

1 tsp olive oil

1 Tbsp lite margarine

1 green onion, chopped

1 cup (250ml / 70g) Portobello mushroom caps, sliced

1/2 cup (125ml) dry sherry

freshly ground pepper

1 Simmer green beans in water for about 5 minutes, until crisp tender.

2 Drain green beans and return skillet to medium heat.

3 Add oil and margarine to the pan.

4 Add onions and sauté 2-3 minutes.

5 Add mushrooms and season with black pepper.

6 Sauté mushrooms with onions, about 3-5 minutes; add green beans back to the skillet.

7 Heat green beans through and add sherry.

8 Cook for 1-2 minutes.

Sassy
❖ Sides

Peppers & Mushrooms

meals in minutes

2 *servings*

■ SERVING SIZE:
  1 CUP (250ML)
■ COUNTS AS:
  2 VEGETABLES

▶ *size according to plan*

☀ Ingredients

3 Tbsp low-sodium vegetable broth

1 onion, cut into wedges

2 garlic cloves, crushed

1 green bell pepper, cut into 1/4 inch strips

1 sweet red pepper, cut into 1/4 inch strips

1/2 pound (224g) mushrooms, sliced

3 sweet chili peppers, chopped

6 cilantro leaves, chopped

freshly ground pepper

1 Tbsp fresh parsley, chopped

1 Heat broth in a skillet; add onion and garlic and sauté until onion is translucent.

2 Add peppers, mushrooms and cilantro.

3 Stir-fry until peppers are tender.

4 Add freshly ground pepper and cook 1 minute.

5 Sprinkle with parsley and serve.

Herbed Eggplant

family fare

4 *servings*

■ SERVING SIZE:
  1/2 CUP (125ML)
  1 VEGETABLE

▶ *size according to plan*

☀ Ingredients

1 medium eggplant

2 tomatoes, chopped

1/4 cup (60ml / 40g) chopped onion

2 tsp coriander

2 tsp parsley

1 tsp cilantro

nonfat cooking spray

1 Cut eggplant in half and bake at 325°F for 20 minutes, or until soft. Remove eggplant from oven.

2 Mash eggplant with fork or potato masher.

3 Coat medium skillet with nonfat cooking spray and heat over medium flame.

4 Sauté onions until translucent.

5 Stir in tomato and cilantro; cook 1-2 minutes.

6 Stir in eggplant. Cook 4-5 minutes or until all liquid has evaporated.

7 Remove from heat and sprinkle with coriander and parsley.

Sassy
❖ Sides

Vegetables in Peanut Sauce

2 *servings*

SERVING SIZE: 1/2 OF RECIPE
COUNTS AS:
1/2 PROTEIN
2 VEGETABLES

ze according to plan

☀ Ingredients

1/4 pound (112g) bean sprouts

1/4 head (112g) cabbage, shredded

1/4 pound (112g) fresh spinach

1/4 cup (60ml) water

1 tsp skim milk or plain, enriched soymilk

1/4 tsp red pepper flakes or chili powder

2 packets brown sugar artificial sweetener

2 Tbsp peanut butter

1 Bring a large pot of water to a boil; add cabbage and cook 1 minute.

2 Then add spinach, cook 1 minute. Add bean sprouts and cook another minute.

3 Drain vegetables.

4 To make sauce, bring another 1/4 cup (60ml) water to a boil in small sauce pan.

5 Add milk, red pepper, artificial sweetener and peanut butter.

6 Mix well until ingredients form a smooth sauce.

7 Bring to a boil and remove from heat.

8 Place vegetables on platter, top with sauce.

Sweet Cole Slaw

1 *serving*

SERVING SIZE: 1 RECIPE
COUNTS AS:
2 VEGETABLES

ze according to plan

☀ Ingredients

1 cup (250ml / 70g) shredded cabbage

1/4 cup (60m / 30g) shredded carrot

1 Tbsp chopped sweet pepper

1 Tbsp rice vinegar

1 packet artificial sweetener

1/2 tsp low-sodium soy sauce

1 Combine all ingredients in a bowl.

2 Toss together to mix well.

3 Chill at least 30-60 minutes before serving.

"The cookbook is great because it gives you the food exchange for every recipe."

- F. Grove

Sassy ❖ Sides

Grilled Tomatoes & Eggplant

 4 *servings*

- **SERVING SIZE:**
  2 TOMATO HALVES,
  1/2 CUP (125ML) COOKED EGGPLANT
- **COUNTS AS:**
  2 VEGETABLES
  1 FAT

▶ *size according to plan*

☀ Ingredients

1 pound (448g) eggplant, trimmed and cut crosswise into 1-inch slices

1 pound (448g) tomatoes, sliced

freshly ground pepper

3 Tbsp chopped parsley

1 Tbsp olive oil

1 large garlic clove, pressed

3 Tbsp shredded lite or reduced-fat Romano cheese

nonfat cooking spray

1 Spray both sides of eggplant and tomato slices with olive-oil flavored, nonfat cooking spray.

2 Sprinkle with freshly ground pepper to taste.

3 Grill eggplant slices until brown and tomato halves are charred.

4 Combine parsley, olive oil and garlic in a small bowl; pour over eggplant and tomatoes.

5 Top with grated cheese.

Stuffed Summer Squash

family fare

 8 *servings*

- **SERVING SIZE:**
  1/4 OF A ZUCCHINI
  1/4 OF A SQUASH
- **COUNTS AS:**
  2 VEGETABLES

▶ *size according to plan*

☀ Ingredients

2 large yellow summer squash

2 large zucchini

2 heads radicchio, roughly chopped

6oz (168g) baby spinach

1 Tbsp balsamic vinegar

1 Tbsp olive oil

1 tsp minced garlic

freshly ground pepper

nonfat cooking spray

1 In a medium bowl, whisk together the oil, vinegar, garlic and freshly ground pepper. Set aside.

2 Cut summer squash and zucchini in half lengthwise.

3 With a melon-baller or small spoon, scoop out center of each section, leaving only the skins. Reserve the flesh for another use.

4 Coat large saucepan with nonfat cooking spray. Heat over medium flame and add radicchio.

5 Stir and cook for 30 seconds; next add baby spinach, cover and turn off heat

6 Allow to steam for 1 minute, or until just wilted.

7 Season with pepper, to taste.

8 Drizzle inside of squash and zucchini shells with marinade, then stuff with radicchio and baby spinach.

9 Prepare grill and preheat to medium high.

10 Placed stuffed shells on grill and cook for 2-3 minutes or until bottoms are crisp-tender and slightly charred and filling is heated through.

Sassy
❖ Sides

Buttermilk Biscuits

dozen biscuits

SERVING SIZE: 1 BISCUIT
COUNTS AS:
1 STARCH
1 FAT

ze according to plan

family fare

☀ Ingredients

2 1/2 cups (625ml / 315g) all
  purpose flour

1 Tbsp sugar

1 Tbsp artificial sweetener

1/2 tsp baking powder

1/2 tsp salt

4 Tbsp cold butter, cubed

4 Tbsp cold lite margarine, cubed

1/4 cup (60ml) warm water

1 package active dry yeast

3/4 cup (200ml) warm low-fat
  buttermilk

1. In large bowl, combine flour, sugar, artificial sweetener, baking powder and salt.

2. Cut in butter and margarine to flour mixture, using a pastry blender or 2 knives, until mixture resembles coarse crumbs, set aside.

3. Place warm water in a small bowl; sprinkle in yeast and stir until dissolved.

4. Add yeast mixture and warm buttermilk to flour mixture, stir until blended well.

5. Turn out dough onto a floured surface. Knead dough until smooth. Form into a ball.

6. With a rolling pin, roll out dough to 3/4 to 1 inch thickness.

7. Cut biscuits with a 2 or 2 1/2 inch biscuit cutter.

8. Place biscuits onto a baking sheet coated with nonstick cooking spray. Cover biscuits and let rest until doubled in size, about 30-45 minutes.

9. Meanwhile, preheat oven to 400°F.

10. Bake in oven for approximately 15 minutes or until lightly browned.

Glazed Carrots

servings

SERVING SIZE:
6 CARROTS
COUNTS AS:
1 VEGETABLE
1 FAT

ze according to plan

family fare

☀ Ingredients

24 cooked baby carrots

2 packets artificial sweetener

1 Tbsp grated orange peel

1 Tbsp orange juice

4 Tbsp lite margarine

dash of cinnamon

1. Melt margarine in small saucepan. Add orange peel and juice.

2. Add carrots and artificial sweetener; cook over low heat, stirring occasionally, until carrots are glazed and heated through.

Sassy
❖ Sides

Cauliflower & Potatoes

■ SERVING SIZE: 1 RECIPE
■ COUNTS AS:
  1 STARCH
  2 VEGETABLES

▶ *size according to plan*

✳ Ingredients

1 cup (250ml / 100g) raw cauliflower

1/2 potato

1/4 tsp cumin seeds

1/4 tsp ginger

1 garlic clove

1/4 cup (60ml) water

1/4 tsp turmeric

1/4 tsp red chili powder

1 tomato, diced

1/2 tsp garam masala

1/2 tsp coriander powder

1/2 tsp parsley

nonfat cooking spray

1. Chop cauliflower and potato into a large dice.

2. Heat a medium sauté pan coated with nonfat cooking spray.

3. Sauté cumin seeds for 1 minute.

4. Add ginger, garlic and potato.

5. Cook 1-2 minutes, stirring continuously, over medium high heat.

6. Add water, turmeric, chili powder and tomato.

7. Simmer for 5 minutes while stirring.

8. Add cauliflower and continue to cook 1 minute on medium high. Lower heat and cover.

9. Allow to simmer 10-15 minutes, or until cauliflower and potatoes are tender.

10. Garnish with parsley.

11. Serve hot.

Rosemary Rigatoni

■ SERVING SIZE:
  2/3 CUP (170ML)
■ COUNTS AS:
  1 STARCH
  1 FAT

▶ *size according to plan*

✳ Ingredients

3 Tbsp lite margarine

2 Tbsp fresh rosemary, chopped

1 Tbsp lemon zest

1 tsp lemon juice

1 cup (250ml / 140g) cooked rigatoni

1/4 tsp lite salt

1. Melt margarine in small saucepan. Add garlic and spinach; stir over low heat until spinach is wilted down.

2. Add artichokes, pasta and dressing. Mix well.

3. Sprinkle with pine nuts and cheese. Serve immediately.

Sassy
❖ Sides

Hoppin' John

3 servings

SERVING SIZE:
3/4 CUP (200ML)
COUNTS AS:
1/2 PROTEIN
1 STARCH

ze according to plan

☀ Ingredients

1 Tbsp olive or canola oil

1oz (28g) low-sodium Canadian bacon, diced

1/2 cup (125ml / 80g) onion, diced

1/2 medium green pepper, diced

1 celery stalk, diced

2 garlic cloves, minced

3 cups (750ml / 495g) cooked black-eyed peas

1 cup (250ml / 15g) cooked rice

1/4 tsp lite salt

1/8 tsp freshly ground pepper

1/8 tsp cayenne pepper

1 Heat 1 tbsp olive oil in a Dutch oven over medium-high flame. Add Canadian bacon and cook for approximately 2-3 minutes or until lightly browned.

2 Next add onion, green pepper, celery and garlic. Cook, stirring, until just tender.

3 Add black-eyed peas, rice and seasonings; toss to combine.

4 Reduce heat to medium, and cook until heated through. Add a small amount of water if becomes too dry or starts to burn.

Stir-Fried Asparagus

1 serving

SERVING SIZE:
1 CUP (250ML) COOKED
COUNTS AS:
2 VEGETABLES

ze according to plan

good source of fiber

☀ Ingredients

1 1/2 cups (375ml / 201g) fresh asparagus

1 tsp cornstarch

1 tsp cold water

1/4 cup (60ml) low-sodium chicken broth

1/2 cup (125ml / 35g) fresh mushrooms, sliced

1 tsp garlic powder

nonfat cooking spray

1 Cut asparagus on an angle 1/2-inch pieces.

2 Mix cornstarch and cold water; reserve.

3 Coat skillet with nonfat cooking spray. Heat skillet over medium-high flame.

4 Add asparagus and mushrooms; sprinkle with garlic powder. Stir-fry until asparagus is crisp-tender, about 3 minutes.

5 Stir in broth; heat to boiling.

6 Stir cornstarch mixture; cook and stir until thickened, about 10 seconds.

Sassy
❖ Sides

8 *servings*

- **SERVING SIZE:**
  1/2 CUP (125ML)
- **COUNTS AS:**
  1 STARCH

▶ *size according to plan*

good source of fiber

Succotash

☀ Ingredients

1 package (16oz / 448g) frozen
lima beans

1 package (16oz / 448g) frozen
whole kernel corn

1/4 tsp lite salt

1 cup (250ml) water

1 tomato, diced

1/2 cup (125ml / 80g) diced white
onion

1 In medium saucepan, combine corn, lima beans, salt
and water.

2 Bring to a boil and then reduce heat.

3 Add tomato and onion to mixture; simmer 5 minutes
until all vegetables are tender.

"Easy-Appetizing-Flavorful"
- Paula R.

---

3 *servings*

- **SERVING SIZE:**
  1/3 CUP (85ML)
- **COUNTS AS:**
  1 STARCH

▶ *size according to plan*

family fare

Lemon **Pilaf**

☀ Ingredients

2 tsp dried minced onion

1-2 garlic cloves, finely chopped

1/2 cup (125ml / 96g) raw brown
or white rice

1 cup (250ml) low-sodium
chicken broth

1 tsp lemon zest, minced

nonfat cooking spray

1 Coat saucepan with nonfat cooking spray. Sauté onion
and garlic until soft.

2 Add remaining ingredients. Heat to boiling, stirring
once or twice. Reduce heat to low and cover tightly.

3 Simmer approximately 20 minutes, or until all liquid is
absorbed.

4 Remove from heat; fluff with fork and serve.

Sassy
❖ Sides

Fried Cabbage

serving

SERVING SIZE: 1 RECIPE
COUNTS AS:
3 VEGETABLES

ze according to plan

good source of fiber

⁂ Ingredients

2 cups (500ml / 140g) cabbage, shredded

5 green onions, chopped

1/4 tsp onion powder

1/8 tsp lemon pepper

1/4 tsp lite salt

nonfat cooking spray

1 Tbsp water

1. Coat skillet with nonfat cooking spray; heat over low flame.

2. Add all ingredients to skillet.

3. Cover and cook over low until all vegetable are tender.

4. Add water, 1 Tbsp at a time, if mixture becomes dry while cooking.

5. Serve hot.

Asparagus with Dijon Sauce

servings

SERVING SIZE: 1/2 CUP (125ML)
COUNTS AS:
1 VEGETABLE

⁂ Ingredients

1 pound (448g) frozen asparagus spears, thawed

1 cup (250ml) low-sodium chicken broth

2 Tbsp Dijon mustard

2 Tbsp grated reduced-fat romano cheese

nonfat cooking spray

1. Coat large skillet with nonfat cooking spray. Heat over high flame.

2. Add asparagus to pan. Pour broth over asparagus and reduce heat; cover and steam over medium heat until crisp-tender, about 4 minutes.

3. Remove asparagus to serving plate with slotted spoon; keep warm.

4. Add mustard to skillet; increase heat to high and bring to a boil, stirring constantly.

5. Pour over asparagus; sprinkle with cheese.

Sassy
♣ Sides

Breadcrumbs

6 *servings*

- SERVING SIZE: 1/3 CUP (85ML)
- COUNTS AS:
  1 STARCH

▶ *size according to plan*

☀ Ingredients

6 slices lite bread

1/4 tsp lite salt

1/2 tsp onion powder

1/2 tsp garlic powder

1/4 tsp oregano

1/4 tsp basil

1. Toast bread lightly to remove any moisture.

2. Allow toast to cool.

3. Crumble toast into crumbs over large plate.

4. Mix salt, onion powder, oregano, basil and garlic powder into crumb mixture.

5. Adjust seasonings to taste.

Pad Thai Noodles

8 *servings*

family fare

- SERVING SIZE:
  1/2 CUP (125ML) COOKED
- COUNTS AS:
  1 STARCH
  1 VEGETABLE

▶ *size according to plan*

☀ Ingredients

1 package (6.75oz / 190g) dry rice noodles

1 cup (250ml / 83g) raw bean sprouts

1 Tbsp chopped red pepper

3 green onions, chopped

1 Tbsp chopped white onion

1 tsp lemon juice

1 Tbsp low-sodium soy sauce

1 tsp rice wine vinegar

1/4 tsp sugar

1 clove minced garlic

2 Tbsp chopped peanuts

1 egg

nonfat cooking spray

1. Soak noodles in hot water for 15-20 minutes, or until soft. Drain and set aside.

2. Coat wok with nonfat cooking spray. Heat over medium-high flame.

3. Add red pepper, white onion and garlic; sauté for 1 minute. Remove from wok and set aside.

4. Place egg in wok and scramble. Add onion and pepper mixture back to wok. Add noodles, bean sprouts, soy sauce and vinegar. Heat through.

5. Add green onion, lemon juice, sweetener and peanuts. Mix well.

Sassy
✤ Sides

skewers

SERVING SIZE: 1 RECIPE
COUNTS AS:
1 VEGETABLE
1 FAT
1/2 DAIRY

ze according to plan

family fare

Tandoori Cauliflower

☀ Ingredients

2 cups (500ml) plain nonfat yogurt

1 1/2 pounds (672g) cauliflower

3 garlic cloves, minced

1 1/2 Tbsp ginger, freshly grated

2 Tbsp olive oil

1 tsp cayenne pepper

1/2 tsp freshly ground pepper

1 tsp cumin, ground

1/2 tsp coriander, ground

2 tsp fresh lemon juice

2 Tbsp whole wheat flour

1. Wrap the yogurt in cheesecloth, twist and suspend from a wooden spoon over a bowl.

2. Leave suspended in the refrigerator for 24 hours to drain the excess liquid from the yogurt.

3. Using a small grinder, blend the garlic, ginger and oil until you get a paste like substance. Place this mixture into a bowl.

4. Add cayenne, pepper, coriander, cumin, yogurt, lemon juice and flour to thicken into a paste.

5. Separate the cauliflower into florets. Using a fork, prick florets in several places.

6. Place cauliflower into a plastic bag and pour the yogurt marinade overtop. Refrigerate for a minimum of 2 hours.

7. Soak some bamboo skewers in water for a minimum of 30 minutes.

8. Preheat the grill to medium high.

9. Remove the cauliflower and divide them among the skewers. Place the skewers on the middle burner and cook using indirect heat for 25 minutes with the lid closed.

10. Lift the lid and turn the heat up to high.

11. Move florets over to sit directly over the heat. This will crisp the outside of the florets.

12. Remove from heat once crisp and serve hot.

Corn with Basil

servings

SERVING SIZE:
1/2 CUP (125ML) COOKED
COUNTS AS:
1 STARCH

ze according to plan

☀ Ingredients

1 (10oz / 280g) package frozen, whole kernel corn

5 green onions, chopped

1 large celery stalk, thinly sliced

1 garlic clove, minced

1 tsp fresh basil, chopped, or 1/4 tsp dried basil leaves

nonfat cooking spray

1. Cook corn by steaming or microwaving.

2. Coat skillet with nonfat cooking spray. Cook and stir corn, onion, celery and garlic, over low heat, until onion is tender about 10 minutes.

3. Stir in basil; reduce heat.

4. Cover and cook until corn is tender, 3 minutes.

Sassy
❖Sides

Marinated Cucumbers

 serving

- **SERVING SIZE: 1 RECIPE**
- **COUNTS AS:**
  1 VEGETABLE

▶ *size according to plan*

☀ Ingredients

1 Tbsp apple cider vinegar

1 Tbsp water

1/2 packet artificial sweetener

1/4 tsp freshly ground pepper

1/4 tsp dill, minced

1/4 medium cucumber, peeled and thinly sliced

1 Stir together vinegar, water, artificial sweetener and pepper until dissolved.

2 Stir in dill and set aside.

3 Add cucumbers to marinade. Toss and chill before serving.

Green Onions & Carrots

 serving

- **SERVING SIZE: 1 RECIPE**
- **COUNTS AS:**
  2 VEGETABLES

▶ *size according to plan*

☀ Ingredients

5 green onions, chopped

2 thin slices fresh ginger, finely chopped

1 garlic clove, finely chopped

1/2 medium carrot, shredded

1/4 tsp lite salt

1/8 tsp fresh ground pepper

nonfat cooking spray

1 Coat pan with nonfat cooking spray; add onion, ginger and garlic; stir fry for approximately 2 minutes, or until onions are crisp-tender.

2 Stir in carrots and salt; sprinkle with pepper.

"The recipes taste as good as in the picture!"

- Sandy S.

Sassy ❖ Sides

Peas & Onions

SERVING SIZE:
1/2 OF RECIPE
COUNTS AS:
1 STARCH

ze according to plan

good source of fiber

☀ Ingredients

1/2 cup (125ml) water

1/2 tsp lite salt

1 cup (250ml / 144g) frozen peas, thawed

1/2 cup (125ml / 80g) sliced white onion

1/4 tsp dried thyme leaves

1 In small saucepan, bring water and salt to a boil.

2 Add peas, onions and thyme.

3 Heat to boiling; reduce heat. Cook, uncovered, 5 minutes or until onions are tender.

4 Drain before serving.

Apple Chutney

servings

SERVING SIZE: 1/6 OF RECIPE
COUNTS AS:
1 FRUIT

ze according to plan

☀ Ingredients

2 tart apples, peeled, cored and finely chopped

1/8 yellow onion, quartered

1/2 (1 inch) piece fresh ginger root, peeled

2 Tbsp and 1/4 tsp white wine vinegar

1 Tbsp and 1/2 tsp white sugar

1 Tbsp and 1/2 tsp brown sugar

1/8 tsp cinnamon

1/8 tsp white pepper

1/8 tsp ground cardamom

1/8 tsp ground nutmeg

1 In a saucepan, mix the apples, onion, ginger, vinegar, white sugar, brown sugar, cinnamon, white pepper, cardamom and nutmeg.

2 Bring to a boil, reduce heat and cover.

3 Simmer 30 minutes, stirring frequently, until the apples are tender. Mix in some water if necessary to keep the ingredients moist.

4 Remove the onion and ginger, and store in the refrigerator until ready to serve.

Sassy
❖ Sides

Veal ❖ Deal Plus

From delectable Veal Involtini and Tangy Glazed Pork Chops to Stuffed Lamb and Buffalo Burgers, this unique section truly has something for everyone. No matter what your favorite dish, you'll find many new and easy ways to create delightful meals that will keep the whole family coming back for seconds every time.

Mediterranean Veal Chops recipe can be found on page 169

Cuts of Veal

Veal is a term used to describe a young calf or cow that is approximately 1-3 months old. When shopping for veal, choose a piece that has a somewhat pale pink flesh; veal that is turning red means that the calf was likely older than 3 months. The texture should be firm, finely grained and smooth.

- **Roast** — A large cut of meat that is large enough to serve multiple people. Popular roasts include loin, shoulder, rib, breast and crown roasts.

- **Breast** — Cuts from the breast region of a young calf, such as a boneless breast roast.

- **Shanks** — Cut from the front leg of the calf. It is a very flavorful cut, but because of large amounts of connective tissue, it can be a tough cut of meat. Moist heat methods such as braising or stewing are used to prepare shank cuts. Osso buco is a popular dish made with veal shanks.

- **Round** — Cuts of meat from the leg. Popular cuts from the leg include cutlets, round steaks, rump roasts and round roasts.

- **Chops** — Cut of meat usually from the rib section and may also include part of the rib. Chops may also come from the loin.

- **Ground Veal** — This can come from various parts of the calf, so the fat content will vary depending on which cuts are ground. Ground veal is often used in conjunction with other ground meats to make dishes such as meatballs or meatloaves.

- **Loin** — A tender cut that comes from either side of the backbone. The loin may be cut into steaks, chops or roasts.

Basic Veal Roast

Place roast (4-5 pounds) into shallow pan and roast at 325°F, until internal temperature reads 150°F. Remove from oven and allow to rest for 10 minutes to allow juices to redistribute throughout the roast. Slice and serve.

TIP!

For more tender cuts of veal, choose loin roast, rib roast, rump roast and loin chop.

The less tender cuts great for marinating are shanks, shoulder roasts, breasts and riblets.

Lamb

Lamb is the meat from a sheep that is less than 1 year old. Meat from an animal that is older than 2 years is called mutton; mutton has a stronger flavor, but is less tender than lamb. Lamb is traditionally tender, with the exception of leg cuts. Baby lamb, which is from an animal younger than 8 weeks, should be pale pink when raw; other lamb cuts should be reddish-pink.

Lamb is a staple in many cultures, especially in Greece, Turkey, the Middle East, North Africa, India and beyond. Common flavors and spices you may see in lamb recipes include rosemary, lemon, garlic, mint and thyme, as well as cumin, coriander, cinnamon and turmeric.

Cuts

■ **Roast** — A large cut of meat that is large enough to serve multiple people. Popular roasts include shoulder, shank leg, loin, loin eye and crown roasts.

■ **Chops** — Cut of meat usually from the rib section; it may also include part of the rib. Chops may also come from the shoulder, rib or loin.

■ **Ground Lamb** — Ground lamb can come from various parts of the lamb; therefore, the fat content will vary depending on which cuts are ground.

■ **Legs** — Any cut of meat from the leg area. Leg cuts, such as a shank, are flavorful cuts of meat, but may be very tough. These are best suited for moist cooking methods, such as braising.

■ **Loin** — A tender cut that comes from either side of the backbone. The loin may be cut into chops or roasts.

■ **Rib** — A cut of meat from the rib section. It is a tender cut that may available as chops or roasts.

Fresh Pork Cuts

Place roast (4-5 pounds) into shallow pan and roast at 325°F, until internal temperature reads 150°F. Remove from oven and allow to rest for 10 minutes to allow juices to redistribute throughout the roast. Slice and serve.

■ **Chops** — Cut of meat from the rib section and will usually also include part of the rib.

■ **Ground Pork** — Ground pork can come from various parts of a pig, so the fat content will vary depending on which cuts are used. Ground pork is often used in conjunction with other ground meats to make meatballs and meatloaves.

■ **Loin** — Cut from either side of the backbone, from the shoulder to the leg, of the pig. This is a tender cut of meat that can be cut in to chops, tenderloin or roasts.

■ **Ribs** — A cut of meat that is long and narrow, taken from the lower portion of the loin. This cut is usually a fatty cut of pork. These include "baby-back" ribs, spare ribs and country style ribs.

■ **Roast** — A large cut of meat that is large enough to serve multiple people. Popular roasts include loin roasts, crown roasts and rib roasts.

TIP!

Cooking foods quickly in a small amount of fat in a skillet over direct heat. This works well for pork cutlets and chops.

Pork and Pineapple Stir-Fry

1 *serving*

- **SERVING SIZE: 1 ENTRÉE**
- **COUNTS AS:**
  1 PROTEIN
  3 VEGETABLES
  1 FRUIT

▶ *size according to plan*

good source of fiber

☀ Ingredients

4 or 6oz (112 or 168g) pork tender loin, size according to plan

2 tsp cornstarch

2 tsp low-sodium soy sauce

1 cup (250ml) low-sodium chicken broth

1/8 tsp ground cumin

3 green onions, diced

1 cup (250ml / 83g) bean sprouts

3/4 cup (200ml / 115g) fresh pineapple, cut into bite-size chunks

1/2 small tomato, diced

1 cup (250ml / 47g) shredded romaine

nonfat cooking spray

1. Partially freeze meat. Thinly slice across the grain into bite-size strips. Set aside.

2. Mix chicken broth, cornstarch, soy sauce and cumin. Set aside.

3. Coat skillet or wok with nonfat cooking spray. Add pork and stir fry until no longer pink; set aside.

4. Over medium heat, add green onion and stir fry 1 minute. Add bean sprouts and stir fry another minute, or until vegetables are tender.

5. Add pork to vegetable mixture. Stir soy sauce mixture into pork and vegetables. Cook and stir until thickened.

6. Add tomato and pineapple. Toss to coat with sauce. Heat through.

7. Serve over shredded romaine lettuce.

BBQ Pulled Pork

8 *servings*

- **SERVING SIZE: 3 OR 5OZ (84 OR 140G) COOKED**
- **COUNTS AS:**
  1 PROTEIN
  1 VEGETABLE

▶ *size according to plan*

family fare

☀ Ingredients

2-3 pounds (896g-1360g) pork loin, diced, size according to plan

1 can (16oz / 996g) low-sodium stewed tomatoes

2/3 cup (175ml) barbeque sauce

1/2 cup (125ml) water

1 onion, diced

2 Tbsp vinegar

1/2 green pepper, diced

3 packets artificial sweetener

4 garlic cloves, minced

1/3 cup (85ml) hot water

1. Preheat oven to 375°F.

2. In a large casserole dish, combine all ingredients.

3. Bake 3-4 hours, or until pork is tender enough to be shredded with a fork.

4. Stir casserole every 30 minutes, if liquid evaporates, add additional hot water, 1/3 cup (85ml) at a time.

5. Once pork is tender, remove from oven. Use 2 large forks to shred all pork.

Veal ✿
Deal Plu

Sausage Patties

2 servings

SERVING SIZE: 2 PATTY

COUNTS AS:
1 PROTEIN
1 STARCH

ze according to plan

☀ Ingredients

10 green onions, finely chopped

1/2 cup (125ml / 54g) breadcrumbs (see recipe on pg 154)

1/2 cup (125ml) skim milk

2-3 pounds (996g-1360g) ground lean pork, according to plan

1 tsp white pepper

1/4 tsp freshly ground pepper

1/4 tsp ground cayenne

1 tsp finely chopped fresh thyme

1 tsp finely chopped fresh sage

nonfat cooking spray

1. Coat skillet with nonfat cooking spray and heat over medium heat.

2. Cook onion, stirring occasionally, until softened and beginning to brown. Remove from heat and cool 10 minutes.

3. While onions are cooling, stir together bread crumbs and milk in a large bowl and let stand until crumbs absorb the milk.

4. Add onions and remaining ingredients to crumb mixture and stir with a fork until blended well.

5. Preheat oven to 250°F.

6. Form sausage patties into 1/2-inch thick patties, with dampened hands, and arrange on a wax paper lined tray.

7. Make into 12 patties.

8. Coat heavy skillet with nonfat cooking spray; heat over medium-high flame. Cook patties, turning once, until browned and just cooked through, about 4-6 minutes per batch.

9. Transfer to shallow baking pan and keep warm, covered with foil, in oven while cooking remaining batches.

Grandma E's Pork & Sauerkraut

3 servings

SERVING SIZE: 3 OR 5OZ (84 OR 140G) COOKED PORK WITH 1/2 CUP (125ML) SAUERKRAUT

COUNTS AS:
1 PROTEIN
1 VEGETABLE

ze according to plan

8-12 servings, depending weight of meat

☀ Ingredients

1 pork loin (2-3 pounds / .89-1.3kg loin)

2 large cans sauerkraut, low-sodium if available

2 apples, peeled, cored and chopped

2 garlic cloves, minced

1/4 cup (60ml) apple juice

nonfat cooking spray

1. Cut pork loin into large chunks.

2. Spray casserole dish with nonfat cooking spray.

3. Combine pork, sauerkraut, apples, juice and garlic in casserole dish.

4. Cover dish and bake in a preheated 300°F oven for approximately 1 hour.

5. Stir after 1 hour and cover, bake additional 30 minutes.

6. Remove cover, turn up heat to 350°F, and bake 30-45 minutes or until pork is cooked.

Veal ♣ Deal Plus

Pork Tenderloin & Peppers

2 *servings*

- SERVING SIZE: 1/2 OF RECIPE
- COUNTS AS:
  - 1 PROTEIN
  - 2 VEGETABLES

▶ *size according to plan*

☀ Ingredients

1/2 tsp dried thyme leaves

2 garlic cloves, crushed

8 or 12oz (224 or 336g) pork tenderloin

1/3 cup (85ml) water

1/2 medium red pepper, cut into 1/4-inch strips

1/2 medium green pepper, cut into 1/4-inch strips

1/2 medium yellow pepper, cut into 1/4-inch strips

3 green onions, thinly sliced

1/4 tsp lite salt

1 Tbsp cold water

2 tsp cornstarch

nonfat cooking spray

1 Mix together thyme and garlic; rub over pork.

2 Coat large skillet with nonfat cooking spray. Add pork to skillet and cook until no longer pink.

3 Remove pork and cover loosely with foil to keep warm.

4 Add water, peppers, and onion to skillet; cover and simmer, until vegetables are tender.

5 Mix cold water and cornstarch; stir into pepper mixture. Cook, stirring, until slightly thickened.

6 Cut pork into strips and add back to vegetable mixture. Heat through and serve.

Roast Pork with Rosemary

6 *servings*

- SERVING SIZE: 3 OR 5OZ COOKED PORK
- COUNTS AS:
  - 1 PROTEIN

▶ *size according to plan*

family fare

☀ Ingredients

1 or 2 pounds (448 or 896g) pork loin roast, size as according to plan

1 tsp lite salt

1 tsp freshly ground pepper

3 Tbsp dried rosemary leaves, crushed

3 garlic cloves, crushed

1 Sprinkle meat with salt and pepper; rub with rosemary and garlic.

2 Place pork roast in roasting pan. Roast, uncovered, in a 325°F oven until internal temperature of 160°F, about 30 minutes per pound.

Veal ❖
Deal Plu

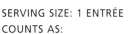 *serving*

family fare

Pork Piccata

SERVING SIZE: 1 ENTRÉE
COUNTS AS:
1 PROTEIN
1 STARCH
1 FAT

ze according to plan

☀ Ingredients

4 or 6oz (112 or 168g) pork*
  tenderloin, size according to plan

1/3 cup (85ml / 36g) breadcrumbs
  (see recipe on pg 154)

1/4 tsp lite salt

1 Tbsp capers

freshly ground pepper

1 tsp garlic powder

1 Tbsp lite margarine

1 Tbsp lemon juice

1 Tbsp dry white wine

nonfat cooking spray

1 With a meat mallet, pound tenderloin to 1/4 inch thickness.

2 Mix together breadcrumbs, salt, pepper and garlic powder. Dampen meat lightly with water, then coat with breadcrumb mixture.

3 Coat skillet with nonfat cooking spray. Heat skillet over medium flame. Add pork to skillet and cook, turning once, until done, about 7-8 minutes.

4 Remove pork from skillet; add lemon juice, butter, capers and wine into skillet; heat to boil and serve over pork.

♣ Veal or chicken could be substituted for pork.

Italian Pork Chops

serving

SERVING SIZE: 1 COOKED
PORK CHOP
COUNTS AS:
1 PROTEIN

ze according to plan

☀ Ingredients

4 or 6oz (112 or 168g)
  boneless pork loin chop

2 Tbsp fat-free Italian dressing

1 Tbsp parmesan cheese

1 Tbsp hot water

1 Use fork to pierce holes in pork chop to tenderize.

2 Place pork chop in plastic sandwich bag and pour salad dressing over chop. Place in fridge and allow to marinate 1 hour.

3 Coat medium skillet with nonfat cooking spray.

4 Over high heat, brown both sides of pork chop.

5 Turn down heat and continue to cook approximately 10 minutes, turning occasionally.

6 Add hot water, 1 Tbsp at a time, to prevent pork from sticking to pan.

7 Sprinkle with cheese just before serving.

Veal ♣
Deal Plus

Roast Lamb

1 *serving*

- SERVING SIZE: 1 LOIN
- COUNTS AS:
  1 PROTEIN

▶ *size according to plan*

good source of fiber

✳ Ingredients

4 or 6oz (112 or 168g) lamb loin,
  size according to plan

One of the following rubs:

Rosemary Garlic Rub

2 tsp dried rosemary, crushed

1 garlic clove, minced

1/8 tsp lite salt

freshly ground pepper

OR

Lemon Thyme Rub

2 tsp dried thyme

1 Tbsp lemon zest

1 Tbsp lemon juice

1/8 tsp lite salt

nonfat cooking spray

1 Preheat broiler.

2 Rinse lamb; pat dry. Combine ingredients for one of the herbal rubs in a small bowl.

3 Liberally apply the herbs to the loin, pressing the rub into the surface. Allow to rest 5-10 minutes.

4 Spray a broiler pan with nonfat cooking spray; place loin on pan.

5 Cook until desired doneness, approximately 7-11 minutes for medium rare or 15-19 minutes for medium; or to a temperature of 145°F for medium rare or 160°F for medium.

Pork al'Orange

1 *serving*

- SERVING SIZE: 1 ENTRÉE
- COUNTS AS:
  1 PROTEIN
  1 FRUIT

▶ *size according to plan*

✳ Ingredients

1 Tbsp water

1/3 cup (85ml) orange juice

1 tsp cornstarch

1 tsp low-sodium soy sauce

1/4 tsp ground ginger

2 tsp dried onion

4 or 6oz (112 or 168g)
  pork tenderloin

1 Mix water, orange juice, cornstarch, soy sauce, ginger and onion in saucepan. Cook sauce over medium heat until thickened. Set aside.

2 Coat skillet with nonfat cooking spray. Add pork; cook until pork is no longer pink. Add sauce to pan, heat through.

Veal ♣
Deal Plu

Stuffed Lamb

family fare

SERVING SIZE: 3 OR 5OZ
(84 OR 140G) COOKED
LAMB WITH 1-2 TBSP SAUCE
COUNTS AS:
1 PROTEIN
2 VEGETABLES

ize according to plan

☀ Ingredients

1 or 1 1/2 pound (448 or 672g) lamb roast, size according to plan, untied

1/4 tsp lite salt

1/8 tsp freshly ground pepper

2 medium carrot, diced

2 large celery stalks, diced

1/2 cup (125ml / 80g) yellow onion, diced

3 Tbsp fresh mint, chopped

3 Tbsp lemon juice

1 1/2 cup (375ml) water

1 Tbsp cornstarch

1 Tbsp cold water

nonfat cooking spray

1. Season lamb with salt and pepper.
2. Spray skillet with nonfat cooking spray. Add carrots, celery and onion; cook, stirring often, until vegetables are tender.
3. Stir in mint and lemon juice.
4. Spread vegetable mixture evenly over lamb. Roll lamb over stuffing; secure with butchers string.
5. Place lamb in roasting pan with rack, sprayed with nonfat cooking spray.
6. Bake in 325°F oven, uncovered, for approximately 40-45 minutes for medium, or until desired doneness.
7. Remove meat from pan; cover loosely with foil to keep warm.
8. Place roasting pan on stovetop. Add 1/2 cup (125 ml) water to pan; heat to a boil.
9. In a small bowl, mix cornstarch and cold water; add to roasting pan and heat until thickened.
10. To serve, slice meat and top with sauce.

Tangy Glazed Pork Chops

SERVING SIZE: 1 ENTRÉE
COUNTS AS:
1 PROTEIN
1 VEGETABLE

ize according to plan

☀ Ingredients

4 or 6oz (112 or 168g) pork chop (bone and fat removed), size according to plan

1 cup (250ml / 130g) zucchini, sliced

1 Tbsp ketchup

2 tsp low-sodium soy sauce

1 Tbsp water

1/8 tsp ground ginger

dash garlic powder

nonfat cooking spray

1. Coat skillet with nonfat cooking spray. Cook pork chop over medium heat, about 10 minutes, or until meat is tender and no longer pink.
2. Meanwhile, steam zucchini for 5-6 minutes, or until crisp-tender.
3. Mix ketchup, soy sauce, water, ginger and garlic powder. Pour over pork chops in skillet; cover and heat through.

Veal ♣ Deal Plus

Lamb Kabobs

1 *serving*

■ SERVING SIZE: 1 ENTRÉE
■ COUNTS AS:
  1 PROTEIN
  3 VEGETABLES

▶ *size according to plan*

✴ Ingredients

4 or 6oz (112 or 168g) boneless lamb, size according to plan, cut into 1-inch cubes

1/4 cup (60ml) lemon juice

1/2 tsp dried oregano leaves

1/8 tsp pepper

1/2 medium green pepper, cut into 1-inch pieces

5 green onions

1 cup (250ml / 82g) eggplant, cut into 1-inch pieces

1. Place lamb cubes into non-metal bowl.

2. In a separate bowl, mix lemon juice, oregano and pepper; toss lamb cubes with marinade.

3. Cover and refrigerate lamb for 30 minutes to 2 hours.

4. Preheat broiler.

5. Thread lamb cubes onto long metal skewer(s), leaving space between each. Broil 3-inches from heat and cook until desired level of doneness. Turn and brush with reserved marinade while cooking.

6. Meanwhile, prepare vegetables onto 2 or 3 more skewers, alternating the green pepper, onion and eggplant, leaving space between each piece. Broil until vegetables are crisp-tender; brush with marinade while cooking.

Veal & Mushrooms

meals in minutes

1 *serving*

■ SERVING SIZE: 1 ENTRÉE
■ COUNTS AS:
  1 PROTEIN
  1 VEGETABLE

▶ *size according to plan*

✴ Ingredients

5 or 7oz (140 or 196g) veal cutlet, unbreaded, size according to plan

1 cup (250ml / 70g) fresh mushrooms, sliced

1 garlic clove, minced

1 tsp garlic powder

1 Tbsp water

1 tsp flour

1/8 tsp lite salt

freshly ground pepper

1 Tbsp fresh parsley, chopped

2 Tbsp dry white wine

nonfat cooking spray

1. Pound veal to 1/4-inch thickness.

2. In skillet coated with nonfat cooking spray, sauté garlic, mushrooms and garlic powder, until tender.

3. Add veal to skillet and cook through. Remove veal and vegetables; keep warm.

4. In a small bowl, mix water and flour, until dissolved.

5. Add water-flour mixture, salt and pepper to meat juices in skillet and stir until thickened.

6. Add parsley and wine; heat through.

7. Before serving, veal and mushrooms with sauce.

Veal ✤
Deal Plu

Mediterranean Veal Chops

servings

SERVING SIZE: 1 CHOP AND APPROXIMATELY 1/2 CUP (125ML) SAUCE

COUNTS AS:

1 PROTEIN
2 VEGETABLES

ze according to plan

family fare

☀ Ingredients

4 boneless veal chops, 5 or 7oz (140-196g) each, size according to plan

1/4 tsp lite salt

1/8 tsp freshly ground pepper

2 tsp olive oil

1 garlic clove, minced

1 cup (250ml / 56g) baby spinach

1/4 cup (60ml) white wine

1 cup (250ml / 49g) grape tomatoes, halved

1 cup (250ml / 168g) artichoke hearts, roughly chopped

1 Tbsp capers, rinsed

2 Tbsp lemon juice

nonfat cooking spray

1 Preheat oven to 350°F.

2 Trim any excess fat from chops. Season with salt and pepper.

3 Coat a large oven-proof skillet with nonfat cooking spray. Heat over a medium-high flame.

4 Add chops to pan; sear chops on each side until lightly browned, about 3-4 minutes per side. Remove from pan; set aside.

5 Add olive oil and garlic to skillet; heat over a medium flame. Cook for 1 minute — do not allow garlic to burn.

6 Add spinach to pan; pour wine over spinach leaves. Toss together to wilt spinach.

7 Next add tomatoes, artichokes, and capers. Cook until heated through, about 3 minutes.

8 Return veal chops to pan; spoon spinach-artichoke sauce over chops.

9 Cover pan loosely with foil and place in the oven. Finish cooking in oven, approximately 25 minutes.

10 Remove from oven; sprinkle each chop with lemon juice just before serving. Allow to rest 5-10 minutes.

Veal Swiss Steak

serving

SERVING SIZE: 1 VEAL CUTLET WITH VEGETABLES

COUNTS AS:

1 PROTEIN
1 STARCH
2 VEGETABLES

ze according to plan

meals in minutes

☀ Ingredients

5 or 7oz (140 or 196g) veal cutlet, unbreaded, size according to plan

1 Tbsp flour

1/2 tsp dry mustard

1/4 tsp lite salt

1/2 small tomato, diced

1/4 tsp garlic powder

1 cup (250ml) water

1/2 medium green pepper, sliced into strips

5 green onions, thinly sliced

1 If necessary, pound veal 1/4-inch thick, with a meat mallet.

2 In a small dish, combine flour, dry mustard, and salt.

3 Coat each side of the veal with flour mixture.

4 Coat skillet with nonfat cooking spray. Cook veal over medium-high heat until browned; remove from pan and keep warm.

5 Add tomatoes, onion, green pepper, garlic powder and water. Bring to a boil; reduce heat.

6 Cover and simmer until vegetables are tender.

7 Return veal to pan to heat through before serving.

Veal ♣ Deal Plus

Italian-Style Veal

1 *serving*

- SERVING SIZE: 1 CUTLET WITH VEGETABLES AND CHEESE
- COUNTS AS:
  1 PROTEIN
  4 VEGETABLES
  1/2 DAIRY

▶ *size according to plan*

meals in minutes

☀ Ingredients

5 or 7oz (140 or 196g) veal cutlet, unbreaded, size according to plan

1/2 (125ml / 35g) cup fresh mushrooms, sliced

1/2 cup (125ml / 80g) white onion, finely chopped

1/2 medium red pepper, chopped

1/2 large celery stalk, finely chopped

1 garlic clove, minced

1 small tomato, seeded and diced

1/4 tsp dried basil, crushed

1/8 tsp crushed red pepper (optional)

1oz (28g) reduced-fat mozzarella cheese, shredded

nonfat cooking spray

1. Coat oven-safe skillet with nonfat cooking spray. Brown both sides of veal over medium high heat. Remove from pan and keep warm.

2. Add mushrooms, onion, red pepper, celery and garlic to pan. Cook until tender.

3. Add tomatoes, basil, oregano and red pepper (optional); toss to combine.

4. Return veal to pan. Simmer until meat is heated through.

5. Top veal and vegetables with cheese. Broil, 3 inches from heat, until cheese is melted.

Dijon Lamb Chops

1 *serving*

- SERVING SIZE: 1 ENTRÉE
- COUNTS AS:
  1 PROTEIN
  3 VEGETABLES

▶ *size according to plan*

meals in minutes

☀ Ingredients

4 or 6oz (112 or 168g) boneless lamb chop(s), size according to plan

1 Tbsp Dijon mustard

1/2 tsp dried thyme

1/4 tsp lite salt

1/2 medium carrot, sliced into thin strips

1 cup (250ml / 130g) zucchini, sliced into thin strips

1 cup (250ml / 100g) cauliflower florets

nonfat cooking spray

1. Preheat broiler.

2. In a small bowl, mix mustard, thyme and salt.

3. Place lamb chop on broiler pan, coated with nonfat cooking spray. Brush lamb chop with half of the marinade.

4. Broil chop, 3-inches from heat, about 6 minutes. Turn chop over and brush with remaining marinade. Broil another 5-8 minutes.

5. Meanwhile, steam vegetables lightly until tender. Season to taste.

6. Serve vegetables with lamb chop.

Veal ❖
Deal Plu

Veal Involtini

servings

SERVING SIZE: 1/4 OF THE RECIPE OR 1 INVOLTINI
COUNTS AS:
1 PROTEIN
1 VEGETABLE
1/2 DAIRY

ize according to plan

✳ Ingredients

1 1/4–1 3/4 pounds (560-784g) veal scaloppini, size as according to plan

1/8 tsp lite salt

1/8 tsp freshly ground pepper

1 cup (250ml / 56g) baby spinach leaves, rinsed

4oz (112g) lite mozzarella cheese, sliced thin

2 tsp olive oil

2-3 garlic cloves, crushed

1 cup (250ml) white wine

1. Preheat oven to 350°F.

2. Rinse veal; pat dry. Season with salt and pepper.

3. Arrange veal scaloppini on a cutting board. Onto each veal cutlet, place a few spinach leaves, 3-4 per piece. Top spinach with a slice of mozzarella.

4. Roll each veal scaloppini, enclosing spinach and cheese. Secure with a toothpick or with some butcher's string.

5. Heat an oven-proof skillet over a medium-high flame. Add olive oil and garlic, sauté 30 seconds.

6. Add veal rolls (involtini) to pan, sear until lightly brown on all sides, about 2 minutes per side. Pour wine over veal.

7. Put pan in oven to finish cooking, about 15 minutes. Remove from oven, loosely cover with foil; allow to rest 5-10 minutes before serving.

Veal Goulash

serving

SERVING SIZE: 1 RECIPE
COUNTS AS:
1 PROTEIN
2 VEGETABLES

ize according to plan

✳ Ingredients

5 or 7oz (140 or 196g) veal, any boneless cut, such as a chop, cubed, into bite-sized pieces, size according to plan

1/8 teaspoon lite salt

freshly ground pepper

1/2 cup white onion, sliced

1 small tomato, seeded and diced

1/2 Tbsp flour

1/4 cup (60ml) low-sodium beef broth

1 Tbsp lemon juice

1/2 tsp paprika

1/4 tsp caraway seeds

nonfat cooking spray

1. Season veal cubes with salt and pepper.

2. Spray skillet with nonfat cooking spray; brown veal over medium-high heat.

3. Add onion and tomato; cook, uncovered, approximately 15 minutes.

4. Sprinkle veal and vegetables with flour. Stir, while cooking, for about 1 minute.

5. Stir in beef broth, lemon juice, paprika and caraway seeds.

6. Cover and reduce heat. Simmer 20 minutes or until veal is tender.

Veal ♣
Deal Plus

Balsamic Lamb Chops

4 servings

- SERVING SIZE: 1/4 OF RECIPE
- COUNTS AS:
  1 PROTEIN

▸ *size according to plan*

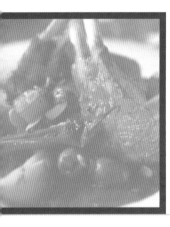

☀ Ingredients

1 tsp dried rosemary

1/4 tsp dried basil

1/4 tsp dried oregano

1/2 tsp dried thyme

freshly ground pepper

1 or 1 1/2 pounds (448 or 672g) boneless lamb chops, size according to plan

1 Tbsp olive oil

2 shallots, minced

1-2 garlic cloves, minced

1/3 cup (85ml) balsamic vinegar

2/3 cup (170ml) low-sodium chicken broth

1/3 cup (85ml) water

1 tsp butter

nonfat cooking spray

1. Combine rosemary, basil, oregano, thyme and pepper in a small bowl. Rub herb mixture onto lamb chops, on both sides; allow to rest 15-30 minutes, covered.

2. Heat olive oil in a large skillet or grill pan over medium-high flame.

3. Cook chops, approximately 3-4 minutes per side, for medium-rare doneness, or to desired temperature. Remove from pan and set aside, keeping warm.

4. Coat the same pan with nonfat cooking spray, allowing pan to reheat. Add shallots and garlic; cook until golden brown.

5. Next, add in balsamic vinegar, stirring constantly, scrapping to remove any browned bits from the bottom of the pan. Add in chicken broth and water, stirring to combine, and continue to cook approximately 5 minutes or until slightly thickened and reduced by half.

6. Remove sauce from heat and stir in butter.

7. Drizzle each chop with sauce; garnish with fresh rosemary and lemon slices.

Buffalo Burgers

4 servings

- SERVING SIZE: 1 BURGER PATTY
- COUNTS AS:
  1 PROTEIN

▸ *size according to plan*

☀ Ingredients

1 -1 1/2 pounds (448-672g) ground buffalo, size according to plan

1/2 jalapeño, seeded and minced

1/8 tsp lite salt

freshly ground pepper

dash of garlic powder

1. Combine all ingredients in a large bowl, mix until just combined.

2. Form into 4 patties. Cover and refrigerate until ready to use.

3. Preheat grill or broiler. Cook burgers for approximately 6 minutes on each side, or until desired doneness.

Veal ❦
Deal Plu

Veal Meatloaf

servings

SERVING SIZE: 1/4 RECIPE
COUNTS AS:
1 PROTEIN
1 FAT
1 STARCH

ze according to plan

☼ Ingredients

1 or 1 1/2 pounds ground veal, size as according to plan

1/2 cup egg substitute

1/2 cup dry bread crumbs

1/4 cup warm water

1/2 (1oz) envelope dry onion soup mix

1 large carrot, grated

1 small shiitake mushroom, sliced

1 Preheat oven to 350°F.

2 In a bowl, mix the ground veal, egg substitute, dry bread crumbs, water, soup mix, carrots and shiitake mushrooms. Transfer to a 9 x 5 inch loaf pan.

3 Bake 1 hour in the preheated oven, or to a minimum internal temperature of 160°F.

Venison Chili

servings

family fare

SERVING SIZE:
1 CUP (250ML)
COUNTS AS:
1 PROTEIN
2 VEGETABLES

ze according to plan

☼ Ingredients

1 Tbsp canola or other vegetable oil

4 garlic cloves

2 cups (500ml / 320g) chopped yellow onion

1 cup (250ml / 148g) chopped green pepper

1 jalapeño, seeded and chopped

2 pounds (896g) ground venison

2 Tbsp chili powder

1 tsp ground cumin

1 tsp cayenne pepper

1 (28oz / 784g) can diced tomatoes, no salt, undrained

3 cups (750ml) low-sodium chicken or beef broth

2 Tbsp tomato paste, no salt

nonfat cooking spray

1 Coat large pot with nonfat cooking spray; heat over medium flame. Add oil and garlic, sauté until just golden.

2 Add onion, green pepper and jalapeño; cook until soft.

3 Stir in venison, chili powder, cumin and cayenne. Cook the meat and spices with the vegetables, stirring, until browned, about 5-6 minutes.

4 Add tomatoes and liquid, broth and tomato paste to chili base; stir to combine. Bring to a boil; reduce heat and simmer at least 30-45 minutes before serving.

Veal ♣
Deal Plus

Under the ❖ Sea

There are lots of delicious recipes found Under the Sea and you'll find plenty to choose from inside the *L A Lite Cookbook*! From mouthwatering Ginger Salmon to Citrus Grilled Swordfish, you'll want to dive in to our unique seafood blends. Plus, you'll also discover the numerous health benefits of a variety of fish and the healthiest methods for selection, preparation and cooking.

Shrimp Fried Rice recipe can be found on page 183

How to select fish

When purchasing whole fish look for:

- Clear, bright eyes, not sunken eyes.

- Bright red gills.

- Intact scales that are firmly attached to the skin; scales should not be missing.

- Moist, shiny skin, but not slimy.

- Tail should be stiff and the flesh should be firm.

- Should not smell!

- Refrigerate fish for only 1 or 2 days.

When purchasing fish filets, look for:

- White fish should have a white translucent color with no discoloration.

- Flesh should be firm.

- Should not smell!

- Refrigerate fish for only 1 or 2 days.

How to purchase frozen fish:

- Frozen hard with no signs of thawing.

- Packaging should not be damaged.

- No evidence of freezer burn.

When purchasing shellfish/mollusks:

- Clear, bright eyes for crabs or lobsters.

- Shellfish should not smell!

- Check mollusks before cooking for freshness: avoid broken shells. Also the fish or shellfish should be alive — make sure they are responsive if pressure is applied to their shells.

- Once cooked, discard any mollusks which shells do not open after adequate cooking.

- Refrigerate shellfish on ice, for only 1-2 days maximum.

TIP!

Fish is a good source of potassium, vitamins, and other mineral. Potassium in your diet will help regulate blood pressure and proper muscle functions.

Cuts of fish

- **Whole dressed** — A whole fish with tail and head still attached, though typically your fish monger will have cleaned it already.

- **Pan dressed** — A whole fish with head, tail and fins removed.

- **Filets** — To filet a fish is to remove the filets from the bones. Typically, it is sold in a full length or may be cut into individual servings.

- **Steaks** — A cross-cut piece of the body of a larger fish. Steaks may contain small pieces of the backbone.

Basic cooking methods

It is important to cook fin fish thoroughly, but do not overcook it. Proper cooking allows the fish to develop the flavors and soften the connective tissue. Cooking fish at too high a temperature and cooking it too long will destroy the flavor, texture, and moisture of the fish. Fish is fully cooked when the flesh becomes opaque. White fish should also flake easily with pressure from a fork. Fish should be cooked to an internal temperature of 130° - 145°F.

Common methods for cooking fish

- **Poaching** — Fish simmered in liquid, serve hot or cold.

- **Steaming** — Fish is cooked from the steam of boiling water or any other liquid.

- **Broiling or Grilling** — Fish is cooked by dry heat from above, as in the oven or under a salamander or a grill.

- **Oven baking** — Fish is baked in an oven and basted usually with a small amount of fat or liquid, and sometimes in a pouch of paper or foil.

- **Pan-frying** — Cooking fish quickly in a small amount of fat on a skillet over direct heat.

TIP!

• Fish offers the same quality and quantity of protein as meat but often with fewer calories. Fish is generally low in cholesterol and is healthy for the heart.

Under the ❖ Sea

1 *serving*

- **SERVING SIZE: 1 FILET**
- **COUNTS AS:**
  1 PROTEIN

▸ *size according to plan*

meals in minutes

Poached **Fish**

☀ Ingredients

2 cups (500ml) water

1 cup (250ml) white wine

1/4 tsp lite salt

1/4 tsp dried thyme

1/4 tsp dried tarragon

1 tsp peppercorns

4 sprigs of parsley

1 bay leaf

5 or 7oz (140 or 196g) filet of
fish, such as cod or halibut, size
according to plan

1 Heat water, wine, salt, thyme, tarragon, peppercorns,
parsley and bay leaf to a boil, in a deep skillet; reduce
heat. Cover and simmer 5 minutes.

2 Place fish in skillet; add water, if necessary, to cover.
Again, heat to boiling; then reduce heat.

3 Simmer fish, uncovered, until it flakes easily with a
fork.

4 Carefully remove fish with slotted spatula, allowing to
drain.

5 Add to broth and heat until boiling, stirring frequently.

6 Boil one minute then turn off.

7 Add pepper and parsley.

8 Ladle soup into bowls and sprinkle with bacon pieces.

---

1 *serving*

- **SERVING SIZE: 1 FILET**
- **COUNTS AS:**
  1 PROTEIN
  1 STARCH

▸ *size according to plan*

meals in minutes

Oven Fried **Fish**

☀ Ingredients

5 or 7oz (140 or 196g) fish
filet, such as flounder or
tilapia, size according to plan

1/2 cup (125ml / 54g)
breadcrumbs (see recipe on
page 154)

1/8 tsp lite salt

1/8 tsp paprika

dash of dried dill

freshly ground pepper

butter flavor cooking spray

nonfat cooking spray

1 Preheat oven to 350°F.

2 In a shallow bowl, combine breadcrumbs, salt, paprika,
dill and pepper.

3 Rinse fish in cold water. Lightly pat dry.

4 Dip fish filet into breadcrumb mixture, coating each
side.

5 Coat baking pan with nonfat cooking spray. Place fish
on baking sheet.

6 Bake fish, uncovered, until easily flakes, approximately
20 minutes.

Under
the ❧ Se.

Vegetable Stuffed Sole

serving

SERVING SIZE:
1 STUFFED FILET
COUNTS AS:
1 PROTEIN
2 VEGETABLES

ze according to plan

☀ Ingredients

5 or 7oz (140 or 196g) sole filet, size according to plan

1/4 tsp lite salt

1/2 tsp dried dill

1/4 tsp freshly ground pepper

1/2 medium carrot, cut into strips

1/2 medium red pepper, cut into strips

1/4 cup (60ml) dry white wine

nonfat cooking spray

1 Preheat oven to 350°F. Coat a small baking dish with nonfat cooking spray.

2 In a small bowl, mix salt, dill and pepper; season filets with spice mixture. Place in baking dish.

3 Place carrot and pepper strips in the middle of the sole filet.

4 Roll fish, enclosing the vegetables; secure with toothpicks, if necessary. Place seam side down in baking dish. Pour wine over fish.

5 Cover with aluminum foil and bake until opaque, approximately 20 minutes, or until fish flakes easily with a fork.

Baked Stuffed Fish

serving

SERVING SIZE: 2 FILET PIECES
WITH STUFFING
COUNTS AS:
1 PROTEIN
1 STARCH
2 VEGETABLES

ze according to plan

☀ Ingredients

5 or 7oz (140 or 196g) fish fillet, such as tilapia or flounder, size according to plan

1 slice diet bread, toasted and cut into cubes

1 garlic clove, minced

1 tsp dried minced onion

1/2 cup (125ml / 35g) mushrooms, chopped

1/2 medium carrot, shredded

1 Tbsp lemon juice

1/4 tsp dried marjoram

1/4 tsp freshly ground pepper

1/4 cup (60ml) lemon juice

nonfat cooking spray

1 Preheat oven to 350°F oven. Coat baking dish with nonfat cooking spray.

2 Cut filet into 2 pieces; set aside.

3 Coat skillet with nonfat cooking spray. Add garlic, onions and mushrooms; sauté until tender.

4 Add in carrots, lemon juice, marjoram and pepper; gently toss to combine.

5 Spoon stuffing on top of one piece of filet. Top with remaining piece of filet.

6 Season filet with butter spray; sprinkle with lemon juice. Bake, uncovered, until fish flakes easily with fork, or approximately 30 minutes.

Under the ✿ Sea

Ginger Salmon

1 *serving*

- SERVING SIZE: 1 FILET WITH SAUCE
- COUNTS AS:
  1 PROTEIN
  1 VEGETABLE

▶ *size according to plan*

※ Ingredients

4 or 6oz (112 or 168g) salmon filet, size according to plan

1/2 Tbsp brown sugar artificial sweetener

1/2 Tbsp low-sodium soy sauce

1/2 Tbsp dry white wine

1/2 Tbsp lemon juice

1/2 tsp garlic minced

1/4 tsp fresh ginger, grated

dash of red pepper sauce

5 green onions, sliced

nonfat cooking spray

1. Coat skillet with nonfat cooking spray and heat over medium flame. Add salmon to pan.
2. Cook salmon for 4 minutes on each side.
3. Remove salmon from pan; cover loosely with foil to keep warm.
4. Combine remaining ingredients in a small bowl.
5. Reduce heat to low. Add sauce to skillet and sauté for 1 minute.
6. Return salmon to pan and cook until heated through.

> "Cooking is so easy now with the L A Weight Loss Cookbook."
>
> *- Mandy M.*

Broiled Ginger Scallops

1 *serving*

- SERVING SIZE: 1 RECIPE
- COUNTS AS:
  1 PROTEIN

▶ *size according to plan*

※ Ingredients

4 or 6oz (112 or 168g) scallops, size according to plan

2 Tbsp low-sodium soy sauce

1 garlic clove, minced

1 Tbsp ginger, minced

2 Tbsp lemon juice

1 Tbsp brown sugar artificial sweetener

nonfat cooking spray

1. Arrange scallops in a single layer in a baking dish.
2. Heat soy sauce in a small saucepan, over a medium flame. Add garlic, ginger, lemon juice, and brown sugar; simmer 2-3 minutes. Allow to cool to room temperature.
3. Pour cooled sauce over scallops. Cover and refrigerate at least 2 hours.
4. Preheat broiler.
5. Remove scallops from marinade. Place scallops, in a single layer, on a broiler pan coated with nonfat cooking spray.
6. Broil 4 inches from heat until opaque, approximately 6-8 minutes, turning once during cooking.

Under the ✤ Sea

Shrimp Jambalaya

serving

SERVING SIZE: 1 RECIPE
COUNTS AS:
1 PROTEIN
1 STARCH
3 VEGETABLES

ze according to plan

☀ Ingredients

1/2 cup (125ml / 80g) white onion, chopped

1/2 medium green pepper, chopped

1 garlic clove, minced

5 or 7oz (140 or 196g) fresh shrimp, peeled and deveined, size according to plan

1 cup (250ml) low-sodium chicken broth

1/4 tsp lite salt

1/8 tsp freshly ground pepper

1/8 tsp ground thyme

1/8 tsp hot pepper sauce

1 bay leaf

1 small tomato, seeded and chopped

2 1/2 Tbsp uncooked brown rice

nonfat cooking spray

1. Coat a saucepan oven, over medium heat, with nonfat cooking spray. Add onion, green pepper and garlic; cook until tender.

2. Add shrimp; cook until opaque and turning pink. Remove shrimp and vegetables from pan; set aside.

3. Next, add rice, chicken broth, salt, pepper, thyme, hot pepper sauce, bay leaf and tomato. Heat to boiling. Reduce heat; cover and simmer, until rice is tender.

4. Return shrimp and vegetables to saucepan oven. Cover again, and cook until heated through.

> "The Shrimp Jambalaya is my favorite, flavorful & easy."
>
> *- J. DeBow*

Boiled Lobster Tails

serving

SERVING SIZE: 1 TAIL
COUNTS AS:
1 PROTEIN

ze according to plan

☀ Ingredients

2 quarts (1L) water

1/4 tsp lite salt

1 lobster tail, with shell, size according to plan, to yield 4 or 6oz (112 or 168g) cooked

nonfat cooking spray

1. Bring water and salt to a boil in a large pot. Add lobster tail.

2. Return water to boiling. Cover and reduce heat; simmer 10 minutes. Drain.

3. Slice thin under-shell of tail down the middle and gently open tail; trim away shell, as needed. Pull meat out of tail to expose.

4. Place tail on broiler rack. Season with nonfat cooking spray.

5. Broil 3-inches from heat until hot, approximately 2-3 minutes.

6. Serve with lemon and 1 tsp of melted butter, to count as 1 fat, as desired.

Under the ❧ Sea

Lemon Shrimp Stir-fry

1 *serving*

- SERVING SIZE: 1 ENTRÉE
- COUNTS AS:
  - 1 PROTEIN
  - 3 VEGETABLES
  - 1 FRUIT

▶ *size according to plan*

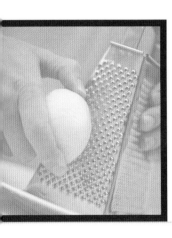

☀ Ingredients

5 or 7oz (140 or 196g) fresh or fresh-frozen shrimp, peeled and deveined, size according to plan

1 Tbsp cornstarch

1 tsp artificial sweetener

1 Tbsp low-sodium soy sauce

freshly ground pepper

1/2 cup (125ml) water

1/2 tsp lemon zest, minced

1 1/2 Tbsp lemon juice

1 large celery stalk, sliced on the bias

1/2 medium green or red pepper, sliced

1/2 cup (125ml / 35g) mushrooms, sliced

3 green onions, sliced

1/4 cup (60ml / 8g) fresh bean sprouts

nonfat cooking spray

1. In a bowl, combine cornstarch, artificial sweetener, soy sauce, pepper, water, lemon zest and lemon juice. Stir to combine; set aside.

2. Spray skillet or wok with nonfat cooking spray. Preheat over medium-high flame. Add celery and cook for 1 minute. Add green pepper and cook for another minute. Finally, add green onion. Stir-fry all vegetables for 1-3 minutes or until crisp-tender. Remove from pan and set aside.

3. Add shrimp to skillet or wok. Stir-fry for 2-3 minutes or until shrimp turns pink. Move shrimp to side(s) of skillet or wok, to keep warm.

4. Add sauce to center of pan; cook, stirring, until slightly thickened.

5. Return vegetables to pan. Add bean sprouts. Cook and stir for 1 minute or until heated through.

6. If desired, serve stir-fry over 1/3 cup (85ml / 55g) brown rice equals 1 Starch.

Steamed Crab

1 *serving*

- SERVING SIZE: 2 CUPS (500ML)
- COUNTS AS:
  - 1 PROTEIN
  - 1 STARCH

▶ *size according to plan*

☀ Ingredients

4 or 6oz (112 or 168g) fresh crab meat, size according to plan, picked for shells

1/2 cup (125ml) water

1/2 cup (125ml) white wine

2-3 slices lemon

1 tsp peppercorns

1/8 tsp lite salt

1 bay leaf

nonfat cooking spray

1. Under a light stream of water, rinse crab in a fine sieve or strainer.

2. Add water, wine, lemon, peppercorns, salt and bay leaf to a medium saucepan. Place steamer basket in pan.

3. Add crab to basket. Gently steam until heated through, about 10 minutes.

4. Serve hot or cold with cocktail sauce, red pepper or other desired condiment.

Under the ♣ Sea

Baked Crab & Broccoli

serving

SERVING SIZE: 1 RECIPE
COUNTS AS:
1 PROTEIN
2 STARCH
2 VEGETABLES
1/2 DAIRY

ze according to plan

good source of fiber

☼ Ingredients

1 cup (250ml / 70g) broccoli florets, trimmed

4 or 6oz (112 or 168g) fresh crab meat, rinsed and picked for shells, size as according to plan

1 cup (250ml / 70g) fresh mushrooms, sliced

1 garlic clove, minced

1/2 cup (125ml) skim milk

1 Tbsp flour

freshly ground pepper

1oz (28g) reduced-fat sharp cheddar cheese, shredded

3 slices Melba toast, finely crushed

1. Steam broccoli until crisp-tender, drain.

2. Arrange broccoli and crab meat in a casserole dish, coated with nonfat cooking spray. Set aside.

3. Spray skillet with nonfat cooking spray. Sauté mushrooms and garlic until tender. Sprinkle vegetables with flour and pepper. Stir in milk.

4. Cook sauce, stirring, until thickened. Add cheddar cheese; stir until melted.

5. Spoon sauce on top of broccoli and crabmeat. Cover with foil.

6. Bake at 400°F for 15-20 minutes, until bubbling. Sprinkle with Melba toast crumbs; return to oven and bake again until golden brown.

Shrimp Fried Rice

serving

SERVING SIZE: 1 ENTRÉE
COUNTS AS:
1 PROTEIN
1 STARCH
3 VEGETABLES

ze according to plan

☼ Ingredients

5 or 7oz (140 or 196g) peeled and deveined raw shrimp, size according to plan

1/2 medium green pepper, diced

2 green onion, diced

1/2 medium carrot, diced

1/2 stalk celery, diced

dash of garlic powder

dash of onion powder

1/4 tsp ground ginger

1 Tbsp low-sodium soy sauce

1/4 tsp lite salt

1/3 cup (85ml / 53g) cooked brown rice

1 egg white, scrambled

nonfat cooking spray

1. Spray skillet or wok with nonfat cooking spray. Over medium-high heat, cook shrimp until pink. Remove from pan; set aside.

2. Return pan to flame. Stir-fry vegetables in wok until crisp-tender.

3. Season vegetables with garlic powder, onion powder, ginger, soy sauce and salt.

4. Add rice, scrambled egg white, and shrimp back to wok. Toss to combine; allow to heat through before serving.

Under the ♣ Sea

Tangy Shrimp Skewers

1 *serving*

- **SERVING SIZE: 2-3 SKEWERS**
- **COUNTS AS:**
  1 PROTEIN
  2 VEGETABLES
  1 FRUIT

▸ *size according to plan*

☀ Ingredients

5 or 7oz (140 or 196g) fresh or fresh-frozen raw shrimp, size according to plan, peeled and deveined

1/2 cup (125ml / 90g) pineapple chunks, canned in juice (drain and reserve juice)

1/2 medium red pepper, cut into 1 inch pieces

1/4 red onion, cut into 1-inch pieces

2 Tbsp low-sodium soy sauce

2 Tbsp water

1 tsp ginger, minced

1-2 garlic clove(s), minced

nonfat cooking spray

1. Preheat broiler or grill.

2. In a small saucepan, combine reserved pineapple juice, soy sauce, ginger and garlic, over a medium flame. Cook, stirring, until slightly thickened.

3. Thread shrimp, pineapple, pepper and onions, onto metal skewers, alternating the ingredients.

4. Place skewers onto grill or broiler pan (coated with nonfat cooking spray). Cook, brushing with sauce, approximately 4-5 minutes per side or until shrimp are opaque and cooked through.

Pan Seared Lemon-Pepper Grouper

1 *serving*

- **SERVING SIZE: 1 FILET**
- **COUNTS AS:**
  1 PROTEIN

▸ *size according to plan*

☀ Ingredients

5 or 7oz (140 or 196g) of fresh grouper, size according to plan

2 Tbsp citrus rub (recipe on page 224)

1 Tbsp lemon juice

1 tsp lemon zest

nonfat cooking spray

1. Combine lemon zest and pepper-herb mix together.

2. Sprinkle herb mixture over both sides of fish.

3. Coat medium skillet with nonfat cooking spray.

4. Fry fish over high heat for 1 minute on each side.

5. Turn down heat to low and cook on each side 5-7 minutes, or until fish flakes with a fork.

6. Drizzle lemon juice over fish, serve hot.

Under the ✤ Sea

Orange Sesame Salmon

1 serving

SERVING SIZE: 1 FILET
COUNTS AS:
1 PROTEIN
2 FRUITS
1 FAT

ize according to plan

✳ Ingredients

4 or 6oz (112 or 168g) raw
salmon filet, size according
to plan

1/3 cup (85ml) orange juice

1/2 cup (125ml / 95g) canned
mandarin oranges, drained

2 tsp sesame seeds

1/4 tsp ginger

nonfat cooking spray

1. Sprinkle ginger over salmon filet.
2. Coat medium skillet with nonfat cooking spray.
3. Place salmon in skillet and sear each side 2 minutes over high heat.
4. Pour orange juice over salmon and reduce heat.
5. Simmer 15 minutes, flipping occasionally to cook evenly.
6. Next, add oranges and sesame seeds, cooking another 1-2 minutes or until oranges are warmed through.
7. Serve hot over rice or salad.

Salmon Stuffed Tomatoes

1 serving

SERVING SIZE:
2 STUFFED TOMATOES
COUNTS AS:
1 PROTEIN
2 VEGETABLES

ize according to plan

✳ Ingredients

4 or 6oz (112 or 168g) fresh
salmon filet, size according to
plan

2 small whole tomatoes

1 tsp olive oil

2 tsp white wine vinegar

2 tsp lemon juice

1/4 tsp lite salt

1 Tbsp chopped cilantro

1/4 tsp onion powder

1. Cook salmon filet, as desired; chill.
2. Chop cooked salmon into small pieces.
3. In medium bowl combine salmon, oil, vinegar, lemon juice, salt and cilantro. Mix well. Chill.
4. While salmon mixture is chilling, cut tops off of tomatoes. Remove seeds and flesh from tomatoes. Chop 1/4 cup of tomato flesh; discard rest.
5. Mix diced tomato into salmon salad.
6. Fill hollowed tomatoes with salmon mixture.
7. Serve chilled, garnish with chopped parsley, if desired.

Under the ♣ Sea

Curried Salmon

1 *serving*

- **SERVING SIZE: 1 FILET**
- **COUNTS AS:**
  1 PROTEIN
  2 VEGETABLES
  1/2 DAIRY

▶ *size according to plan*

meals in minutes

☀ Ingredients

4 or 6oz (112 or 168g) fresh salmon filet, size according to plan

2 Tbsp fat-free evaporated milk

2 Tbsp skim milk

2 tsp curry powder

1/2 carrot, thinly sliced

1/8 tsp ground ginger

1/8 tsp lite salt

1/8 tsp coriander

1 packet artificial sweetener

1/2 small tomato, diced

1 In a small saucepan, combine evaporated milk, skim milk, curry powder, ginger, salt, coriander and artificial sweetener. Heat over medium heat.

2 Chop salmon into small pieces. Add to curried milk mixture.

3 Bring mixture to a simmer; reduce heat to low.

4 Add carrot and tomato and cook 5-10 minutes, or until salmon is cooked.

5 Serve hot over rice or vegetables.

Citrus Grilled Swordfish

1 *serving*

- **SERVING SIZE:**
  1 SWORDFISH STEAK
- **COUNTS AS:**
  1 PROTEIN
  1 FRUIT

▶ *size according to plan*

meals in minutes

☀ Ingredients

5 or 7oz (140 or 196g) raw swordfish steak, size according to plan

1/4 cup (60ml) orange juice

1 Tbsp lemon juice

1 Tbsp lime juice

1 tsp low-sodium soy sauce

1/4 tsp lite salt

1 tsp chopped cilantro

1 Tbsp chives

1/4 tsp onion powder

1/4 tsp garlic powder

1/4 tsp white pepper

1/4 tsp freshly ground pepper

2 slices orange

1 Sprinkle swordfish with salt, pepper, cilantro, chives, garlic powder and onion powder.

2 In a small bowl, combine juices and soy sauce; brush steak with marinade and set aside.

3 Place steak on grill. Cook steak for 5 minutes per side, or until cooked through. Baste steak with citrus marinade while cooking.

4 Garnish with fresh orange. Squeeze juice for orange wedges over fish for a fresh burst of flavor.

Under the ❖ Sea

Salmon with Green Beans

4 servings

SERVING SIZE: 3 OR 5
OUNCES COOKED (84 OR
140G) SALMON, 1/2 CUP
(125ML) GREEN BEANS,
1/4 RECIPE GLAZE
COUNTS AS:
1 PROTEIN
1 VEGETABLE

ize according to plan

☀ Ingredients

4 salmon filets, 4 or 6oz (112 or
168g) each, size according
to plan

1/2 tsp coarse black pepper

1/2 cup (125ml) dry white wine

1/2 cup (125ml) balsamic vinegar

2 Tbsp fresh orange juice

2 tsp lemon juice

2 packets artificial sweetener

1 pound (448g) green beans,
trimmed

nonfat cooking spray

1 Preheat a cast iron pan or heavy bottomed skillet over
medium-high flame coated with nonfat cooking spray.

2 Season filets with pepper, then spray with nonfat
cooking spray.

3 Cook salmon until just cooked through, about
3 minutes on each side.

4 While salmon cooks, bring wine, vinegar, juices and
artificial sweetener to a boil over high heat, in a small
saucepan.

5 Cook glaze 3 or 4 minutes, until reduced and
thickened.

6 Remove from heat. Stir in 1/2 tsp coarse black pepper.

7 In a second skillet, bring 1/2-inch water to a boil with
green beans and pieces of orange rind and/or lemon
rind.

8 Cover the green beans and cook 3-4 minutes.

9 Drain the beans and toss and season with pepper.

10 Drizzle glaze over salmon filets. Serve with green beans
on the side.

Caesar Shrimp Skewers

1 serving

SERVING SIZE: 1 SERVING
COUNTS AS:
1 PROTEIN
1 VEGETABLE

ize according to plan

☀ Ingredients

1 Tbsp fat-free Caesar dressing

2 Tbsp lemon juice

1 Tbsp margarine, melted

1 tsp garlic powder

1 green onion, chopped

1/4 tsp lite salt

5 or 7oz (140 or 196g) fresh
shrimp peeled and deveined,
size according to plan

1 yellow squash, cubed

kabob skewers

nonfat cooking spray

1 In a small bowl, combine dressing, lemon juice,
margarine, chopped onion and half of the garlic
powder.

2 Place shrimp and squash on skewers.

3 Spray finished kabobs with cooking spray, then sprinkle
with salt and remaining garlic powder.

4 Place skewers on grill.

5 Brush with dressing and turn while grilling.

6 Cook until squash begins to soften. Continue to brush
with dressing frequently during cooking.

7 Serve hot over rice.

Under
the ✤ Sea

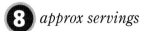

8 *approx servings*

- SERVING SIZE: 3 OR 5OZ
  COOKED (84 OR 100G)
- COUNTS AS:
  1 PROTEIN

▸ *size according to plan*

family fare

Herb **Stuffed Salmon**

☀ Ingredients

freshly ground pepper

1 Tbsp olive oil

2 pounds (896g) salmon filets,
  skin on, scaled and pin bones
  removed

2 lemons

bunch fresh dill

bunch fresh marjoram

bunch fresh basil

nonfat cooking spray

1 Preheat the oven to 400°F.

2 Cut 5 lengths of string and lay them out on the work
   surface next to each another, with less than 1-inch
   space between each.

3 Sprinkle pepper over the work surface, then drizzle
   with olive oil.

4 Lay 1 salmon filet onto work surface, skin side down.
   Sprinkle pepper over the salmon, then, using fine
   grater or microplane, grate the zest of 1 lemon over
   top. Next, season with the marjoram, dill and basil.

5 Season the flesh side of the other salmon filet with
   pepper, and grate the second lemon.

6 Place 1 filet on top of the other, thin end to thick,
   then tie them together and trim the strings.

7 Put the fish on a baking sheet coated with nonfat
   cooking spray.

8 Bake for about 20 minutes, or until fish is flaky.

---

1 *serving*

- SERVING SIZE: 2 TACOS
- COUNTS AS:
  1 PROTEIN
  1 STARCH
  1 VEGETABLE
  1/2 DAIRY

▸ *size according to plan*

good source of calcium

Fish **Tacos**

☀ Ingredients

5 or 7oz (140 or 196g)
  mahi-mahi, size according to plan

1 tsp hot sauce

1 tsp cilantro

1/4 tsp chili powder

1/2 whole wheat flour tortilla

1/4 cup (60ml / 18g) shredded
  lettuce

1/2 tomato, seeded and diced

1 Tbsp salsa

1 Tbsp fat-free sour cream

1oz (28g) reduced-fat shredded
  cheddar cheese

1 Sprinkle fish with hot sauce, cilantro and chili powder.

2 Bake in preheated 375°F oven until flaky,
   approximately 15-20 minutes.

3 Slice tortilla in half.

4 Place fish in tortilla. Top with condiments and
   vegetables.

Under
the ❧ Sea

Spinach Stuffed Sole

servings

SERVING SIZE: 1/4 RECIPE
COUNTS AS:
1 PROTEIN
2 VEGETABLES

ze according to plan

good source of calcium

☀ Ingredients

1.5 - 2 pounds (896g) sole filets, size according to plan

1 tsp olive oil

1/2 pound (224g) fresh mushrooms, sliced

1/2 pound (224g) fresh spinach, chopped

1/4 tsp oregano leaves, crushed

1 garlic clove, minced

2 Tbsp sherry

4oz (112g) part-skim mozzarella cheese, grated

nonfat cooking spray

1 Preheat oven to 400°F.

2 Coat a baking dish with nonfat cooking spray.

3 Heat oil in skillet; sauté mushrooms about 3 minutes or until tender.

4 Add spinach and continue cooking about 1 minute, or until spinach is beginning to wilt.

5 Remove from heat; drain liquid into prepared baking dish.

6 Add oregano and garlic to drained vegetables; stir to mix ingredients.

7 Divide vegetable mixture evenly among filets, placing filling in center of each filet.

8 Roll filet around mixture and place seam-side down in prepared baking dish.

9 Sprinkle with sherry, then grated mozzarella cheese.

10 Bake fish for 15-20 minutes, or until flaky.

Baked Trout

servings

SERVING SIZE: 4 OR 6OZ
(112 OR 168G) COOKED
TROUT
COUNTS AS:
1 PROTEIN
1 VEGETABLES

ze according to plan

family fare

☀ Ingredients

2 pounds (896g) trout filet

3 Tbsp lime juice (about 2 limes)

1 medium tomato, chopped

5 green onions, chopped

3 Tbsp cilantro, chopped

1/2 tsp olive oil

1/4 tsp freshly ground pepper

1/4 tsp cayenne pepper (optional)

nonfat cooking spray

1 Preheat oven to 350°F.

2 Rinse fish and pat dry.

3 Place in baking dish coated with nonfat cooking spray.

4 In a separate dish, mix remaining ingredients together and pour over fish.

5 Bake for 15-20 minutes or until flaky.

Under the ♣ Sea

Scallops & Mushrooms

1 *serving*

- SERVING SIZE: 1 RECIPE
- COUNTS AS:
  - 1 PROTEIN
  - 2 VEGETABLES

▶ *size according to plan*

☀ Ingredients

12 medium Portabella mushroom caps

1 Tbsp low-sodium soy sauce

1 garlic clove, finely diced

1 green onion, finely diced

6 or 8oz (168 or 224g) large scallops, size according to plan

nonfat cooking spray

1 Preheat oven to 325°F degrees.

2 Marinate the mushrooms in the soy sauce, garlic and green onion. Let sit for 30 minutes.

3 Grill or broil mushrooms 2 minutes per side; then bake in the oven for 10 minutes. Allow mushrooms to cool slightly before cutting into thin strips.

4 Pat the scallops dry, then season with pepper.

5 Sear the scallops in a large skillet that has been coated with nonfat cooking spray over high heat for about 1 minute per side, or until browned.

6 Add mushrooms. Cook for 1 minute longer, or until warmed through.

Red Snapper

5 *servings*

family fare

- SERVING SIZE: 4 OR 6OZ (112 OR 168G) COOKED
- COUNTS AS:
  - 1 PROTEIN
  - 1 STARCH
  - 2 VEGETABLES

▶ *size according to plan*

☀ Ingredients

2 Tbsp low-sodium chicken broth

1 green bell pepper, seeded and cut into thin strips

1 yellow bell pepper, seeded and cut into thin strips

1 onion, sliced

1 garlic clove, crushed

1 can (14.5oz / 406g) canned, diced tomatoes, no salt added

1/4 cup (60ml) sliced pimento-stuffed olives

1/4 cup (60ml) green pepper sauce

2 Tbsp lime juice

1 pound (448g) red snapper filets

1/4 cup (60ml) chopped cilantro

1 cup (250ml / 158g) cooked yellow rice

1 In a large skillet, over medium heat, heat the broth to a simmer. Cook peppers and onion until tender-crisp; add garlic.

2 Add diced tomatoes with liquid, olives, green pepper sauce, lime juice and red snapper filets.

3 Heat to boiling; reduce heat to low.

4 Cover and simmer 5-10 minutes, stirring occasionally until fish is tender.

5 Stir in chopped cilantro.

> "The L A Lite Cookbook recipes are such a delight. I savor the dishes bite by bite."
> *— Lynn K.*

Under the ❖ Se

Tuna Tostadas

2 servings

meals in minutes

SERVING SIZE: 1 TOSTADA
COUNTS AS:
1 PROTEIN
1 STARCH
1 VEGETABLE
1/2 DAIRY
1 FAT

ize according to plan

☀ Ingredients

12oz (336g) water-packed, low-sodium tuna, well drained

1-2 tsp pepper sauce

1 small tomato, seeded and chopped

1/2 cup (125ml / 80g) chopped onions

1/2 cup (125ml) finely chopped cilantro

1/4 cup (60ml) fat-free sour cream

2 Tbsp fresh lime juice

1/4 ripe avocado, halved and pitted

corn tortilla, cut in half

2oz (56g) reduced-fat Mexican-style cheese

nonfat cooking spray

1 In a bowl, combine tuna and 1 tsp pepper sauce and mix.

2 Add tomato, onion, cilantro, sour cream and lime juice. Blend and chill.

3 With a spoon, scoop the avocados into a bowl and mash with a fork; add remaining pepper sauce, blend.

4 Preheat oven to 350°F.

5 Spray tortilla lightly with nonfat cooking spray on both sides. Place on a baking sheet; bake until crisp.

6 To assemble, spread half of avocado mixture on each tortilla.

7 Add 1/2 of tuna mixture to each tortilla half.

8 Top each tostada with 1oz (28g) cheese.

Swordfish in Lemon Sauce

4 servings

family fare

SERVING SIZE: 3 OR 5OZ
(84 OR 140G) COOKED
COUNTS AS:
1 PROTEIN

ize according to plan

☀ Ingredients

4 swordfish steaks, 4 or 6oz each (112 or 168g each), size according to plan

6 whole black peppercorns

2 garlic cloves, peeled

1 tsp dried oregano

1/4 tsp dried basil

1/3 cup (85ml) fresh lemon juice

3 Tbsp low-sodium vegetable broth

1 Wash fish and dry with paper towels.

2 In a small bowl, crush peppercorns, garlic, oregano and basil. Add lemon juice and broth.

3 Place fish in a shallow dish.

4 Add the marinade; turn to coat both sides.

5 Cover and set aside for 1 hour, turning once.

6 Coat broiling pan with non stick cooking spray and broil 4 inches from heat.

7 Broil 4-5 minutes per side, brushing with marinade.

Under
the ✿ Sea

Mango **Prawns**

4 *servings*

- SERVING SIZE: 1/4 RECIPE
- COUNTS AS:
  - 1 PROTEIN
  - 1 FRUIT
  - 1 FAT

▶ *size according to plan*

☀ Ingredients

20 or 24oz (560 or 672g) uncooked prawns, size according to plan

1 egg white

2 tsp cornstarch

1 tsp sesame oil

1/2 tsp white pepper

1 pound (448g) mango

2 cups (500ml) water

1 Tbsp fresh ginger, finely chopped

1 Tbsp sesame oil

1 Tbsp dry sherry

2 Tbsp green onion, finely chopped, for garnish

1 Peel the prawns, then wash them and pat them dry.

2 Combine the prawns with the egg white, cornstarch, sesame oil and pepper. Mix well and leave in the refrigerator for 20 minutes.

3 Peel the mangos and cut the flesh into cubes.

4 Add water to a saucepan, bring to a boil.

5 Remove the saucepan from heat, immediately add the prawns, stirring vigorously to prevent them from sticking.

6 After 2 minutes, when the prawns turn white, quickly drain the prawns in a stainless steel colander.

7 Heat the wok or large frying pan over high flame.

8 Add the oil, when slightly smoking, add the ginger and garlic and fry for 10 seconds.

9 Then return the prawns to the wok or pan, together with dry sherry, and pepper.

10 Stir-fry the mixture for 1 minute.

11 Add the mango pieces and stir gently for 1 minute to warm the mango.

12 Garnish with green onions and serve.

Sautéed **Sea Scallops**

2 *servings*

- SERVING SIZE: 1/2 OF RECIPE
- COUNTS AS:
  - 1 PROTEIN
  - 1 VEGETABLE

▶ *size according to plan*

☀ Ingredients

8 or 12oz (224 or 336g) fresh sea scallops, size according to plan

6 mushrooms, sliced

1/2 green pepper, diced

1 tomato, diced

1/4 cup (60ml) dry white wine

2 green onions, chopped

1 tsp dill, dried

1 Rinse scallops and pat dry with a paper towel.

2 Place mushrooms, green pepper, tomato and wine in a large skillet; cook 5 minutes until vegetables are tender.

3 Add onions, scallops and dill.

4 Cook another 5 minutes until scallops are opaque.

Under the ❖ Sea

Lemon Baked **Flounder**

serving

SERVING SIZE: 1 FILET
COUNTS AS:
1 PROTEIN
1 FAT

ze according to plan

meals in minutes

☀ Ingredients

5 or 7oz (140 or 196g) flounder
filet, size according to plan

1 Tbsp lite margarine, melted

1 Tbsp lemon juice

1 tsp all purpose flour

2 tsp fresh parley, chopped

1/4 tsp freshly ground pepper

1/4 tsp paprika

nonfat cooking spray

1 Rinse filet thoroughly in cold water; pat dry with paper towels and set aside.

2 Pre-heat oven to 350°F.

3 Combine melted margarine and lemon juice in a small bowl.

4 Combine flour, chopped parsley, and pepper in a shallow container.

5 Dip filet in margarine mixture, then dredge in flour mixture.

6 Transfer filet to a baking sheet that has been coated with nonfat cooking spray and drizzle any remaining margarine mixture over fish.

7 Sprinkle filets with paprika.

8 Bake in oven for 15 minutes, or until fish is golden brown and flakes easily when tested with a fork.

Tuna **Melt**

serving

SERVING SIZE:
1 TUNA MELT
COUNTS AS:
1/2 PROTEIN
1 STARCH
1 FAT
1/2 DAIRY

ze according to plan

meals in minutes

☀ Ingredients

1 6oz can (168g) low-sodium
tuna, drained

1 Tbsp lite mayonnaise

1/2 English muffin

1oz (28g) lite shredded cheese

1 Mix tuna with mayo.

2 Place tuna on top of English muffin.

3 Sprinkle sandwich with cheese.

4 Place in sprayed skillet over medium heat and cover until cheese is melted.

5 Serve hot.

Under
the ♣ Sea

Tilapia Italiano

serving

- **SERVING SIZE: 1 FILET**
- **COUNTS AS:**
  - 1 PROTEIN
  - 2 VEGETABLES

▶ *size according to plan*

☀ Ingredients

5 or 7oz (140 or 196g) tilapia filet, size according to plan

1 tsp crushed garlic

1/4 tsp lemon pepper

1/2 tsp oregano

lite salt, to taste

2 tomatoes, diced

nonfat cooking spray

1. Rinse tilapia under cold water and pat dry with paper towels.
2. Coat skillet with nonfat cooking spray.
3. Sauté garlic over medium heat for 1 minute.
4. Sprinkle fish with oregano, lemon pepper and salt.
5. Add fish to pan, sauté on each side until opaque. Remove from pan and keep warm.
6. Add tomatoes to pan, heat over medium-high flame until reduced by half.
7. Return fish to pan and heat.
8. Serve hot.

Spiced Shrimp & Rice

serving

- **SERVING SIZE: 1 RECIPE**
- **COUNTS AS:**
  - 1 PROTEIN
  - 1 STARCH
  - 1 VEGETABLE

▶ *size according to plan*

☀ Ingredients

5 or 7oz (140 or 196g) raw shrimp, size according to plan, peeled and deveined

5 green onions, sliced

1 garlic clove, minced

1/4 tsp grated ginger

2 cardamom pods

2 whole cloves

1/2 stick cinnamon

1 cup (250ml) hot water

1/3 cup (85ml / 64g) cooked rice

1 green chile, sliced

1/2 tsp garam masala

1/4 tsp chili powder

1 Tbsp cilantro, chopped

nonfat cooking spray

1. Coat a medium saucepan with nonfat cooking spray; heat over a medium high flame.
2. Cook shrimp, turning once, until pink, approximately 5 minutes. Remove from saucepan and set aside.
3. Add onion, garlic and ginger to saucepan. Cook, stirring, until onion is translucent.
4. Add cardamom, cloves and cinnamon stick; cook and stir for 1 minute.
5. Return shrimp to sauce pan. Next add water, rice, green chile, garam masala and chili powder.
6. Bring to a boil. Reduce heat to low and cover; cook for 20 minutes, or until most of the water is absorbed.
7. Remove cardamom pods and cinnamon sticks. Garnish with cilantro, before serving.

Under the ✤ Sea

Shrimp Creole

4 servings

SERVING SIZE:
APPROX 1 1/2 CUPS
COUNTS AS:
1 PROTEIN
2 VEGETABLES

size according to plan

☀ Ingredients

1 Tbsp canola oil

1-2 garlic cloves, minced

1/2 cup (125ml / 80g) onion, diced

1/2 cup (125ml / 74g) green pepper, chopped

1 celery stalk, diced

2 Tbsp flour

1/2 cup (125ml / 122g) tomato sauce, low-sodium or no salt added

1-2 cups (250-500ml) water

dash of hot pepper sauce

2-3 tomatoes, seeded and chopped

1 1/2 or 3/4 pounds (672 or 784g) shrimp, peeled and deveined, size according to plan

1. Heat a large skillet coated with oil over a medium flame. Add garlic, onion, pepper and celery; sauté until tender.

2. Sprinkle with flour. Stir to coat all vegetables. Cook, until flour is lightly browned, approximately 5 minutes.

3. Add tomato sauce, water and hot pepper sauce. Stir to combine.

4. Bring to a boil; reduce heat.

5. Add tomatoes and shrimp. Cook, stirring occasionally, until shrimp are pink and cooked through.

Ginger Poached Cod

1 serving

SERVING SIZE: 1 RECIPE
COUNTS AS:
1 PROTEIN
2 VEGETABLES

size according to plan

☀ Ingredients

2 cups (500ml) water

2 Tbsp fresh ginger, thinly sliced

1 small tomato, seeded and chopped

1/4 cup (60ml / 30g) white onion, sliced

5 or 7oz (140 or 196g) cod filet, size according to plan

1 cup (250ml / 70g) bok choy, leaves and stems, chopped

1/4 tsp lite salt

1/8 tsp freshly ground pepper

1. In a large saucepan, simmer sliced ginger, tomato and onion in 2 cups of water, over medium heat, until onions are tender.

2. Reduce heat to low; add fish and poach for 3-4 minutes, until just becoming opaque.

3. Add bok choy; gently stir while cooking, for approximately 1-2 minutes, allowing bok choy to wilt.

4. Serve immediately.

Under the ✿ Sea

Go Meatless

Vegetarian diets are those that exclude animal products, mainly that of meat, fish or poultry origin. There are several types of diets classified under this term, though the basis of all these diets are plant-based foods, including protein, fruits, vegetables and starches. For vegetarians, the *L A Lite Cookbook* is a fantastic resource of unique food preparation, combinations, storage and more!

Vegetable Ziti Bake recipe can be found on page 208

Complete Proteins and Complementary Proteins

Protein is built of amino acids; there are essential and nonessential amino acids. Essential amino acids cannot be made in the body, therefore it is essential to get these from foods. Nonessential amino acids can be made in the body, so it is not pertinent to eat foods containing them. An example of an essential amino acid is tryptophan; tyrosine is a nonessential amino acid.

A complete protein is one that contains all the essential amino acids for the human body and in approximately the adequate amount needed. Most animal proteins are considered complete (with the exception of gelatin). Most plant-based proteins tend to be limiting only in one or two amino acids, such as vegetables, grains and legumes; some plant proteins, like corn, are known to be incomplete, while soy protein is complete.

As you can tell, most vegetable proteins are of lower quality than animal proteins, but if you pair your foods correctly to replace the missing "links" or amino acids, you can somewhat create a complete protein. The foods that supply the missing links to each other are complementary proteins; the strategy of combining two protein foods in a meal is called mutual supplementation. Some examples would be peanut butter and toast and rice and black beans.

But this is not a necessary action for you to achieve optimal health; in most instances, a vegetarian person will obtain the necessary and essential amino acids over the course of one day, provided he/she eats a variety of foods, such as grains, seeds, legumes, etc.

TIP!

Ever come across a recipe that called for dried herbs when you'd rather use fresh ones? Feel free to use the fresh herbs, just triple the amount that the recipe calls for that specific herb. Better yet, try to add in the herbs in the final cooking stages so their unique flavor stays bold.

Glossary of Vegetarian Cooking

- **Tofu** — also known as soybean curd or bean curd; produced from curdled soy milk as extracted from ground, cooked soybeans, in which the curds are drained and pressed, similarly done as in cheese-making; it has a bland, nutty flavor that tends to take on the flavor of what it is cooked with or in; may be firm or soft.

- **Tempeh** — a fermented soy bean cake, similar in texture to soft tofu, though with a slightly nutty texture.

- **Seitan** — a protein rich meat substitute made from wheat gluten; it has a firm texture that is chewy and meat-like; also called "wheat meat"; also picks up the flavors that is cooked in or with; can be found in cakes or tubs.

- **Miso** — a fermented soybean paste and comes in many flavors; its flavor is influenced by the amount of salt, amount of aging, and koji (mold cultivated in barley, rice or soybean); can be used in many different menu items, soups, salads, entrees and dips; it is high in protein and B vitamins.

- **Textured Vegetable Protein** — typically found in powdered form, this is produced grinding soy beans and extruding them to obtain just protein; appears as a flour and easily prepared by mixing with water; may also be found flaked or in frozen form; make sure to use low fat version — it is basically defatted soy flour.

- **Edamame** — Japanese name for soybeans; may be fresh or fresh-frozen; may be eaten in the pod or out of the pod; generally steamed or boiled as an appetizer in Japanese restaurants.

❀TIP!

Want to keep your spices lasting longer? First, move your spice rack from above your stove. Store your spices in a cool, dark place. Humidity, light and heat are all flavor losing factors in your spice rack. To make the most of your spices, stash them in an airtight container or in the freezer in tightly sealed containers.

Preparing

Use an electric coffee grinder to grind up nuts, seeds and spices. It saves time preparing and cooking so you don't have to crush them yourself. Just make sure to clean it out before you put coffee beans in, or your coffee will go nuts!

When buying garlic for cooking always looks for heads that are firm with plenty of flaky paper covering.

Storing

Once you open the tofu package, rinse and cover the leftover with water to store in your refrigerator. Change the water daily and use the food within 7 days.

Keep your fresh herbs staying fresh longer in the refrigerator. Place any stem bunches in water. Store loose leaves in perforated bags in the coldest part of your fridge. Remember to shake them before you store them. To absorb extra moisture place a paper towel in the bag under the herbs.

Cooking

To help the oil heat faster when using a wok, add the oil so that it circles around the sides before reaching the bottom.

When stir-frying vegetables, cook them according to density. Stir-fry the densest veggies, such as carrots and eggplant, first because they take the longest. Green leafy vegetables require less cooking time.

❀ Go Meatless

1 *serving*

■ SERVING SIZE: 1 RECIPE
■ COUNTS AS:
  2 VEGETABLES
  1 FRUIT

▶ *size according to plan*

good source of fiber

Red Kidney Bean Curry

✳ Ingredients

1 cup (250ml / 177g) cooked red kidney beans

1/4 cup (60ml / 40g) white onions, chopped

1/2 green chili, sliced

1/2 tsp ginger, grated

1/2 tsp turmeric

1/2 tsp cumin seeds

1 small tomato, seeded and chopped

1 Tbsp lemon juice

1/2 tsp garam masala

1/4 tsp lite salt

1 Tbsp chopped cilantro

nonfat cooking spray

1 Coat skillet with nonfat cooking spray. Add onion, chili, ginger, turmeric and cumin seeds. Cook, stirring, until onion is soft and lightly browned. Add tomato; cook until soft.

2 Add beans to onion mixture; toss to combine. Add lemon juice, garam masala and salt. Cook, stirring, uncovered for 5 minutes.

3 Garnish with cilantro.

---

1 *serving*

■ SERVING SIZE: 1 RECIPE
■ COUNTS AS:
  2 VEGETABLES
  1 FRUIT

▶ *size according to plan*

family fare

Red Beans & Rice

✳ Ingredients

1 Tbsp olive or canola oil

2 garlic cloves, minced

2 celery stalks, chopped

1 cup onion, chopped

1 medium green pepper, chopped

1 jalapeño, seeded and deveined, chopped

1 pound (448g) dried red beans, rinsed and picked over

2 quarts (1L) low-sodium chicken or vegetable broth

1/4 tsp freshly ground pepper

1/4 cup (60ml) flat leafed Italian parsley, chopped

2 cups (500ml / 330g) rice, cooked

1 Place beans in a large bowl; cover with water by one inch. Soak overnight. Drain and set aside.

2 In large soup pot, heat olive oil over medium flame. Add garlic, celery, onion and peppers. Sauté until soft, about 10 minutes.

3 Add broth and beans. Bring to a boil over medium-high heat. Reduce heat.

4 Continue to cook over low heat until beans are soft, about 2 hours. Stir occasionally while cooking.

5 Garnish with parsley and serve over hot cooked rice.

✤ Go
Meatle

Scrambled Tofu

4 servings

SERVING SIZE: 1/4 OF RECIPE
COUNTS AS:
1/2 PROTEIN
1 VEGETABLE

ze according to plan

☼ Ingredients

1/2 cup (125ml / 80g) onion,
  finely chopped

1 pound (448g) firm tofu,
  crumbled

1 Tbsp low-sodium soy sauce

1 tsp basil or cilantro

1/4 tsp garlic powder

1/4 tsp freshly ground pepper

nonfat cooking spray

1 Sauté onions in a skillet coated with nonfat cooking
  spray until tender; next, add remaining ingredients.

2 Cook until tofu starts to brown and heated through.

3 Serve with toast.

Indian-Style Chickpeas

4 servings

SERVING SIZE: 1/4 OF RECIPE
COUNTS AS:
1/2 PROTEIN
3 VEGETABLES

ze according to plan

☼ Ingredients

1 medium onion

3 garlic cloves, coarsely chopped

1 Tbsp cumin seeds

1 Tbsp turmeric

2-inch long piece of fresh peeled
  ginger, chopped

1/2 cup (125ml) lite tomato sauce

chilies, cayenne powder, or
  chopped fresh jalapeños
  (optional and to taste)

2 carrots, diced

1 can (15.5oz / 434g) chickpeas,
  rinsed and drained

1 Place the first 6 ingredients and pepper (optional) in a
  blender and blend until smooth, add water if it is too
  thick to mix properly.

2 Pour the paste into a saucepan on medium high heat
  and stir until it begins to darken and gains aroma.

3 Stir constantly to prevent burning.

4 Add the diced carrots and stir the mixture to coat the
  carrots with the paste; add a small amount of water if
  there is no liquid at the bottom of the pan and allow
  the vegetables to steam until nearly done.

5 Add chickpeas and mix well, heating through.

❖ Go
Meatless

Vegetarian Chili

10 *servings*

- **SERVING SIZE: 1 CUP (250ML)**
- **COUNTS AS:**
  - 1/2 PROTEIN
  - 2 VEGETABLES

▶ *size according to plan*

❋ Ingredients

1 large onion, finely chopped

1 green pepper, seeded and finely chopped

6 cups (1.5L) canned low sodium stewed tomatoes

2 cups (500ml / 480g) canned pinto beans, drained and rinsed

2 cups (500ml / 512g) canned kidney beans, drained and rinsed

1/8 tsp ground cloves

dash of allspice

2 Tbsp chili powder

1 Tbsp cumin

nonfat cooking spray

1 Sauté onion and green pepper in a Dutch oven coated with nonfat cooking spray.

2 Add the remaining ingredients and simmer until flavors are blended.

3 Heat and serve.

Jalapeño Red Bean Burgers

good source of fiber

4 *servings*

- **SERVING SIZE: 1 PATTY**
- **COUNTS AS:**
  - 1/2 PROTEIN
  - 1 STARCH
  - 1 VEGETABLE

▶ *size according to plan*

❋ Ingredients

1 can (16oz / 448g) kidney beans, drained and rinsed

1 small onion, finely chopped

1 small tomato, chopped

1 jalapeño chili, seeded and chopped

1 garlic clove, finely minced

1 tsp chili powder

1/4 cup (60ml) barbecue sauce

1/3 cup (85ml / 36g) bread crumbs (see recipe on pg 154)

nonfat cooking spray

1 In a bowl, mash beans with a fork.

2 Add first 5 ingredients.

3 Add bread crumbs, enough so that mixture can be formed into patties that hold together.

4 Make 4 patties.

5 Grill in a skillet coated with nonfat cooking spray, until heated through.

"Try this with the sweet cole slaw."

❖ Go
Meatle

BBQ Tofu

serving

SERVING SIZE: 1 RECIPE
COUNTS AS:
1 PROTEIN

ze according to plan

☀ Ingredients

1/2 or 1 cup (125 or 250ml) firm tofu, size according to plan

1 Tbsp low-sodium soy sauce

1 packet artificial sweetener

1 tsp water

1/2 tsp dry mustard

1 garlic clove, minced

1 tsp onion powder

nonfat cooking spray

1 Cut tofu into strips.

2 In medium bowl, combine soy sauce, artificial sweetener, water, mustard, garlic and onion powder.

3 Marinade tofu in sauce 1 hour.

4 Cook tofu in wok that has been coated with nonfat cooking spray until heated through.

Pizza Bagel

serving

SERVING SIZE: 1 RECIPE
COUNTS AS:
1 STARCH
1 VEGETABLE
1 DAIRY

ze according to plan

good source of calcium

☀ Ingredients

1/2 small bagel

1 small tomato

fresh basil

2oz (56g) part-skim shredded mozzarella cheese

1 Cut tomato in to 2-3 slices.

2 Place tomato on bagel.

3 Sprinkle basil and cheese on top of tomato.

4 Place on baking sheet and place in 375°F oven, until cheese is melted.

☘ Go
Meatless

4 *servings*

- SERVING SIZE:
  1/2 OR 3/4 CUP (125 OR 200ML) COTTAGE CHEESE
- COUNTS AS:
  1 PROTEIN

▶ *size according to plan*

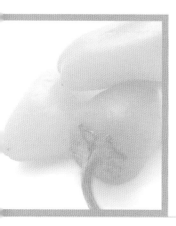

good source of calcium

Silken Delight

☀ Ingredients

2 cups (500ml) 1% cottage cheese

1 cup (250ml) boiling water

1 envelope sugar free flavored gelatin*

1 In a small bowl, combine gelatin powder and 1/4 cup (60ml) water, allow to soften.

2 In a blender, combine cottage cheese, gelatin mixture and remaining water. Process until smooth.

3 Divide into serving cups and refrigerate until firm.

4 Serve with fresh fruit.

*Unflavored gelatin can be used in place of fruit flavored, add 1 tsp vanilla extract and artificial sweetener to add flavor.

Vegetarian Pepper Quesadillas

2 *servings*

- SERVING SIZE: 1 RECIPE
- COUNTS AS:
  1 STARCH
  2 VEGETABLES
  1/2 DAIRY

☀ Ingredients

1/2 green pepper, chopped

1/2 red pepper, chopped

10 small green onions, chopped

2oz (56g) reduced-fat shredded cheese, such as cheddar

1 corn or flour tortilla

salsa

lite salt

freshly ground pepper

cumin

1 Sauté onion and pepper in skillet.

2 Stir in salt, pepper and cumin.

3 Remove from heat.

4 Spoon cheese onto tortilla. Top with pepper mixture.

5 Place on baking sheet and bake in 350°F oven for 5-10 minutes until cheese is melted.

6 Top with salsa before serving.

GC
Meatle

Meatless Sloppy Joe

servings

SERVING SIZE: 1 RECIPE
COUNTS AS:
2 VEGETABLES
1 FRUIT

ze according to plan

✳ Ingredients

1/2 cup (125ml / 48g) green onion, chopped

1/2 cup (125ml / 74g) green pepper, chopped

1 tsp garlic, minced

3/4 cup (200ml / 53g) fresh mushroom, sliced

1/2 cup (125ml) reduced-sodium ketchup

2/3 cup (170ml) water

2 Tbsp brown sugar artificial sweetener

1 Tbsp mustard

1 tsp celery seed

1/2 tsp chili powder

12oz (336g) textured vegetable protein

nonfat cooking spray

1. Coat medium saucepan with nonfat cooking spray; heat over medium flame until hot.

2. Sauté onion, green pepper, and garlic until tender, 5-8 minutes. Stir in mushroom, ketchup, water, brown sugar, mustard, celery seed and chili powder; heat to boiling.

3. Stir in vegetable protein; reduce heat and simmer, covered, 10 minutes.

4. Season to taste with lite salt and pepper.

Tofu-Bacon

servings

SERVING SIZE: 1/4 RECIPE
COUNTS AS:
1/2 PROTEIN
1 VEGETABLE

ze according to plan

✳ Ingredients

1/3 cup (85ml) low-sodium soy sauce

2 Tbsp water

1 Tbsp nutritional yeast flakes

1 Tbsp maple syrup

1/2 Tbsp liquid smoke

8oz (224g) extra-firm tofu

1. Mix the soy sauce, water, yeast flakes, maple syrup and liquid smoke together in a shallow, flat container.

2. With a cheese slicer, shave the tofu into thin slices.

3. Marinate in the mixture for 24 hours.

4. To cook, heat a nonfat griddle over medium-high heat.

5. Fry the tofu slices until golden brown and almost crispy on both sides, scraping underneath the slices as you turn them with a sturdy spatula.

6. Serve hot.

✤ Go
Meatless

Mediterranean Pasta Bake

1 *serving*

SERVING SIZE: 1 RECIPE
COUNTS AS:
1 STARCH
2 VEGETABLES
1 FAT
1/2 DAIRY

▶ *size according to plan*

※ Ingredients

2 garlic cloves, minced

2 Tbsp onion, diced

1/4 cup (60ml / 28g) thinly sliced zucchini

1/2 tomato, diced

1 tsp flour

1/4 cup (60ml) skim milk

1 Tbsp tomato paste

1/3 cup (85ml / 53g) cooked pasta

1oz (28g) lite feta cheese

9 kalamata olives, halved

nonfat cooking spray

1 Coat medium skillet with nonfat cooking spray. Sauté garlic and onion over medium heat for 1 minute.

2 Add zucchini and tomato; cook until zucchini is tender.

3 Sprinkle flour into zucchini mixture and mix well.

4 Stir in milk and tomato paste; heat to a simmer.

5 Toss in pasta. Top with cheese and olives.

Eggplant Parmigiana

2 *servings*

SERVING SIZE: 1/2 OF RECIPE
COUNTS AS:
1 STARCH
2 VEGETABLES
1 DAIRY

▶ *size according to plan*

good source of calcium

※ Ingredients

1/2 cup (125ml) lite tomato sauce

1 small tomato

1/2 cup (125ml) water

1 tsp dried onion

1 tsp garlic powder

dash of dried parsley flakes

dash of lite salt

dash of oregano

freshly ground pepper

1/2 eggplant, sliced

1/2 cup (125ml) egg substitute

1/2 cup (125ml / 54g) breadcrumbs

4oz (112g) part-skim, shredded mozzarella cheese

nonfat cooking spray

1 In small saucepan, combine tomato sauce, tomato, water, dried onion, garlic powder, parsley flakes, salt, oregano and pepper. Heat to a simmer and set aside.

2 Dip eggplant slices in egg, then into bread crumbs.

3 Coat skillet with nonfat cooking spray and heat over medium flame. Lightly brown each side of eggplant.

4 Coat casserole dish with nonfat cooking spray. Arrange half of the eggplant slices in a single layer in casserole dish.

5 Top with half of the tomato sauce. Sprinkle with 2oz (56g) of the cheese.

6 Repeat process with remaining eggplant, sauce and cheese

7 Bake, uncovered, in a 400°F oven for 10-15 minutes, or until cheese is melted.

❖ Go
Meatle

Italian Style "Vegetarian Meatballs"

6 servings

family fare

SERVING SIZE:
4 MEATBALLS AND 1/4 CUP
(60ML) SAUCE
COUNTS AS:
1 PROTEIN
1 VEGETABLE

ze according to plan

✳ Ingredients

12oz (336g) frozen vegetable protein crumbles, thawed

1/2 cup (125ml) egg substitute

1/4 cup (125ml / 27g) breadcrumbs (see recipe on page 154)

2 garlic cloves, minced

2 Tbsp grated reduced-fat parmesan cheese

2 tsp Italian herbs

1/2 tsp fennel seed, crushed

1 1/2 cups (375ml) lite tomato sauce

1 tomato, chopped

2 Tbsp onion, diced

1 tsp basil

1/2 tsp oregano

1. Combine vegetable crumbles, egg substitute, breadcrumbs, garlic, parmesan cheese, Italian herbs and fennel. Mash mixture lightly with fork. Form into 24 balls.

2. Bake in baking pan at 350°F until firm, about 10 minutes.

3. To make sauce, combine tomato sauce, chopped tomato, onion, basil and oregano in small saucepan. Bring to a boil, then lower heat and simmer 5 minutes.

4. Serve sauce over hot meatballs.

Mock-Sausage

2 servings

SERVING SIZE: 1 PATTY
COUNTS AS:
1/2 PROTEIN

ze according to plan

✳ Ingredients

3/4 cup (200ml) boiling water

2 Tbsp low-sodium soy sauce

1 cup (250ml) textured vegetable protein (TVP) granules

1/2 cup (125ml) mashed firm tofu

2 tsp marjoram

1/2 tsp minced garlic

1/2 tsp onion powder

1/2 tsp thyme

1/2 tsp red cayenne flakes

1/2 tsp liquid smoke

1/2 cup (125ml / 63g) unbleached flour

nonfat cooking spray

1. In a bowl, pour the water and soy sauce over the TVP.

2. When soft, add the remaining ingredients, except flour and mix well.

3. When the mixture is cooled, add the flour.

4. Mix well with your hands and form into 12 thin patties

5. In a heavy skillet coated with nonfat cooking spray, fry until firm and browned, 7-10 minutes per side.

6. These can be refrigerated or frozen for later use.

Vegetable Ziti Bake

2 servings

- **SERVING SIZE:**
  1 CUP (250ML)
- **COUNTS AS:**
  1 STARCH
  2 VEGETABLES
  1 DAIRY

▶ *size according to plan*

good source of calcium

☀ Ingredients

1/4 cup (60ml / 40g) diced onion

2 garlic cloves, minced

1/4 cup (60ml / 30g) thinly sliced carrots

1/4 cup (60ml / 18g) sliced mushrooms

1/4 cup (60ml / 28g) thinly sliced zucchini

1/2 tsp garlic powder

1/2 cup (125ml / 28g) fresh spinach

2/3 cup (175ml / 106g) cooked ziti

1/4 cup (60ml) lite tomato sauce

1/2 cup (125ml) part-skim ricotta cheese

1/2 tomato, diced

2oz (56g) part-skim mozzarella cheese

nonfat cooking spray

1 Coat skillet with nonfat cooking spray; heat over medium flame.

2 Add onion, garlic and carrots to skillet and sauté 1-2 minutes, or until onions begin to soften.

3 Add mushrooms, zucchini and garlic powder, and sauté 2 minutes. Add spinach and cook until wilted. Remove vegetables from heat and set aside.

4 In large mixing bowl, combine ziti, ricotta cheese, tomato sauce and vegetable mixture.

5 Coat casserole dish with nonfat cooking spray. Pour ziti mixture into casserole and top with diced tomato.

6 Cover and bake in 350°F oven for 20 minutes.

7 Remove from oven and top with mozzarella cheese. Bake, uncovered, 10 minutes, or until cheese is melted.

Edamame

3 servings

- **SERVING SIZE: 1 CUP (250ML) COOKED**
- **COUNTS AS:**
  1 PROTEIN

good source of fiber

☀ Ingredients

1 pound frozen edamame

1 lemon

1 Tbsp kosher salt

1 In medium sized pot, boil edamame for 5-8 minutes until tender, do not overcook.

2 Drain in colander and pat dry.

3 Place edamame in serving bowl.

4 Squeeze lemon juice on edamame and sprinkle with kosher salt.

▶ *size according to plan*

Go
Meatle

Tofu Manicotti

☀ Ingredients

2 manicotti shells

1/4 cup (60ml / 18g) fresh mushroom, chopped

1/4 cup green onion (60ml / 24g), chopped

1 tsp snipped fresh parsley

1/4 tsp dried Italian seasoning

dash of paprika and garlic powder

4oz (112g) tofu, drained

1 Tbsp reduced-fat parmesan cheese

1/2 cup (125ml) skim milk

1/2 Tbsp flour

1/8 tsp lite salt

1/8 tsp freshly ground pepper

1oz (28g) reduced-fat mozzarella cheese, shredded

1 Cook pasta shells according to package directions. Rinse in cold water; drain.

2 Coat medium skillet with nonfat cooking spray. Add mushroom and onion; cook until tender. Stir in parsley, Italian seasoning and paprika. Cool slightly.

3 Mash tofu in a bowl. Stir in parmesan cheese, mushroom and onion mixture.

4 Stuff each shell with 1/2 of the mixture. Arrange stuffed shells in baking pan.

5 For the sauce, combine milk, flour, garlic powder, salt and pepper in a medium saucepan. Cook, stirring, until slightly thickened. Pour sauce over shells.

6 Bake, covered, and in a 350°F oven for 20-25 minutes, or until heated through.

7 Sprinkle with cheese and bake, uncovered, 2 minutes longer or until cheese is melted.

Baked Macaroni & Cheese

☀ Ingredients

3 Tbsp butter

3 Tbsp all-purpose flour

2 1/2 cups (625ml) skim milk

freshly ground pepper

8oz (224g) shredded reduced-fat cheddar cheese

1 pound (448g) raw macaroni

nonfat cooking spray

1 Over medium heat, melt butter in medium saucepan. Add flour and stir until a paste forms.

2 Remove from heat and add the cold milk a little at a time, stirring well with each addition.

3 Return to heat once all the milk is added and the mixture is smooth. Stir over medium heat until sauce comes to a boil and slightly thickens. Pepper to taste.

4 Remove from heat and add the grated cheddar. Stir until cheese melts. Preheat broiler.

5 Meanwhile, cook macaroni in rolling boiling water according to package directions. Drain and toss with cheese sauce.

6 Transfer to a medium baking dish that has been coated with nonfat cooking spray.

7 Place under broiler until browned and bubbly, about 3-4 minutes.

♣ Go
Meatless

Vegetable Shepherd's Pie

4 *servings*

■ **SERVING SIZE: 1/4 OF RECIPE**
■ **COUNTS AS:**
  1/2 PROTEIN
  1 STARCH
  3 VEGETABLES

▶ *size according to plan*

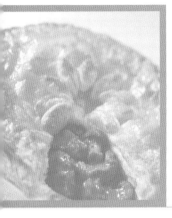

☀ Ingredients

2 cups (500ml) water, divided

1/2 cup (120ml / 96g) uncooked lentils

1/4 cup (60ml / 46g) uncooked barley

1 medium carrot, diced

1 small onion, finely chopped

8oz (224g) low-sodium canned, diced tomatoes

1 garlic clove, crushed

1 tsp flour

1 tsp parsley

3 small potatoes, cooked and mashed

freshly ground pepper

1 Heat 1-1/4 cups (310ml) water; add lentils and barley simmer 30 minutes.

2 Heat remaining water in a separate saucepan, add carrot, onion and garlic; cook until tender, then add tomatoes, parsley and pepper, to taste.

3 Mix the flour with a little water and add to saucepan; cook, stirring, over low heat until thickened.

4 Combine vegetable mixture with cooked lentils and barley, place in ovenproof baking dish, cover with mashed potatoes.

5 Bake at 350°F for 30 minutes.

Hot & Spicy Dahl

1 *serving*

good source of fiber

■ **SERVING SIZE: 1 RECIPE**
■ **COUNTS AS:**
  1 PROTEIN
  3 VEGETABLES

▶ *size according to plan*

☀ Ingredients

1-2 cups (250ml / 198g) cooked red lentils, size according to plan

1 Tbsp minced ginger

2 Tbsp cilantro

2 tomatoes, seeded and chopped

1/2 tsp mustard seeds

5 green onions, chopped

2 jalapeños, seeded and chopped

2 tsp ground coriander

2 tsp ground cumin

3 garlic cloves, minced

2/3 cup (170ml) water

nonfat cooking spray

1 Coat skillet with nonfat cooking spray and heat over medium flame.

2 Add mustard seeds and cook 1-2 minutes.

3 Add onion, ginger, jalapeño and garlic.

4 Cook on medium heat until garlic browns.

5 Add cumin, coriander and tomatoes. Continue to sauté until tomatoes are cooked.

6 Add water, boil 5-6 minutes.

7 Add cooked lentils, stir well.

8 Add cilantro to mixture and remove from heat.

9 Serve immediately.

❖ Gc
Meatle

Tofu & Vegetable Stir-fry

1 serving

SERVING SIZE: 1 ENTREE
COUNTS AS:
1 PROTEIN
1 STARCH
2 VEGETABLES

ize according to plan

✳ Ingredients

1/2 cup (125ml) water

1/4 cup (60ml) dry sherry

1 Tbsp cornstarch

2 Tbsp low-sodium soy sauce

1 packet artificial sweetener

1 tsp very low-sodium bouillon granules

3/4 tsp ground ginger

1/2 medium carrot, thinly sliced

1 garlic clove, minced

1 cup (250ml / 70g) broccoli florets

1/2 or 1 cup (124 or 248g) tofu, cubed

1/3 cup (85ml / 53g) cooked brown rice

1 Tbsp sesame seeds, toasted

nonfat cooking spray

1. For sauce, stir together water, dry sherry, cornstarch, soy sauce, sugar substitute, bouillon and ginger. Set aside.

2. Coat wok or skillet with nonfat cooking spray. Preheat over medium-high flame. Add carrot and garlic and stir-fry for 2 minutes. Add broccoli; stir-fry for another 3-4 minutes, or until all vegetables are crisp-tender. Push vegetables from center of skillet to the side.

3. Stir sauce and add to center of skillet. Cook, stirring, until thickened. Add tofu.

4. Toss ingredients together to coat with sauce.

5. Serve with hot cooked brown rice. Sprinkle with sesame seeds.

Asparagus Soup

4 servings

SERVING SIZE: 1/4 RECIPE
COUNTS AS:
1 STARCH
1 VEGETABLE
1 FAT

ize according to plan

✳ Ingredients

1 onion, chopped

2 Tbsp butter

1 pound fresh asparagus, trimmed and coarsely chopped

1 cup vegetable broth

1 dash garlic powder

1 dash white pepper

1 cup 1% milk

1. Microwave onion and butter on high for 2 minutes

2. Add asparagus, vegetable broth, garlic powder and white pepper.

3. Microwave, covered, on high for 10-12 minutes.

4. Puree in blender.

5. Return mixture to microwave safe dish, stir in milk and microwave until heated through.

✤ Go
Meatless

Add
a little
♣ Zest

The *L A Lite Cookbook* shows you just how to add a little spice to life. You'll find all the information you need for increasing flavor and decreasing fat with fresh herbs, spicy sauces and a variety of seasonings. These zesty recipes will keep your appetite satisfied and your taste buds tantalized!

Add a little Zest

Hot Spice Mix (Garam Masala)

Cajun Spice Seasoning

Teriyaki Sauce

Chocolate-Orange Sauce

Seasoned Margarine

Soy-Sesame Marinade

Spicy Curry Powder

Lemon Seasoning

Mushroom Sauce

Italian-Style Tomato Sauce

Margarita Marinade

Orange-Ginger Marinade

Chili Powder

Indian Spice Blend

Hot Citrus Rub

Vegetable Sauce

Plum Sauce

Basil Mayonnaise

Spicy Flavor Blend

Seasoned Salt

Herb Blend

Taco Seasoning Mix

Citrus Rub

Five Spice Powder

Fajita Seasoning Marinade

Teriyaki Marinade

Glossary of Sauce Terms

- **Roux** — a cooked mixture of equal parts fat and flour, such as butter and flour, which is cooked until desired color and flavor is reached; used as a base of many sauces and also to thicken soups, stews and other sauces.

- **Mayonnaise** — an emulsion of egg yolk, oil and lemon juice or vinegar.

- **Aioli** — a garlic mayonnaise, commonly served with fish or vegetables.

- **Pesto** — a puree of fresh herbs, such as basil, with olive oil, pine nuts and garlic; may also be available with sun-dried tomatoes or artichokes.

- **Hollandaise** — a rich sauce blend of egg yolks, butter and tarragon.

- **Bechamel** — a roux-thickened milk sauce.

- **Demi-glace** — a rich reduction of beef or veal broth into a velvety brown sauce.

- **Mornay** — a cheese and milk sauce made combining a roux with milk and adding parmesan or gruyere cheese.

- **Chutney** — originated from India; a relish of fruits and spices, most common is a spicy mango chutney.

- **Tomato** — a common base sauce, in which garlic and vegetables are sautéed in olive oil and then tomatoes are added and simmer together .

- **Salsa** — Spanish for "sauce"; commonly thought of as a raw sauce of tomatoes and/or fruits or other vegetables, combined with garlic, herbs and olive oil.

Cut the fat...

- Choose vegetable or broth based sauces.

- Keep the sauce on the side to control how much you use with each bite.

- Use sauces and seasonings that are high in flavor—they are more satisfying to the stomach and taste buds.

- Use low fat milk or evaporated nonfat milk in place of cream.

Increase the flavor...

- Use fresh herbs at the end of the recipe or dried herbs at the beginning for optimum flavor.

- Select herbs and spices that will complement foods, such as rosemary or mint for lamb, nutmeg for spinach or dill for eggs.

- In place of salt, try fresh lemon juice to heighten flavors in a recipe.

- Roast vegetables with olive oil and garlic to bring out the natural sweetness.

Add
a little
❖ Zest

Hot Spice Mix (Garam Masala)

☀ Ingredients

4oz (112g) coriander seeds

1oz (28g) cumin seeds

1oz (28g) freshly ground pepper

1/2oz (14g) black cumin seeds

1/4oz (7g) black cardamom

1/4oz (7g) cloves

1/4oz (7g) cinnamon

1/4oz (7g) bay leaves

1/2oz (14g) dry ginger

1 Dry roast all ingredients, except ginger, by cooking the spices in a hot skillet, sliding the spices back and forth over the burner. Cook lightly until aromas are released.

2 Cool to room temperature. Add ginger to mixture; grind to fine powder in a spice/coffee grinder.

3 Store in an air tight container. (Unlimited use)

Cajun Spice Seasoning

SERVING SIZE: 1 TSP

☀ Ingredients

3/4 cup (200ml / 200g) lite salt

1/4 cup (60ml) ground cayenne pepper

2 Tbsp ground white pepper

2 Tbsp freshly ground pepper

2 Tbsp paprika

2 Tbsp onion powder

2 Tbsp garlic powder

1 Combine all ingredients and mix well.

2 Place in an airtight jar.

Spice up the Roast Chicken with a Cajun twist.

215

Add
a little
♣ Zest

Teriyaki Sauce

10 *servings*

- SERVING SIZE: 2 TBSP
- COUNTS AS:
  1 FRUIT

▶ *size according to plan*

☼ Ingredients

1 cup (250ml) low-sodium
soy sauce

1/4 cup (60ml) canola or
soybean oil

4 tsp ground ginger

4 tsp dry mustard

1 garlic clove, minced

1 packet artificial sweetener

1 Combine all ingredients and whisk vigorously to
combine.

2 Use to flavor beef, chicken, pork or other meats.

Chocolate-Orange Sauce

6 *servings*

- SERVING SIZE: 3 TBSP
- COUNTS AS:
  1 FRUIT
  1 FAT

▶ *size according to plan*

☼ Ingredients

1/2 cup (125ml / 100g) artificial
sweetener

1 cup (250ml) evaporated skim
milk

1 Tbsp lite corn syrup

2 squares (1oz / 28g)
unsweetened or semi-sweet
chocolate (for a sweeter sauce)

2 Tbsp butter flavor vegetable
shortening

1 Tbsp orange zest

1/2 tsp orange extract

1 Combine artificial sweetener, evaporated milk and corn
syrup in a 2 quart saucepan.

2 Heat to a full boil over medium-high flame; cook for
1 minute, at a boil, stirring constantly.

3 Reduce heat to low; add chocolate and stir until
smooth.

4 Remove from heat.

5 Stir in vegetable shortening, orange zest and extract.

6 Serve with fruit, or as desired.

Add
a little
✿ Zest

Seasoned Margarine

4 servings

SERVING SIZE: 1 TBSP
COUNTS AS:
2 FAT

...ze according to plan

☀ Ingredients
1/4 cup (60ml / 56g) lite margarine, melted

1. Mix with one of the following seasonings, then chill until solid.
   - ▸ Basil: 1/4 tsp dried basil leaves.
   - ▸ Chive-Parsley: 1 Tbsp snipped chives and 1 Tbsp snipped parsley.
   - ▸ Curry: 1/4 tsp curry powder.
   - ▸ Garlic: 1/4 tsp garlic powder.
   - ▸ Lemon: 1 Tbsp grated lemon peel, 2 Tbsp lemon juice.
   - ▸ Cinnamon: 1 tsp cinnamon and 1 packet of artificial sweetener.

Soy-Sesame Marinade

1 serving

SERVING SIZE: 1 RECIPE
COUNTS AS:
1 FAT

...ze according to plan

☀ Ingredients
2 Tbsp low-sodium soy sauce

2 Tbsp water

1 tsp sesame oil

2 garlic cloves, crushed

1 tsp artificial sweetener or brown sugar artificial sweetener

1. In medium bowl, combine all ingredients; whisk vigorously.
2. Add desired meat, poultry or seafood; toss to combine.
3. Cover and marinate in refrigerator 20 minutes before preparing as desired.

Marinate the Chicken Kabobs with this sassy seasoning.

Add a little ♣ Zest

Spicy Curry Powder

☀ Ingredients

- 20 green cardamom pods
- 2 cinnamon sticks, broken into pieces
- 5 bay leaves
- 1/2 tsp whole cloves
- 1/4 tsp grated nutmeg
- 2 Tbsp anise seeds
- 1 tsp black peppercorns
- 5 dried red chilies
- 10 dried curry leaves
- 6 Tbsp coriander (cilantro) seeds
- 3 Tbsp cumin seeds
- 3 Tbsp ground turmeric
- 1 Tbsp fenugreek seeds
- 2 Tbsp black mustard seeds

1. Roast the spices in a small, heavy-bottomed pan over a medium heat for 4-5 minutes, stirring constantly until lightly darkened and fragrant.

2. Remove the spices from the pan and grind to a fine powder in a spice or coffee grinder.

3. Store in an airtight jar for up to 6 months. (Unlimited use)

Lemon Seasoning

☀ Ingredients

- zest from 1/2 of a lemon
- 2 tsp dried parsley
- 1/2 tsp dried parsley
- 1/2 tsp garlic powder
- 1/2 tsp dried oregano
- 1/2 tsp dried marjoram leaves, crushed
- 1/2 tsp pepper

1. Combine all ingredients. Toss.

2. Refrigerate in covered, air-tight container. (Unlimited use).

Add a little lemon seasoning to the Herbed Chicken Recipe.

218

Add
a little
❖ Zest

Mushroom Sauce

 servings

family fare

SERVING SIZE:
1/4 CUP (60ML)
COUNTS AS:
2 VEGETABLES
1 FRUIT

...ze according to plan

☀ Ingredients

1 Tbsp lite margarine

1 1/2 Tbsp flour

1/4 tsp lite salt

1/8 tsp white pepper

1 cup (250ml) skim milk

1/2 cup (125ml / 78g) cooked
   mushrooms, sliced

1 In a medium saucepan, melt margarine over medium heat.

2 Stir in flour, salt and pepper.

3 Add milk slowly, stirring constantly. Cook, over medium-low flame, until thickened.

4 Add mushrooms. Continue to cook, until heated through.

Italian-Style Tomato Sauce

servings

family fare

SERVING SIZE:
1/2 CUP (125ML)
COUNTS AS:
2 VEGETABLES

...ze according to plan

☀ Ingredients

1 Tbsp olive oil

1/2 cup (125ml / 80g) white or
   yellow onion, diced

2 garlic cloves, minced

1 tsp dried basil

1 tsp dried oregano

1/4 tsp lite salt

1 bay leaf

3oz (85ml) full-bodied red wine,
   such as Burgundy

1 (28oz / 784g) can crushed
   tomatoes, no salt added

1 In a large saucepan, heat olive oil over a medium flame. Add onion and garlic; sauté until begins to become translucent and soft.

2 Add basil, oregano, salt and bay leaf. Cook, stirring constantly, for approximately 1 minute.

3 Add wine, stirring to combine; cook to reduce volume of wine by half.

4 Reduce heat to medium-low flame. Add tomatoes; cook, stirring occasionally for approximately 20-30 minutes.

Add
a little
❖ Zest

Margarita Marinade

1 *serving*

- SERVING SIZE: 1 RECIPE
- COUNTS AS:
  1 FRUIT
  1 FAT

▶ *size according to plan*

※ Ingredients

2 Tbsp fresh lime juice

1 tsp vegetable oil

2 Tbsp water

1oz tequila

1-2 garlic cloves, crushed

1 In a small bowl, combine all ingredients. Whisk vigorously to combine.

2 Add desired meat, poultry, seafood or vegetables. Toss to coat all pieces.

3 Cover and refrigerate for 20-30 minutes, turning occasionally, before cooking.

Orange-Ginger Marinade

 serving

- SERVING SIZE: 1 RECIPE
- COUNTS AS:
  1 FRUIT

▶ *size according to plan*

※ Ingredients

1/4 cup (60ml) orange juice

1/4 cup (60ml) low-sodium soy sauce

2 Tbsp dry sherry

1-2 garlic cloves, minced

1/2 tsp ground ginger

1 In a measuring cup, combine all ingredients. Whisk vigorously.

2 Pour marinade into a large zip-top bag; add desired meat, poultry or seafood. Shake to coat.

3 Refrigerate, turning over occasionally, for 20-30 minutes.

Try this marinade with the Ginger Chicken with Apricots.

Add
a little
❉ Zest

Chili Powder

✳ Ingredients
- 2 Tbsp paprika
- 2 tsp oregano
- 1 1/4 tsp cumin
- 1 1/4 tsp garlic powder
- 1 1/4 tsp cayenne pepper
- 3/4 tsp onion powder

1. Mix all ingredients. Place in an airtight spice jar. (Unlimited use)

Indian Spice Blend

✳ Ingredients
- 8 tsp cumin
- 4 tsp ground ginger
- 2 tsp ground coriander
- 2 tsp cayenne pepper
- 4 tsp turmeric
- 2 tsp freshly ground pepper

1. Combine all ingredients in an airtight spice jar. (Unlimited use)

Hot Citrus Rub

✳ Ingredients
- 1 Tbsp lemon zest
- 1 Tbsp orange zest
- 1 tsp artificial sweetener
- 1 tsp lite salt
- 2 tsp garlic powder
- 1 tsp cayenne pepper

1. Combine all ingredients in a small bowl.
2. Use to grill all your favorite foods. (Unlimited use)

Add
a little
✤ Zest

Vegetable Sauce

12 *servings*

- **SERVING SIZE: 2 TBSP**
- **COUNTS AS:**
  - 1 FAT

▶ *size according to plan*

☀ Ingredients

1/3 cup (85ml) fat-free sour cream

1/3 cup (85ml) parsley, chopped

2 1/2 Tbsp red wine vinegar

1 tsp Worcestershire sauce

1 tsp dry mustard

1 garlic clove, minced

1 cup (250ml) fat-free mayonnaise

2 Tbsp chives, chopped

1 Mix all ingredients well.

2 Refrigerate for at least 30-60 minutes before serving. Use on raw or cooked vegetables.

Plum Sauce

2 *servings*

- **SERVING SIZE: 2 TBSP**
- **COUNTS AS:**
  - 1 FRUIT
  - 1 FAT

▶ *size according to plan*

☀ Ingredients

2 Tbsp plum jam

2 Tbsp low-sodium soy sauce

1/2 tsp hot chili oil

2 tsp sesame oil

1/4 tsp ginger, fresh, grated

1 Combine all ingredients and whisk vigorously to combine.

2 Use to flavor beef, chicken, pork or other meats.

Paint a little Plum Sauce on the Lamb Kabobs to add a little zing.

Add
a little
✿ Zest

Basil Mayonnaise

6 *servings*

SERVING SIZE:
1 1/2 TBSP
COUNTS AS:
1 FAT

ze according to plan

✳ Ingredients

1 cup (250ml) lite mayonnaise

1/2 cup (125ml / 2g) fresh basil,
roughly chopped

freshly ground pepper

1 Place all ingredients in a blender or food processor.
Puree or blend until smooth.

2 Use immediately or refrigerate.

Spicy Flavor Blend

✳ Ingredients

1 Tbsp dry mustard

2 1/2 tsp onion powder

1 3/4 tsp curry powder

1 1/4 tsp white pepper

1 1/4 tsp ground cumin

1 tsp garlic powder

1 Mix all ingredients together in a small bowl.

2 Place into shaker and use as desired. (Unlimited)

Seasoned Salt

✳ Ingredients

1 tsp lite salt

1 tsp paprika

1 tsp turmeric powder

1 tsp onion powder

1 tsp oregano

1 tsp pepper

3/4 tsp garlic powder

1/2 packet artificial sweetener

1 Mix all ingredients together in a small bowl.

2 Place into shaker and use as desired. (Unlimited)

Add
a little
❖ Zest

Herb Blend

☀ Ingredients

1 Tbsp garlic powder

1 tsp dried oregano

1 tsp freshly ground pepper

1 Tbsp parsley flakes

1 Tbsp dried basil

1 Mix all ingredients together.

2 Place in shaker and use as desired. (Unlimited)

Taco Seasoning Mix

☀ Ingredients

2 Tbsp chili powder

2 tsp paprika

2 tsp cumin

2 tsp oregano

1/2 tsp onion powder

1/2 tsp garlic powder

1/2 tsp cayenne pepper

1 Combine all ingredients in an airtight spice jar. (Unlimited use)

Citrus Rub

☀ Ingredients

1 Tbsp lemon zest

1 Tbsp orange zest

1 tsp artificial sweetener

1 tsp lite salt

1 Combine all ingredients in a small bowl.

2 Use to grill all your favorite foods. (Unlimited use)

Add
a little
❖ Zest

Five Spice Powder

✳ Ingredients

- 2 Tbsp black peppercorns
- 3 star anise
- 2 tsp fennel seeds
- 2 3-inch cinnamon sticks, broken into small pieces
- 6 whole cloves

1. Dry-roast the peppercorns in a small skillet, sliding the skillet back and forth over the burner to prevent charring, until a pleasant aroma, 1-2 minutes.
2. Transfer to a bowl and set aside to cool.
3. Repeat this process, one ingredient at a time, with the remaining ingredients.
4. Put all the ingredients into a spice grinder and grind to a fine powder.
5. Transfer to a glass jar with a tight-fitting lid. Mixture will keep for up to 1 month. (Unlimited use)

Fajita Seasoning Marinade

SERVING SIZE: 2 TBSP
COUNTS AS:
FREE FOOD

✳ Ingredients

- 1/4 cup (60ml) red wine vinegar
- 1 packet artificial sweetener
- 1/2 tsp oregano
- 1/2 tsp chili powder
- 1/4 tsp garlic powder
- 1/8 tsp freshly ground pepper
- 1/4 tsp lite salt

1. Combine all ingredients.
2. Use as a marinade for chicken or beef.

serving

SERVING SIZE: 1 RECIPE
COUNTS AS:
1 FAT

ize according to plan

Teriyaki Marinade

✳ Ingredients

- 1-2 tsp brown sugar artificial sweetener
- 3 Tbsp dry sherry
- 3 Tbsp low-sodium teriyaki sauce
- 2 tsp dark sesame oil
- 2 garlic cloves, crushed
- 1/2 tsp ground ginger

1. In small bowl, combine all ingredients; whisk to combine.
2. Add desired meat, poultry, fish or vegetables to bowl, tossing to coat.
3. Cover and refrigerate 20 minutes before cooking.

225

Add
a little
✤ Zest

Sweet Surrenders

Tasty treats can bring an instant smile to anyone, from smoothies and shakes to pudding, pies and crepes. Unfortunately, many of these treats are high in fat and/or sugar. But there are ways to cut the fat and calories while saving the flavor. For instance, fruit-based desserts that are high in fiber and low in fat are still a sweet treat!

Fruit and Yogurt Parfait recipe can be found on page 233

Sugar Substitutes

■ **Sweet 'N Low**® (Saccharin) — earliest form of sugar substitute; 300-500 times sweeter than sugar; it is not stable at high temperatures and results in a bitter taste, best used at the end of recipes; 2 teaspoons Sweet 'N Low = 1/4 cup granulated sugar.

■ **Equal**® (Aspartame) — made of 2 amino acids, the building blocks of protein; 180-200 times sweeter than sugar; breaks down and loses its sweet taste when heated, best for used in cold recipes; in recipes, you may use 1/4 cup Equal in place of 1/4 cup sugar; new Equal Sugar Lite is a product made especially for baking that is half sugar and half encapsulate Equal (making it heat stable).

■ **Splenda**® (Sucralose) — made from sugar so its taste is closest to sugar; may be used teaspoon for teaspoon in place of sugar; heat stable and may be used in all types of recipes; also available in a sugar blend, called "Splenda for Baking," which is half sugar, half Splenda.

■ **Stevia** — a natural, non-caloric sweetener, derived from the plant, Stevia rebaudiana, which is an herb; native to Paraguay; only can be sold as a "dietary supplement" in the US and therefore is not labeled as a "sweetener"; in its natural state is 300 times sweeter than sugar, and even more so when processed; it is heat stable and may be used in cooking; 1/2 teaspoon stevia is equivalent to 2 teaspoons sugar.

TIP!

Keep brown sugar substitute soft when you buy it in a plastic bag. After you open the package store it in a plastic zippered bag to seal in the freshness.

Baking Substitutions

- Use fruit puree, such as unsweetened applesauce or prune puree, in place of some of the fat.

- Replace some of the whole eggs with egg whites or pasteurized egg substitute; it is best to keep some of the whole eggs in the recipe to maintain texture.

- To cut back on sugar, use one-half or one-third sugar substitute — this will maintain flavor but cut back on calories.

- Use evaporated milk in place of heavy cream.

- If cutting out some of the sugar, add extra spices, such as cinnamon, nutmeg, cardamom and ginger, to enhance the flavor.

- When making bread, increase the fiber by using whole wheat flour for all or half the flour.

TIPS!

• When baking pies, cover the edges of the crust with foil to prevent the baked edges from browning. If the top of the pie is browning too much, place foil on top but pierce a hole in the center so the crust stays crisp.

• For the most delicious desserts, bake cakes, muffins and breads on the middle oven rack. Use the lower rack for yeast breads and pies.

• The best way to freeze baked goods is to wrap them in plastic wrap and then in freezer bags or sealed containers. When you want to thaw the dessert, keep it in the bag or container to let any moisture reabsorb if lost during freezing.

Sweet Surrenders

Applesauce Oatmeal Cookies

3 *dozen cookies*

- **SERVING SIZE: 2 COOKIES**
- **COUNTS AS:**
  1 STARCH

▶ *size according to plan*

☀ Ingredients

1/4 cup (60ml) packed brown sugar

1/4 cup (60ml) artificial sweetener

1/2 cup (125ml) unsweetened applesauce

1/4 cup (60ml) egg substitute

1 cup (250ml / 125g) all-purpose flour

1 tsp baking powder

1/2 tsp salt

1 tsp cinnamon

1 cup (250ml / 81g) oats

1/4 cup (60ml / 39g) raisins

1 In a large mixing bowl, mix together the brown sugar, sugar substitute and applesauce.

2 In a separate bowl, sift the flour, baking powder, salt and cinnamon; stir into the applesauce mixture.

3 Add the rolled oats and raisins. Stir until well combined.

4 Drop by spoonfuls onto the prepared cookie sheet.

5 Bake for 10 minutes in a preheated 350°F oven.

6 Allow cookies to cool slightly before removing from the baking sheet.

Apricot Custard

1 *serving*

- **SERVING SIZE: 1 RECIPE**
- **COUNTS AS:**
  1/2 PROTEIN
  1 FRUIT
  1/2 DAIRY

▶ *size according to plan*

good source of fiber

☀ Ingredients

3 medium apricots chopped

1 egg beaten

1/2 cup (125ml) skim milk

1 packet artificial sweetener

1/4 tsp vanilla

dash ground nutmeg

1 Divide chopped apricots into custard cups or soufflé dishes. Place cups in a shallow baking pan.

2 In a small mixing bowl, combine the egg, milk, artificial sweetener and vanilla. Pour egg mixture over apricots. Sprinkle with nutmeg.

3 Place the baking pan containing the cups on the oven rack. Pour boiling water around custard cups in baking pan to depth of 1-inch.

4 Bake in a 325°F oven for 30-35 minutes, or until knife inserted in the center comes out clean.

 ❖Sweet
Surrende

Sparkling Fruited Gelatin

4 servings

SERVING SIZE: 1 CUP (250ML)
COUNTS AS:
1 FRUIT

size according to plan

family fare

☀ Ingredients

2 apples

1/2 cup (125ml / 98g) canned, crushed pineapple, drained

1 tsp lemon juice

10 grapes

1 package (3oz / 84g) sugar-free mixed fruit flavored gelatin mix

1 cup (250ml) hot water

6oz (200ml) diet ginger ale

1. Peel and core apples; cut in to thin slices.
2. Place apple slices in medium bowl. Add pineapple and lemon juice.
3. Slice grapes in half and add to fruit mixture.
4. In a separate bowl, mix gelatin and hot water. Stir until gelatin is dissolved.
5. Once dissolved, pour ginger ale into gelatin.
6. Refrigerate 30 minutes, or until gelatin mixture is the consistency of raw egg whites.
7. Add the fruit mixture to gelatin and fold in gently.
8. Refrigerate until firm.
9. Serve chilled.

Chocolate Banana Crunch Parfait

1 serving

SERVING SIZE: 1 PARFAIT
COUNTS AS:
1 STARCH
2 FRUITS
1 FAT

size according to plan

☀ Ingredients

1 packet L A Lite Chocolate Pudding mix

4oz (125ml) cold water

1/2 small banana, sliced

10 peanuts, crushed

1. Add pudding mix to water and stir thoroughly until smooth.
2. In a tall glass, layer one half of the pudding, then top with half of the banana slices and then half of the crushed peanuts.
3. Repeat layering steps.
4. Place in refrigerator until cold, and serve.

"These recipes are so much fun to create."

- Bella N.

231

❖ Sweet
Surrenders

Chocolate Truffles

1 *serving*

- SERVING SIZE: 6 TRUFFLES
- COUNTS AS:
  1 DAIRY

▶ *size according to plan*

☀ Ingredients

1 egg

1 cup (250ml) skim milk

1 Tbsp artificial sweetener

1 tsp vanilla

1/4 tsp salt

1-2 Tbsp orange or lemon zest

nutmeg for garnish, optional

1. Break egg into small mixing bowl and beat slightly.
2. Add milk, artificial sweetener, vanilla, zest and salt; beat well.
3. Pour into damp custard cups and sprinkle with nutmeg.
4. Bake in 350°F oven, in a shallow pan, of water for 40-50 minutes.
5. When custard is set, a knife inserted to the center will come out clean.

> "The desserts definitely satisfied my sweet tooth... and my husband's too."
>
> *- Sharon M.*

Baked Custard

2 *servings*

- SERVING SIZE: 1/2 CUP (125ML)
- COUNTS AS:
  1 DAIRY

▶ *size according to plan*

☀ Ingredients

1 egg

1 cup (250ml) skim milk

1 Tbsp artificial sweetener

1 tsp vanilla

1/4 tsp salt

1-2 Tbsp orange or lemon zest

nutmeg for garnish, optional

1. Break egg into small mixing bowl and beat slightly.
2. Add milk, artificial sweetener, vanilla, zest and salt; beat well.
3. Pour into damp custard cups and sprinkle with nutmeg.
4. Bake in 350°F oven, in a shallow pan, of water for 40-50 minutes.
5. When custard is set, a knife inserted to the center will come out clean.

❖ Sweet
Surrende

Fruit and Yogurt **Parfait**

serving

SERVING SIZE: 1 PARFAIT
COUNTS AS:
1 STARCH
1 FRUIT
1 DAIRY

ze according to plan

good source of fiber

☀ **Ingredients**

9 small strawberries, sliced

8oz (250ml) vanilla nonfat yogurt

1/4 cup (60ml / 36g) blueberries

1/3 cup (85ml / 20g) high fiber cereal

1 packet artificial sweetener

1 Dice 1 strawberry. Fold into yogurt.

2 In a bowl, toss remaining berries with artificial sweetener.

3 In parfait glass layer the yogurt, strawberries, blueberries and cereal.

4 Serve chilled.

Baked Apple **á la Mode**

serving

SERVING SIZE: 1 APPLE
COUNTS AS:
1 STARCH
1 FRUIT

ze according to plan

☀ **Ingredients**

1 small apple

1/4 cup (60ml) diet black cherry soda

1 tsp cinnamon

1/2 cup (125ml) fat-free sugar-free vanilla ice cream or frozen yogurt

1 Core apple and place in microwave-safe dish.

2 Pour soda in to middle of apple.

3 Sprinkle cinnamon over top.

4 Cook in microwave, on high, for 3-5 minutes, or until soft.

5 Top with ice cream.

"These recipes are just as good as any other cookbook I've used...even better."

- Lauren L.

Apple-Raspberry **Crepe**

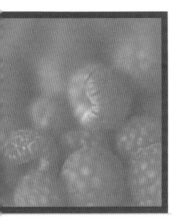

1 *serving*

■ SERVING SIZE: 1 CREPE
■ COUNTS AS:
  1 STARCH
  1 FRUIT

▶ *size according to plan*

☀ Ingredients
1/4 cup (60ml / 3g) raspberries

1 packet artificial sweetener

1/4 cup (60ml) unsweetened applesauce

1 crepe (see page 11 for recipe)

1 Place raspberries and sweetener in microwave safe dish.

2 Heat on high 2-3 minutes, or until hot.

3 Stir in applesauce.

4 Place filling over one half of crepe and fold over filling.

> "The cookbook desserts are so delicious, I feel guilty eating them."
>
> *- Lynn K.*

Frozen Fruit **Pops**

family fare

3 *servings*

■ SERVING SIZE: 1 POP
■ COUNTS AS:
  1 FRUIT

▶ *size according to plan*

☀ Ingredients
24 strawberries

1/2 cup (125ml) unsweetened applesauce

1/4 cup (60ml) apple juice

1 packet artificial sweetener

1/2 cup (125ml) boiling water

1/2 tsp sugar free cherry gelatin mix

1 Place fruits, apple juice and sweetener in blender. Puree 1 minute. There may still be small chunks of fruit in the mixture.

2 In medium mixing bowl, dissolve gelatin in boiling water.

3 Once dissolved, add gelatin to fruit mixture and toss to combine.

4 Pour mixture into plastic ice pop molds.*

5 Place in freezer. Serve frozen.

* If ice pop molds are unavailable, pour mixture in to plastic cups and place in freezer. Once mixture begins to freeze, place ice pop sticks in to cups.

❖ Sweet
Surrende

Peanut Butter Sundae **Parfait**

1 *serving*

SERVING SIZE: 1 PARFAIT
COUNTS AS:
1/2 PROTEIN
1 STARCH
1/2 DAIRY
1 LA LITE

ize according to plan

☀ Ingredients

1 packet L A Lite Chocolate
  Pudding mix

1/4 cup (60ml) cold water

1/4 cup (60ml) cold skim milk

2 Tbsp fat-free whipped topping

1 Tbsp peanut butter

1 Whisk pudding mix, milk and water together until smooth.

2 In a separate bowl, mix together peanut butter and fat-free whipped topping.

3 Layer pudding and peanut butter mixture in a glass.

4 Chill at least 1 hour before serving.

> "When it comes to desserts,
> these are guilt-free."
>
> *- Karen D.*

Rice **Pudding**

2 *servings*

SERVING SIZE: 1/2 OF RECIPE
COUNTS AS:
1 STARCH
1 FRUIT
1/2 DAIRY

ize according to plan

☀ Ingredients

1 Tbsp lite margarine

1 Tbsp flour

1/2 cup (125ml / 96g) raw rice

3/4 cup (200ml) skim milk

1 tsp vanilla extract

4-6 packets of artificial
  sweetener

1/4 cup (60ml / 39g) raisins

dash of allspice

1/4 tsp cinnamon

1 In medium saucepan melt margarine; add flour to melted butter, stirring constantly to make a roux.

2 Gradually stir in 1/2 cup (125ml) milk, mix well; heat over medium flame until warm.

3 Add rice, artificial sweetener, allspice and cinnamon.

4 Reduce heat and simmer.

5 Slowly add remaining milk during cooking until rice is tender.

6 Add vanilla and cook additional 1-2 minutes on low heat.

7 Pour in to bowls and refrigerate.

8 Serve chilled.

❖ Sweet
Surrenders

Peach Melba Crepe

 serving

- **SERVING SIZE: 1 CREPE**
- **COUNTS AS:**
  1 STARCH
  1 FRUIT

▶ *size according to plan*

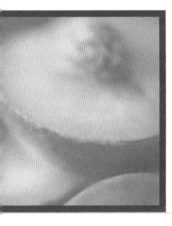

☀ Ingredients

1/2 peach, diced

1 packet artificial sweetener

1/4 tsp ginger

1 Tbsp sugar free raspberry jelly or jam

1/4 cup (60ml / 31g) raspberries

1 Tbsp fat-free whipped topping

1 crepe (see recipe on page 11)

1. Place diced peach, ginger and 1/2 packet of artificial sweetener in microwave safe dish.
2. Heat on high 2-3 minutes, or until hot.
3. Spread raspberry jelly over crepe.
4. Place peach mixture over half of the crepe and fold over filling.
5. Sprinkle remaining artificial sweetener over raspberries.
6. Top crepe with raspberries and whipped topping.

Watermelon Ice

 serving

- **SERVING SIZE: 1 RECIPE**
- **COUNTS AS:**
  2 FRUITS

▶ *size according to plan*

☀ Ingredients

1 1/2 cups (375ml / 228g) watermelon cubes

1 packet artificial sweetener

2 Tbsp apple juice, chilled

2 ice cubes

1. Freeze watermelon overnight.
2. Once frozen, remove melon from freezer and place in blender.
3. Add remaining ingredients in to blender.
4. Blend on medium until smooth.
5. Serve immediately.

> "You can eat desserts on the L A Weight Loss program and still lose weight. I did."
>
> *- Keri K.*

 ❖ Sweet Surrende

8 servings

SERVING SIZE: 1 SLICE
COUNTS AS:
1 STARCH
1 FRUIT

ize according to plan

family fare

Lemon Glazed Cheesecake

☀ Ingredients

Cheesecake

2 - 8oz (224g, each) packages
  fat-free cream cheese, softened

3/4 cup (200ml) artificial sweetener

1 Tbsp flour

2 tsp vanilla extract

1/2 tsp fresh lemon peel, finely
  grated

1/2 cup (125ml) fat-free sour cream

3 egg whites

1/2 cup (125ml) graham cracker
  crumbs

2 cup (500ml) berries of choice

Lemon glaze

1/3 cup (85ml) artificial sweetener

1 1/2 Tbsp arrowroot or cornstarch

1 1/2 Tbsp fresh squeezed lemon
  juice

1/2 tsp fresh lemon peel, finely
  grated

1/3 cup (85ml) water

1 Blend first 5 ingredients with electric mixer.

2 Blend in sour cream and egg whites.

3 Spray 9-inch pie pan with nonfat cooking spray;
   sprinkle with graham cracker crumbs.

4 Pour in cheese mixture and bake at 325°F for
   40 minutes.

5 Cool to room temperature, then refrigerate for
   3 hours.

6 For glaze, stir sugar substitute and arrowroot or
   cornstarch together in a small saucepan then add the
   lemon juice, lemon peel and water.

7 Whisk until smooth.

8 Heat, stirring constantly, until mixture is clear and
   thick.

9 Spread evenly over cheesecake; allow to set at room
   temperature, briefly.

10 Top with berries.

11 Slice pie into 8 slices.

---

1 serving

SERVING SIZE: 9 CHERRIES
COUNTS AS:
1 FRUIT
1 L A LITE

ize according to plan

Chocolate Covered Cherries

☀ Ingredients

1 packet L A Lite Chocolate
  Drink mix

9 medium cherries, pitted

1 Mix L A Lite Chocolate Drink Mix with 1/2 cup (125ml)
   water.

2 Dip cherries into chocolate mixture and place on wax
   paper.

3 Chill for 1 hour before serving.

❖ Sweet
Surrenders

Mango-Passion Fruit Frozen Yogurt

 9 *servings*

■ **SERVING SIZE: 3/4 CUP (200ML)**
■ **COUNTS AS:**
   1 FRUIT
   1/2 DAIRY

▶ *size according to plan*

☀ Ingredients

4 medium mangoes, peeled and cubed

1 cup (250ml) passion fruit pulp

1/3 cup (85ml) artificial sweetener

1/2 tsp vanilla extract

2 cups (500ml) vanilla nonfat yogurt

1 In a food processor or blender, puree the mango; strain through a sieve.

2 Add the remaining ingredients; mix to combine.

3 Pour the mixture into a shallow 9-inch baking pan.

4 Cover with foil or plastic wrap.

5 Freeze until solid (1-2 hours).

6 Break the frozen mixture into pieces.

7 Puree in a food processor, until soft, but not completely melted.

8 Repeat the freezing and pureeing once more.

9 Serve or return to the freezer for later use.

Low-Fat Brownies

8 *servings*

■ **SERVING SIZE:**
   1/8 OF RECIPE
■ **COUNTS AS:**
   2 STARCH

▶ *size according to plan*

☀ Ingredients

3/4 cup sugar

1/2 cup flour

1/2 tsp baking soda

2 egg whites, lightly beaten

1 tsp vanilla

2/3 cup unsweetened applesauce

1/4 cup unsweetened cocoa powder

1 Preheat oven to 350°F.

2 Spray a square nonstick baking pan (8-inch x 8-inch) with cooking spray.

3 Combine the ingredients in a large mixing bowl, blend well.

4 Pour batter into pan and bake in preheated oven 20-30 minutes until baked.

5 To test if batter is done, insert a toothpick. If it comes out clean, brownies are done.

6 Remove from oven and let cool for 5 minutes in pan.

7 Gently remove from pan; place on wire rack and when cool.

8 Cut into 8 squares.

❧Sweet
Surrende

Lemon Sorbet

0 servings

SERVING SIZE: 1/2 CUP (125ML)
COUNTS AS:
1 FRUIT

ze according to plan

☀ Ingredients

1 envelope unflavored gelatin

2 1/4 cups (560ml) water, divided

1/3 cup (80ml / 67g) granulated sugar, divided

1 Tbsp artificial sweetener

2/3 cup (170ml) freshly squeezed lemon juice

2 large egg whites

2 tsp grated lemon peel

1. In small saucepan, sprinkle gelatin over 1 cup (250ml) water; let stand 5 minutes to soften gelatin.
2. Add 1/3 cup (85ml) sugar and 1 1/4 tsp artificial sweetener.
3. Cook over low heat, stirring until gelatin and sugar dissolve completely.
4. Pour into large bowl; add remaining water and lemon juice.
5. Chill syrup, about 2 1/2 hours.
6. In a bowl, beat egg whites with remaining artificial sweetener, until stiff, but not dry.
7. Fold into syrup mixture with lemon peel.
8. Pour into aluminum loaf pan or rectangular baking pan.
9. Cover with foil and freeze 2 hours or until frozen 1-inch around edges.
10. Spoon into large bowl and beat until smooth.
11. Return to aluminum pan, cover and freeze 3 hours.
12. Transfer to bowl and beat again.
13. Return to pan, cover and freeze until firm, several hours or overnight.
14. To serve, let sorbet stand at room temperature about 15 minutes for easier scooping.

Bread Pudding

0 serving

SERVING SIZE: 1 RECIPE
COUNTS AS:
1/2 PROTEIN
1 STARCH

ze according to plan

good source of fiber

☀ Ingredients

1/4 cup (60ml) egg substitute

2 tsp skim milk

1/2 tsp cinnamon

1 tsp vanilla extract

1-2 packets of artificial sweetener

1 slice lite bread

1. In a bowl, mix eggbeaters, skim milk, cinnamon and vanilla extract.
2. Tear bread into small pieces and add to mixture.
3. Place in custard cup. Set cup in baking dish containing 1-inch water.
4. Bake at 350°F for 30 minutes.

❖ Sweet Surrenders

Stuffed Baked Apple

1 *serving*

SERVING SIZE: 1 APPLE
2 FRUITS
1 FAT

▶ *size according to plan*

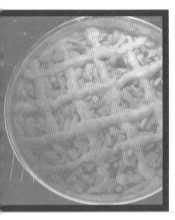

good source of fiber

✷ Ingredients

1 apple

2 Tbsp dried oatmeal

1 Tbsp raisins

1 Tbsp lite margarine

1 Tbsp egg substitute

1 packet artificial sweetener

1 tsp cinnamon

1 Core apple and peel a 1-inch strip of skin around center of apple.

2 Place in a baking dish and set aside.

3 In a medium mixing bowl, combine oatmeal, raisins, egg substitute, artificial sweetener and margarine.

4 Stuff mixture into core of apple.

5 Sprinkle with cinnamon.

6 Pour water into baking dish, approximately 1/4-inch depth.

7 Bake uncovered in 350°F oven until tender, about 30 minutes.

8 While baking, spoon syrup that forms in pan over the apple.

Raspberry Chocolate Parfait

1 *serving*

SERVING SIZE: 1 PARFAIT
COUNTS AS:
1 STARCH
1 FRUIT

▶ *size according to plan*

good source of fiber

✷ Ingredients

1 packet L A Lite Chocolate Pudding mix

4oz (125ml) cold water

1 cup (250ml / 123g) raspberries

2 Tbsp fat-free whipped topping

1 Blend together pudding mix and water with a spoon.

2 Rinse raspberries and pat dry.

3 In a tall wine glass or narrow bowl, layer half of the pudding, followed by 1/2 cup (125ml) of the fruit, and then 1 Tbsp fat-free whipped topping.

4 Repeat process/layers.

5 Garnish with mint, if desired.

6 Cool in refrigerate and serve.

✿ Sweet
Surrender

Almond Cookies

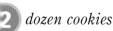 *dozen cookies*

family fare

SERVING SIZE: 1 COOKIE
COUNTS AS:
2 STARCHES
1 FAT

ize according to plan

☀ Ingredients

1 egg yolk

1/3 (80ml / 67g) cup artificial
  sweetener

2 Tbsp sugar

1/2 cup (125ml / 113g) butter

1 tsp almond extract

1 1/2 cups (375ml / 188g) flour

1 Beat the egg yolk, artificial sweetener, butter and
   almond extract in a large bowl.

2 Blend in flour a little at a time.

3 Shape a tablespoonful of dough into a ball.

4 Repeat with the remaining dough.

5 Place the cookies on an ungreased cookie sheet.

6 Bake for 20 minutes, or until lightly golden brown.

Chocolate Dipped Fruit Kabobs

serving

SERVING SIZE: 2-3 KABOBS
COUNTS AS:
1 FRUIT
1 L A LITE

ize according to plan

☀ Ingredients

1 envelope L A Lite Chocolate
  Shake mix

6oz (200ml) cold water

6 small strawberries

1/4 cup (60ml / 4g) pineapple,
  drained

1 Combine pudding mix with cold water, stir well until
   smooth, yet thin, and set aside.

2 Thread strawberries and pineapple onto 2-3 bamboo
   skewers.

3 Place on waxed paper.

4 Cover with pudding mixture.

5 Place in freezer until set.

❖ Sweet
Surrenders

Grapefruit Watermelon Grimatica

4 *servings*

- **SERVING SIZE: 1/2 CUP (125ML)**
- **COUNTS AS:**
  1 FRUIT
  IF USING VODKA, COUNTS AS:
  1 FRUIT
  1 STARCH

▶ *size according to plan*

⁜ Ingredients

1 cup (250ml) fresh squeezed grapefruit juice

1/3 cup (85ml) artificial sweetener

1 cup (250ml) watermelon pulp, seedless

1/4 cup (60ml) vodka (optional)

1 In a saucepan, bring grapefruit juice and artificial sweetener up to a simmer; stir until artificial sweetener is dissolved. Remove from heat and cool.

2 Puree grapefruit syrup with watermelon and strain.

3 Stir in vodka (optional) and place in freezer.

4 After an hour, stir granita. Stir 2 more times before frozen-solid.

5 To serve, scrape up granita granules with a fork and spoon into dessert glasses.

---

family fare

Tiramisu-Rice Dessert

8 *servings*

- **SERVING SIZE:**
  1 CUP (250ML)
- **COUNTS AS:**
  1/2 PROTEIN
  1 STARCH
  1/2 DAIRY

▶ *size according to plan*

⁜ Ingredients

1 cup (250ml / 192g) long grain rice

2 1/2 cups (625ml) skim milk

1 Tbsp instant coffee granules

2 cups (500ml) frozen fat-free whipped topping, thawed

3/4 cup (200ml) fat-free ricotta cheese

1/2 cup (125ml) artificial sweetener

2 Tbsp coffee liqueur

unsweetened cocoa

1 In medium saucepan, combine rice, milk and coffee granules.

2 Stir occasionally until mixture comes to a boil.

3 Reduce heat to simmer; cover and cook 15 minutes or until rice is tender.

4 Cover and refrigerate until chilled.

5 In large bowl, combine rice mixture, whipped topping, ricotta cheese, artificial sweetener and liqueur; mix well.

6 Spoon into individual serving dishes or medium-size serving bowl.

7 Sift cocoa over rice mixture.

8 Cover and refrigerate for at least 1 hour before serving.

❖ Sweet
Surrende

1 *serving*

**SERVING SIZE: 1 RECIPE
COUNTS AS:**
1 STARCH
2 FRUITS

ize according to plan

good source of fiber

Apple Crisp

☼ Ingredients
2 small apples

2-3 packets artificial sweetener

1/4 cup (60ml / 20g) oatmeal

1/4 tsp ground cinnamon

1/4 tsp ground nutmeg

1 Heat oven to 350°F. Arrange apple slices in baking pan, coated with nonfat cooking spray. Mix remaining ingredients sprinkle over apples.

2 Bake until topping is golden brown and apples are tender.

"Oh, the cookbook was key. There was a recipe for every craving – it really helped me stay on target."

- M. Norton

1 *serving*

**SERVING SIZE: 12 BERRIES
COUNTS AS:**
1 STARCH
2 FRUITS
1/2 DAIRY

ize according to plan

Chocolate Covered Strawberries

☼ Ingredients
1 packet L A Lite Chocolate Pudding mix

4oz (125ml) cold skim milk

12 small strawberries

1 Mix chocolate pudding with milk.

2 Dip strawberries in pudding.

3 Place on waxed paper and freeze.

4 Berries are ready to be served once chocolate coating has solidified.

❖ Sweet Surrenders

Strawberry Daiquiri

1 *serving*

- ◼ SERVING SIZE: 1 RECIPE
- ◼ COUNTS AS:
  - 1 STARCH
  - 1 FRUIT
  - 1 L A LITE

▶ *size according to plan*

☀ Ingredients
1 packket L A Lite Vanilla Shake mix

1/2 cup (125ml) water

1 cup (250ml) ice cubes

12 small strawberries

1oz (28ml) rum (or rum extract)

1 Place all ingredients in a blender; puree until smooth.

2 Serve immediately, or freeze until ready to use.

Spiced Coffee

1 *serving*

- ◼ SERVING SIZE: 1 RECIPE
- ◼ COUNTS AS:
  - 1 UNLIMITED BEVERAGE

▶ *size according to plan*

☀ Ingredients
2 cups (500ml) brewed decaffeinated coffee

1 2-inch stick cinnamon

1/4 tsp whole allspice

2 strips of orange zest

1 In a saucepan combine coffee, cinnamon sticks, allspice and orange zest. Bring to boil, reduce heat.

2 Cover and simmer for 5 minutes.

3 Remove solids from coffee with a slotted spoon or by draining over a sieve. If desired, garnish with cinnamon sticks.

Hot Chai Tea

1 *serving*

- ◼ SERVING SIZE:
  1 CUP (250ML) OF SPICED TEA
- ◼ COUNTS AS:
  1/2 DAIRY

▶ *size according to plan*

☀ Ingredients
1/2 cup hot strongly brewed orange spiced tea

1/2 cup fat-free milk

1 Tbsp artificial sweetener

1/4 tsp vanilla

1/8 tsp ground cloves

1 Brew tea.

2 Place milk in glass measuring cup and heat on high for 30-40 seconds.

3 Combine all ingredients in beverage mug and mix until blended.

❖ Sweet
Surrende

Pineapple **Slush**

3 *servings*

SERVING SIZE: 1/3 OF RECIPE
COUNTS AS:
2 FRUITS

ize according to plan

☀ Ingredients

20oz (560g) can crushed
  pineapple

1 cup (250ml) water

2 Tbsp powdered sugar

1 packet artificial sweetener

1 Combine pineapple, water, sweetener and sugar in a
  freezer safe bowl; freeze for a few hours.

2 Remove from freezer and put in a blender.

3 Process at high speed; puree until smooth, about
  3 minutes.

Vanilla Nut **Milk**

1 *serving*

SERVING SIZE: 1 DRINK
COUNTS AS:
1 DAIRY

ize according to plan

good source of calcium

☀ Ingredients

8oz (250ml) skim milk

1 tsp vanilla extract

1/8 tsp almond extract

1 packet artificial sweetener

dash of nutmeg

1 Combine all ingredients in small saucepan.

2 Cook over medium heat until warm stirring frequently;
  do not bring to a boil.

3 Serve hot.

Orange & **Spice Tea**

2 *servings*

SERVING SIZE:
1 CUP (250ML) OF SPICED TEA
COUNTS AS:
1 UNLIMITED BEVERAGE
1 CONDIMENT

ize according to plan

☀ Ingredients

2 cups (500ml) water

1 cinnamon stick, broken into
  pieces

6 whole cloves

2 decaffeinated tea bags

juice from 1 orange

1 In a saucepan, combine water, cinnamon and cloves.
  Bring to a boil; remove from heat.

2 Add tea bags; steep for 5 minutes. Remove tea bags.

3 Stir in juice of 1 orange.

4 Sweeten to taste.

❖ Sweet
Surrenders

Frozen Mocha Drink

 serving

- **SERVING SIZE: 1 DRINK**
- **COUNTS AS:**
  - 1 DAIRY
  - 1 L A LITE

▶ *size according to plan*

good source of calcium

※ Ingredients

1 packet L A Lite Chocolate Shake mix

1 tsp instant coffee (decaf or regular)

1 Tbsp hot water

8oz (250ml) plain nonfat yogurt

1/2 tsp cinnamon

artificial sweetener to taste

1/2 cup (125ml) crushed ice or 4 ice cubes

1 Dissolve coffee in hot water.

2 Add all ingredients to blender.

3 Blend on high until smooth.

4 Pour into container and place in freezer to chill.

Classic Strawberry Shake

 serving

- **SERVING SIZE: 1 SMOOTHIE**
- **COUNTS AS:**
  - 1 STARCH
  - 2 FRUITS
  - 1/2 DAIRY

▶ *size according to plan*

good source of calcium

※ Ingredients

1 scoop L A Lite Strawberry-Banana Smoothie mix

12 small strawberries, sliced

4oz (125ml) skim milk

1/2 cup (125ml) sugar-free or fat-free vanilla frozen yogurt

3 ice cubes

1 Place smoothie mix, milk and berries in blender.

2 Mix well.

3 Add ice cream and blend until smooth.

4 Serve immediately.

❁ Sweet Surrende

Orange Mango **Smoothie**

2 *servings*

SERVING SIZE: 1/2 OF RECIPE
COUNTS AS:
1 FRUIT
1/2 DAIRY

size according to plan

☀ Ingredients

1 cup (250ml) crushed ice

1 cup (250ml / 165g) mango, cubed

1/2 cup (125ml) skim milk

1/2 cup (125ml) fresh squeezed orange juice

1 tsp honey

1 In a blender, combine ice, mango, milk, orange juice and honey; blend until smooth.

2 Pour into 2 glasses and garnish with orange slice.

Peanut Butter **Shake**

1 *serving*

SERVING SIZE: 1 SHAKE
COUNTS AS:
1/2 PROTEIN
1 DAIRY
1 L A LITE

size according to plan

☀ Ingredients

1 Tbsp peanut butter

8oz (250ml) skim milk

1 packet L A Lite Vanilla Shake mix

3 ice cubes

1 Blend all ingredients together; chill.

Cranberry **Blast**

1 *serving*

SERVING SIZE: 1 SMOOTHIE
COUNTS AS:
2 FRUITS

size according to plan

☀ Ingredients

1 scoop L A Lite Mixed Berry Smoothie mix

1/3 cup (85ml) cranberry juice

1/4 cup (60ml) diet cranberry ginger ale

3 ice cubes

1 Place all ingredients in blender, blend until frothy.

2 Serve immediately.

❖ Sweet Surrenders

Coffee Granita

2 servings

SERVING SIZE: 1/2 CUP (125ML)
COUNTS AS:
1 CONDIMENT

▶ *size according to plan*

☀ Ingredients

1-2 packets sugar substitute

2 Tbsp instant espresso coffee powder

1/2 cup (125ml) cold water

2 Tbsp fat-free whipped topping

1. In a bowl, combine sugar substitute and coffee powder. Add boiling water; stir until dissolved. Stir in cold water.

2. Pour mixture into 9 x 5 x 3-inch loaf pan. Freeze for about 2 hours or until firm.

3. Break frozen mixture into small chunks and place in a small chilled mixer bowl. Beat with electric mixer on low speed until fluffy.

4. Freeze mixture for 2 hours, or until firm.

5. To serve, scrape or scoop ice into small dessert dishes. Top with whipped topping.

Chocolate Raspberry Yogurt Shake

1 serving

SERVING SIZE: 1 SHAKE
COUNTS AS:
1 FRUIT
1/2 DAIRY
1 L A LITE

▶ *size according to plan*

good source of fiber

☀ Ingredients

1/2 cup (125ml) skim milk

1/2 cup (125ml) plain fat-free yogurt

1 packet of L A Lite Chocolate Shake mix

1 cup (250ml / 123g) raspberries

1. Place skim milk, yogurt, shake mix and raspberries in blender; cover.

2. Blend until smooth.

3. Serve immediately.

"My kids always ask me for snacks from the L A Lite Cookbook."

- Karen T.

❧ Sweet Surrende

Apple Frappe

serving

SERVING SIZE: 1 DRINK
COUNTS AS:
1 STARCH
1 FRUIT
1 L A LITE

ze according to plan

☀ Ingredients

1/2 cup (125ml / 63g) chopped, cored and peeled apples

1/4 cup (60ml) cup water

ground cinnamon to taste

1/2 cup (125ml) frozen, fat-free and/or sugar-free vanilla yogurt

1 packet L A Lite Vanilla Shake mix

1 In a blender combine the apples, water, cinnamon and Vanilla Shake mix.

2 Process until smooth.

3 Add the frozen yogurt and mix until well-blended.

4 Pour into freezer-safe glass or mug and freeze until ready to use.

5 Serve cold.

Fresh Fruit Ice

serving

SERVING SIZE: 1 DRINK
COUNTS AS:
1 FRUIT

ze according to plan

☀ Ingredients

3/4 cup (200ml) fresh fruit (suggestions: strawberries, raspberries, blueberries, blackberries, mango, watermelon, honeydew and cantaloupe)

1/2 cup (125ml) crushed ice

1 packet sugar substitute

1 Peel, seed and/or core fruit. If necessary, chop roughly.

2 Add fruit, ice and sugar substitute to blender.

3 Blend on high until smooth.

4 Serve in a champagne, cocktail or wine glass.

Home for the Holidays

Holidays are a time of celebrating, gathering with friends and family and enjoying traditions and food. But when it comes to holidays, many of us can become discouraged with all the tempting treats and traditional choices. We may find that our classic styled meals are quite high in calories and fat.

Roasted Turkey with Mushroom Gravy recipe can be found on page 258

Healthy for the Holidays!

The key to successful weight loss and maintenance is moderation, and this includes the holidays. Many people feel that holidays are a time to let free or loose and forgo any diet or healthful eating habits. But with weight maintenance, comes self control and reliance to choose the right foods. Some foods will never be low in fat or calories, but there are many that can be altered to meet your needs. You'll find many of these types of recipes in this section. Remember though, these are still more caloric, sometimes higher fat, food choices, that should be limited to special occasions!

But what if you aren't the one cooking? What if you spend all your holidays visiting friends and family and are never home? There are a few tips to take with you:

■ Offer to bring a dish — this way you can have control over something that will be on the menu! You will know what you are eating and what went into the dish!

■ Make good choices, avoid the things you could have in an everyday setting, such as chips and dip — instead, go for something that is specific to the event or holiday.

■ Fill up on veggies or lower fat/calorie items — if you must try a bit of the richer, creamier items, have a little, but fill up on healthier choices, such as vegetables and dip, salads, lean proteins, such as turkey or lean beef and fruit.

■ Have a snack before you leave for the party, such as a piece of fruit and a glass of water. If you get to the party and you are famished, you are more likely to overindulge!

TIP!

Make good choices, such as vegetables and dip, salads, lean proteins, such as turkey or lean beef, and fruit.

Tips for the Perfect Holiday

Looking for a special gift for the holidays? Home made dishes are a warm, considerate, and much appreciated way to say "happy holidays." You'll find everything you'll need inside the *L A Lite Cookbook*. Here are great ways to wrap up a cake, a plate of cookies, an appetizer or any special dish:

- **Gift Basket** — A gift basket makes a beautiful presentation. Purchasing them can be costly so why not make your own? Colorful tins of Almond and Applesauce Oatmeal cookies and Chocolate Truffles placed in a white basket and wrapped in clear wrap with red and green ribbon is a very festive, fun gift.

- **Holiday Dish** — Why not make a Lemon Glazed Cheesecake and place it in a pretty holiday cake dish or plate…the dish will also be a part of the gift!

- **Holiday Canister** — a fun holiday canister filled with cookies and goodies from the *L A Lite Cookbook* is unique way to spread the holiday cheer!

What wine should I serve when entertaining for the holidays?

Planning a holiday celebration and wondering what wine goes with what? Here's a simple chart to help your remember when to Bordeaux and when you to Chardonnay!

- **Salmon** — A medium bodied wine, red or white like Pinot Noir or White Burgundy is perfect for salmon.

- **Pork** — For pork, try a medium full-bodied white with fruit aromas and a strong acidity like Riesling, Pinot Gris or Pinot Blanc.

- **Roast Beef** — A rich full-bodied red with substantial tannin like Cabernet Sauvignon or Rivera del Duero Red is ideal for Roast Beef.

- **Chicken** — Light chicken dishes go great with a Chardonnay or Pinot Grigio.

- **Turkey** — A medium bodied red like Pinot Noir is an excellent accompaniment to roasted turkey.

(When drinking wine, be sure to count one 3oz glass of wine as one fruit exchange!)

TIPS!

• *Have smaller helpings at dinner so you can try a wider variety of foods and won't feel as bad at the end of the party. Eating only 1/2 as much as you normally would take can prevent overeating.*

• *Save yourself some time by setting the table for the holidays the night before. The holiday will become a little hectic and scrambling for extra place settings and silverware will be the last thing on your mind.*

Home
❖ for the
Holidays

Challah

 18 *servings*

- **SERVING SIZE:**
  1/18 OF BREAD (APPROX 1OZ)
- **COUNTS AS:**
  1 STARCH

▸ *size according to plan*

☀ Ingredients

1 packet or 1 Tbsp active dry yeast

2 Tbsp sugar

1/4 cup (60ml) warm water

2 cups (500ml / 248g) all-purpose flour

2 cups (500ml / 248g) whole wheat flour

1/2 tsp lite salt

1 egg

2 Tbsp vegetable oil

1 1/4 cup (310ml) cold water

1 egg, beaten

1 Tbsp poppy seeds

nonfat cooking spray

1. Dissolve the yeast and sugar in 1/4 cup (60ml) of warm water. Let stand for 5 minutes.

2. Combine flour and salt in a large mixing bowl.

3. Make a well in the center of the flour mixture; add the egg, oil, yeast mixture and cold water. Mix well.

4. Knead the dough on a floured board, adding more whole wheat flour, as needed, until dough is smooth and elastic.

5. Place in an oiled bowl.

6. Cover with a damp towel and let rise until doubled, about 1 hour.

7. Divide the dough into three parts.

8. Roll, by hand, each third into a strip, about 15 inches long.

9. Braid the strips together and place on a baking sheet that has been lightly coated with nonfat cooking spray. Brush with the beaten egg. Sprinkle on the poppy seeds.

10. Cover and let rise until loaf has doubled in size.

11. Bake in a 375°F oven for 40-45 minutes, or until golden brown.

Winter Salad

4 *servings*

- **SERVING SIZE:**
  1/4 OF RECIPE
- **COUNTS AS:**
  2 VEGETABLE
  1 FAT

▸ *size according to plan*

☀ Ingredients

2 heads bibb lettuce

1 bunch watercress

1 apple, chopped

2 Tbsp chopped pecans, toasted

3 Tbsp balsamic vinegar

1 Tbsp Dijon mustard

1 Tbsp olive oil

1 tsp honey

1. Clean and chop lettuces. Toss together and divide among 4 salad plates.

2. Combine apples and pecans; sprinkle over lettuce.

3. Whisk together remaining ingredients; drizzle over salads.

Potato Latkes

2 *servings*

SERVING SIZE: 2 PANCAKES
COUNTS AS:

1 STARCH
2 VEGETABLES

ze according to plan

☀ Ingredients

1 pound (448g) zucchini, peeled

1 pound (448g) potatoes, peeled

2 large onions, chopped

1 pound (448g) fresh spinach

1 large egg

2 egg whites

1/2 cup (125ml / 63g) flour

1/2 tsp ground cumin

1/2 tsp dried ground coriander

ground white pepper

1/4 tsp lite salt

nonfat cooking spray

1 Grate potatoes, zucchini and onion in food processor (work quickly to avoid discoloration). Squeeze out any liquid. Place in a large mixing bowl.

2 Add spinach, egg, flour, cumin, coriander, salt and pepper, to taste. Mix well.

3 Coat large skillet with nonfat cooking spray.

4 Spoon batter into pan, being careful not to crowd.

5 Cook until crisp and brown on one side, then turn over and fry on other side.

6 Keep finished pancakes warm in oven until all pancakes are cooked.

7 Makes 24 pancakes.

Baked Stuffed Zucchini

3 *servings*

SERVING SIZE: 1/4 ZUCCHINI
COUNTS AS:

1 VEGETABLE

ze according to plan

family fare

☀ Ingredients

2 zucchini, cut in half lengthwise

1 small onion, finely chopped

1/4 cup (60ml) lite tomato sauce

1/2 tsp parsley

1 garlic clove, chopped

2 Tbsp matzo meal

1 Scoop out pulp/flesh of the zucchini halves.

2 Heat pulp, onion, sauce, parsley and garlic in a pan for 5 minutes. Add matzo meal to mixture and mix well.

3 Stuff shelled zucchinis with mixture.

4 Place in a baking dish with a little water on bottom.

5 Bake in 450°F oven for 30 minutes, until zucchini shells are soft.

Home
❖ for the
Holidays

Filet Mignon with Mushroom & Wine Sauce

4 *servings*

- **SERVING SIZE: 1 STEAK AND 1/2 CUP (125ML) SAUCE**
- **COUNTS AS:**
  1 PROTEIN
  2 VEGETABLES

▶ *size according to plan*

※ Ingredients

1/3 cup (85ml / 32g) chopped green onion

1/2 pound (224g) fresh shiitake mushrooms, stems removed

1 1/2 cups (375ml) red wine, divided

1 small (10-12fl oz / 310-375ml) can low-sodium beef consommé, undiluted

freshly ground pepper

4 filet mignon steaks (4 or 6oz / 112 or 168g, each), size according to plan

1 Tbsp low-sodium soy sauce

2 tsp cornstarch

1 tsp dried thyme

nonfat cooking spray

1. Coat a skillet with nonfat cooking spray and heat over medium flame.

2. Add onions and mushrooms; sauté for 4 minutes.

3. Add 1 cup (250ml) wine and 3/4 cup (200ml) consommé; cook for 5 minutes, stirring frequently. Remove the mushrooms with a slotted spoon; place in a bowl.

4. Increase heat to high; cook wine mixture until reduced to 1/2 cup (125ml), about 5 minutes.

5. Add reduction to mushrooms; set aside. Wipe pan with paper towel. Sprinkle steaks with pepper.

6. Coat a nonstick skillet with nonfat cooking spray and heat over high flame. Add steaks; cook 3 minutes on each side.

7. Reduce heat to medium-low; continue to cook another 2-4 minutes, or until desired level of doneness.

8. Combine soy sauce with cornstarch.

9. Add 1/2 cup (125ml) wine and remaining consommé to skillet; scrape bottom of skillet to loosen browned bits. Bring to a boil; cook 1 minute.

10. Add mushroom mixture, cornstarch mixture, and dried thyme to skillet; bring to a boil, and cook 1 minute, stirring. Serve sauce over steaks.

Glazed Ham

8 *servings*

- **SERVING SIZE: 3 OR 5OZ (84 OR 140G) COOKED**
- **COUNTS AS:**
  1 PROTEIN

▶ *size according to plan*

※ Ingredients

4-6 pound (1.8 - 2.7kg) ham

1 cup (250ml) apricot halves in lite syrup

3 Tbsp no sugar added apricot preserves

1/2 tsp whole ground cloves

1. Trim all visible fat from ham. Place ham in baking pan.

2. Pour apricot halves and juice over ham. Dot cloves throughout ham, gently pressing into flesh.

3. Heat ham in oven according to package directions.

4. To prepare glaze, place preserves in small dish. Place in microwave 10-20 seconds, until preserves begin to melt.

5. During last 30 minutes of cooking, brush ham with warm glaze. Continue to brush ham every 10 minutes until cooked through.

6. Preserves may need to be re-heated, as needed, before basting.

7. Allow to rest 5 minutes, before slicing.

Home
❖ for th
Holiday

Crown Roast of Pork

5 *servings*

SERVING SIZE: 3 OR 5OZ
(84 OR 140G) COOKED PORK
ROAST AND 1/2 CUP (125ML)
STUFFING

COUNTS AS:
1 PROTEIN
1 STARCH
1 FRUIT

e according to plan

☼ Ingredients

27 pounds (3kg) crown pork roast
   (12 rib)

Stuffing

5 green onions, chopped

2 celery stalks, finely chopped

1 cup (250ml / 126g) red apple,
   peeled and chopped

1 cup (250ml /126g) green apple
   chopped, peeled and chopped

6 slices lite bread, cubed and
   toasted

2 Tbsp dried sage leaves

1/2 tsp dried rosemary

1/2 tsp dried thyme

1/4 cup (60ml) beaten egg
   substitute

1/4 cup (60ml) skim milk

1/4 tsp freshly ground pepper

nonfat cooking spray

Roast

1 Trim all visible fat from roast; season with pepper

2 Cut a piece of aluminum foil into an 8-inch square; place
   on rack in roasting pan.

3 Place roast; bone ends up, on foil-lined rack.

4 Bake in 325°F oven for one hour, before stuffing.

Stuffing

1 Coat skillet with nonfat cooking spray and heat over
   medium heat-high flame; add onion and celery. Cook,
   stirring, until tender.

2 Combine apples, bread cubes and seasonings in a large
   bowl; stir in vegetable mixture, egg and remaining
   ingredients.

3 Spoon stuffing into center of roast; cover with additional
   foil.

4 Insert oven-proof meat thermometer into roast, taking
   care not to touch fat or bone.

5 Bake at 325°F for 1 1/2 hours, or until thermometer
   reaches 150°F.

Minted Leg of Lamb

2 *servings*

SERVING SIZE: 3 OR 5OZ (84
OR 140G) COOKED LAMB

COUNTS AS:
1 PROTEIN

e according to plan

☼ Ingredients

1 tsp lite salt

1-1 1/2 tsp dried mint flakes

1/2 tsp cayenne pepper

9 pounds (4kg) bone-in
   leg of lamb

5 green onions, chopped

3 cups (750ml) dry white wine

1/2 cup (125ml) low-sodium
   chicken broth

1/3 cup (85ml) Dijon mustard

4 garlic cloves, chopped

2 Tbsp low-sodium
   Worcestershire sauce

nonfat cooking spray

1 Combine first 3 ingredients; rub into lamb.

2 Place chopped onion in center of the roasting pan that
   has been coated with nonfat cooking spray; place lamb
   on top of onion.

3 Combine wine and remaining 4 ingredients; pour over
   lamb.

4 Insert oven-proof meat thermometer into thickest part
   of lamb, taking care not to touch bone or fat.

5 Bake at 325°F for 1 hour 45 minutes to 2 hours 30
   minutes, or until thermometer registers 150-160°F.
   Baste lamb every 30 minutes with wine mixture.

6 Let stand 10 minutes before slicing.

Home
✣ for the
Holidays

Roasted Turkey with Mushroom Gravy

10 *servings*

- SERVING SIZE: 4 OR 6OZ (112 OR 168G) COOKED TURKEY AND 1/4 CUP (60ML) GRAVY
- COUNTS AS:
  1 PROTEIN
  2 VEGETABLES

▶ *size according to plan*

☀ Ingredients

Turkey

3 Tbsp chopped fresh rosemary

3 Tbsp chopped fresh thyme

3 Tbsp chopped fresh tarragon

1 Tbsp freshly ground pepper

2 tsp lite salt

20-22 pound (9-10kg) turkey

3 Tbsp lite margarine, melted

4 cups (1L) low-sodium chicken broth

Gravy

1/2 cup (125ml / 48g) finely chopped green onions

1 cup (250ml / 70g) finely chopped fresh mushrooms

2 Tbsp chopped fresh parsley

2 cups (500ml) low-sodium chicken broth

2 Tbsp cornstarch

freshly ground pepper

Turkey

1 Mix first five ingredients in small bowl.

2 Rinse turkey, then pat dry with paper towels; place on rack set in large roasting pan.

3 Place herb mixture into main cavity. Tie legs together loosely to hold the shape of the turkey.

4 Position rack in lowest third of oven and preheat to 425°F.

5 Pour 2 cups (500ml) broth into the pan. Drizzle melted margarine over turkey.

6 Roast turkey for 45 minutes in 425°F oven.

7 Remove turkey from oven and cover breast with foil. Reduce oven temperature to 350°F.

8 Return turkey to oven; roast turkey for 1 hour.

9 Remove foil from turkey; pour remaining 2 cups (500ml) broth into pan.

10 Continue roasting turkey until meat thermometer, inserted in thickest part of thigh, registers 180°F (or until juices run clear when thickest part of thigh is pierced by skewer), basting occasionally with pan juices. Expected cooking time will be about 1-2 hours longer.

11 Transfer turkey to platter; tent with foil.

12 Let stand 30 minutes before slicing.

Gravy

1 In a saucepan, sauté onion, mushrooms, and parsley in 1/4 cup (60ml) broth until vegetables are tender.

2 Combine cornstarch, pepper, and 1/2 cup (125ml) broth; stir until smooth.

3 Add to cornstarch mixture to pan and mix well.

4 Bring to a boil, stirring occasionally. Boil for 2 minutes.

Home
❖ for th
Holiday

Grilled Chicken & Portabellas

servings

SERVING SIZE: 1 CHICKEN
BREAST, 1 MUSHROOM CAP,
AND 2 TBSP SAUCE
COUNTS AS:
1 PROTEIN
2 VEGETABLES

ze according to plan

☀ Ingredients

2 1/4 cups (560ml) Marsala
wine, divided

2 Tbsp reduced/low-sodium
Worcestershire sauce

6-8oz skinless chicken breasts,
size according to plan

1 pound (448g) portabella
mushroom caps

1/4 cup (60ml / 24g) diced
green onion

nonfat cooking spray

1. Combine 2 cups (500ml) wine, Worcestershire sauce, and chicken breast in a large zip-lock bag; seal and marinate in refrigerator 1 hour.

2. Remove chicken from bag, reserving marinade.

3. Prepare grill.

4. Lightly coat mushrooms with nonfat cooking spray.

5. Place mushrooms, top sides down, on grill rack coated with nonfat cooking spray; spoon 1 Tbsp wine into each cap.

6. Add chicken and grill for 6 minutes on each side, or until chicken is done.

7. Cut mushrooms into 1/2-inch thick slices.

8. While the chicken and mushrooms are grilling, place a medium skillet coated with cooking spray over medium-high heat until hot.

9. Add green onions; sauté for 1 minute.

10. Add the reserved marinade and bring to a boil.

11. Reduce heat, and simmer until reduced to 1/2 cup (125ml).

12. Serve chicken and mushrooms with sauce.

Balsamic Roasted New Potatoes

servings

SERVING SIZE: 2 POTATOES
COUNTS AS:
1 STARCH

ze according to plan

☀ Ingredients

2 pounds (896g) new potatoes,
quartered

1 Tbsp minced garlic

1 tsp chopped fresh thyme

1 tsp chopped fresh rosemary

3 Tbsp balsamic vinegar

1/4 tsp freshly ground pepper

nonfat cooking spray

1. Heat large cast iron skillet, coated with nonfat cooking spray, over medium-high flame.

2. Add potatoes and seasonings and heat through.

3. Remove skillet from heat; place in oven, uncovered, at 425°F for 30 minutes, or until potatoes are tender, stirring occasionally.

4. Add vinegar, and toss well.

5. Sprinkle with salt and pepper. Roast, uncovered, 6 more minutes.

6. Serve immediately.

Home
✤ for the
Holidays

Zucchini-Carrot Casserole

3 *servings*

- SERVING SIZE: 1/3 OF RECIPE
- COUNTS AS:
  3 VEGETABLES
  1 DAIRY

▸ *size according to plan*

☀ Ingredients

1 onion, chopped

2 medium zucchinis, thinly sliced

1 medium carrot, thinly sliced

2 garlic cloves, chopped

1/4 cup (60ml) low-sodium chicken broth

1/4 cup (60ml) fat-free sour cream

4oz (112g) reduced-fat shredded cheddar cheese, divided

1/2 tsp basil

1/4 tsp oregano

1/4 tsp onion powder

1/4 tsp lite salt

1/4 tsp freshly ground pepper

4 Melba toasts, crushed

nonfat cooking spray

1. Coat large skillet with nonfat cooking spray and heat over medium-high flame. Add onion to skillet, cook 1 minute.

2. Increase flame to high.

3. Add zucchini, garlic and carrots. Cook 1-2 minutes. Add broth and cook until vegetables are soft.

4. Once veggies are soft and all liquid has evaporated, remove from heat.

5. Stir in sour cream, 3oz (84g) cheese, salt and pepper.

6. Pour mixture into a large greased casserole dish.

7. In separate bowl, combine basil, oregano, onion powder and crushed Melba toast.

8. Top the zucchini mixture with Melba crumb mixture and remaining cheese.

9. Bake at 350°F for 15 minutes, or until cheese is melted. Serve immediately.

Bread Dressing

12 *servings*

- SERVING SIZE: 1/2 CUP (125ML)
- COUNTS AS:
  1 STARCH
  1 VEGETABLE

▸ *size according to plan*

☀ Ingredients

1 cup (250ml / 120g) chopped celery

1 cup (250ml / 160g) chopped onion

1/3 cup (85ml) low-sodium chicken broth

1 tsp ground sage or poultry seasoning

dash of lite salt

freshly ground pepper

12 slices bread cubes (use diet whole wheat bread and lightly toast to remove excess moisture)

1/2-3/4 cup (125-200ml) low-sodium chicken broth

nonfat cooking spray

1. In medium saucepan, cook celery and onion in 1/3 cup (85ml) broth, until tender. Remove from heat.

2. Stir poultry seasoning or sage, pepper and salt.

3. Place dry bread cubes in a large mixing bowl. Add onion mixture.

4. Drizzle with enough broth to moisten, and lightly toss.

5. Coat casserole dish with nonfat cooking spray. Place stuffing in dish and bake at 350°F for 20 minutes, or until browned.

Home
❖ for th
Holiday

Wild Rice Pilaf

servings

SERVING SIZE: 1/2 CUP
(125ML)
COUNTS AS:
1 STARCH
1 VEGETABLE

ize according to plan

☀ Ingredients

1 1/4 cups (310ml) water

3 cups (750ml) low-sodium chicken broth

1 1/2 cups (375ml / 288g) uncooked wild rice

1 Tbsp lite margarine

3 cups (750ml / 210g) sliced mushrooms

1 cup (250ml / 96g) chopped green onions

1/2 cup (125ml / 30g) finely chopped fresh parsley

1/3 cup (85ml / 36g) chopped pecans, toasted

3/4 tsp poultry seasoning

1/2 tsp lite salt

1/4 tsp freshly ground pepper

nonfat cooking spray

1. Bring water and broth to a boil in a medium saucepan.

2. Add wild rice; cover, reduce heat, and simmer 1 hour or until tender. Drain any excess liquid.

3. Preheat oven to 325°F.

4. Melt margarine in a large, nonstick skillet over medium-high heat.

5. Add mushrooms and onion; sauté until tender.

6. Remove from heat; stir in parsley and next 4 ingredients.

7. Combine rice and mushroom mixture in a 2-quart casserole, coated with nonfat cooking spray.

8. Cover and bake at 325°F for 25 minutes.

Southern Peach Shortcake

servings

SERVING SIZE: 1/9 OF CAKE
COUNTS AS:
1 STARCH
1 FRUIT

ze according to plan

☀ Ingredients

3 peaches, sliced

10 packets of artificial sweetener

1/2 tsp almond extract

1/2 tsp cinnamon

1 cup (250ml / 126g) flour

1/3 cup (85ml / 67g) sugar

2 tsp baking powder

2 Tbsp oil

2 egg whites

1/4 cup (60ml) skim milk

1. Place peaches in bottom of well-greased 8-inch baking dish.

2. Sprinkle with 3 packets of artificial sweetener, almond extract and cinnamon.

3. Combine flour, remaining artificial sweetener, sugar and baking powder in mixing bowl. Add oil, egg and milk to flour mixture. Mix well.

4. Spread mixture evenly over peaches.

5. Bake at 400°F for 30 minutes, or until lightly browned.

6. Cool for 15 minutes. To serve, place large serving plate over top of the cake and invert onto plate.

Home
❖ for the
Holidays

New York Cheesecake

8 *serving*

- **SERVING SIZE:** 1/16 OF CAKE
- **COUNTS AS:**
  1 STARCH
  1 FAT
  1 DAIRY

▶ *size according to plan*

☼ Ingredients

50 reduced-fat vanilla wafers, crumbled

4 Tbsp lite margarine, melted

8 Tbsp artificial sweetener

2 packages (8oz or 224g each) reduced-fat cream cheese, softened

1 cup (250ml) reduced-fat sour cream

6 Tbsp sugar

2 eggs

2 egg whites

2 Tbsp cornstarch

1 tsp vanilla

1 pint (500ml / 288g) strawberries, sliced (optional)

1. Mix vanilla wafer crumbles, margarine and artificial sweetener in the bottom of 9-inch springform pan. Set aside 1 Tbsp of crumb mixture.

2. Pat the remaining mixture evenly on bottom and 1/2 inch up side of pan.

3. Bake in preheated 350°F oven until the crust is lightly browned, about 8 minutes or so. Cool on wire rack.

4. Beat cream cheese, sour cream, and sugar in a large bowl until fluffy; then beat in eggs, egg whites, vanilla and cornstarch. Pour mixture into pre-baked crust.

5. Place cheesecake in roasting pan on oven rack; and 1 inch hot water to roasting pan.

6. Bake in preheated 300°F oven just until set in the center, 45-60 minutes.

7. Remove cheesecake from roasting pan, sprinkle with reserved crumbs and return to oven. Turn oven off and let cheesecake cool in oven with door ajar for 3 hours.

8. Refrigerate 8 hours or overnight.

9. Remove sides of pan; place cheesecake on serving cake plate.

10. Serve with strawberries, if desired, to count as an additional fruit serving.

Egg Nog

2 *servings*

good source of calcium

- **SERVING SIZE:** 3/4 CUP (200ML)
- **COUNTS AS:**
  1/2 PROTEIN
  1 DAIRY

▶ *size according to plan*

☼ Ingredients

2 eggs, well beaten

3 packets artificial sweetener

dash of vanilla extract

2 cups (500ml) cold skim milk

dash of nutmeg, to taste

1. Combine egg and artificial sweetener.

2. Add vanilla extract and cold milk and beat well.

3. Pour into glasses or mugs and sprinkle with nutmeg.

Home
❖ for th
Holiday

Crustless Pumpkin Pie

SERVING SIZE: 1/8 OF PIE
COUNTS AS:
1 STARCH
1/2 DAIRY

ize according to plan

✳ Ingredients

1 can (15oz / 420g) pumpkin, no salt added

1 can (12oz / 336g) evaporated skim milk

1/2 cup (125ml) egg substitute

2 egg whites

3/4 cup (200ml / 150g) artificial sweetener

1 tsp ground cinnamon

1/4 tsp ground allspice

1/4 tsp ground ginger

1/8 tsp salt

1/2 cup (125ml / 59g) reduced-fat graham cracker crumbs

nonfat cooking spray

1 In a mixing bowl, combine the pumpkin, milk, egg substitute, egg whites and sweetener, beat until smooth.

2 Add the spices and salt, beat until well combined.

3 Stir in graham cracker crumbs.

4 Pour into a 9-inch pie plate that has been coated with nonfat cooking spray.

5 Bake at 325°F for 50-55 minutes, or until knife inserted near the center comes out clean. Cool before slicing.

Fruit & Nut Crisp

SERVING SIZE: 1-INCH
SQUARE (1/8 OF PAN)
COUNTS AS:
1 STARCH
2 FRUITS

ize according to plan

✳ Ingredients

1/4 cup (60ml / 32g) flour

1/2 cup (125ml / 40g) uncooked instant oatmeal

1/2 tsp allspice

3 Tbsp lite margarine, softened

2 cups (500ml / 362g) canned pineapple chunks, drained

1 mango, peeled and sliced

1/2 banana, peeled and sliced

1 orange, peeled and sliced

3/4 cup (200ml / 115g) sliced papaya

1 kiwi, sliced

2 Tbsp brown sugar

2 Tbsp artificial sweetener

3 Tbsp almonds, chopped

1 Tbsp flour

1 In small bowl, combine flour, oatmeal, brown sugar, and allspice.

2 Add margarine; mix with fork, until a crumbly dough forms.

3 In large mixing bowl, combine all fruits, artificial sweetener, and almonds.

4 Sprinkle with flour and toss to coat.

5 Pour fruit mixture into greased 8-inch square baking pan. Sprinkle oatmeal mixture on top.

6 Bake in preheated oven at 350°F until crust is brown and fruit mixture begins to bubble, about 20-25 minutes.

Home
❖ for the
Holidays

General Information

The *L A Lite Cookbook* has been designed to spice up your L A Weight Loss program. Eating a variety of foods will not only keep you interested in your program, but it will also provide your body with the vitamins, minerals and other nutrients that are essential for balanced nutrition and good health. This cookbook will provide you with healthy and delicious recipes that can be used not only while you are losing weight, and for many years to come. Eating healthy is not only important for weight loss, but it's also important for maintaining your new weight for a lifetime.

Adopting a healthier lifestyle will not only help you lose weight, but can benefit the entire family. This cookbook includes many popular dishes that everyone will enjoy. Start off any meal with an appetizer, soup or salad. Next, with over a hundred entrée recipes, you will be sure to find a delicious entree to suit your mood. Finally, conclude your meal with a tantalizing dessert or delicious beverage.

Depending on the situation, it may make sense to adjust the diet and reduce or exclude the intake of some foods. Here are the most common cases for considering dietary modifications:

Dietary Substitutions

▶ **Lactose intolerant**
Use fat-free or skim Lactaid milk in place of skim milk in recipes. Soymilk may also be used.

▶ **Gluten and wheat free**
Use rice in recipes that call for pasta. Starches such as winter squash and potatoes are also delicious wheat and gluten-free alternatives.

▶ **Vegetarians**
Use your favorite vegetarian protein in place of any meat in a recipe. For example, instead of using beef in the beef teriyaki recipe you can use beans, seitan or textured vegetable protein instead. Tofu and tempeh can be used in place of chicken. Make substitutions accordingly.

▶ **Vegans**
Use soymilk in place of milk in recipes. Cheeses such as mozzarella and cheddar can be replaced with soy cheese. Ricotta and cottage cheese can be substituted with tofu. Animal proteins such as chicken and beef can be substituted with beans, veggie burgers or textured vegetable protein.

To make using this cookbook easier, we have included a number of icons; you will see these throughout the cookbook. Let these icons help guide you in choosing recipes that fit your lifestyle and nutritional needs. An explanation of each is listed below.

Symbol Key

▶ **Good Source of Fiber**

Recipes that contain at least 2.5g of fiber per serving are considered to be good sources of fiber (fiber is a component of foods that can not be fully digested.) Fiber has many health benefits, from improving digestion, relieving constipation, protecting against some types of cancers and lowering blood cholesterol levels. In addition, high fiber foods take longer to digest, keeping you satisfied longer.

▶ **Good Source of Calcium**

Recipes that contain at least 10 percent of the recommended daily value for calcium per serving. Calcium is an essential mineral used to maintain strong bones and teeth. Adequate calcium intake can help prevent osteoporosis and is important for people of all ages.

▶ **Meals in Minutes**

Recipes that will take 20 minutes or less to prepare and reach the table. These recipes are great for people with active lifestyles. You will be able to prepare and cook a delectable meal in less time than waiting for take-out to be delivered!

▶ **Family Fare**

These are recipes that make more than one serving. These recipes were created so everyone can sit down and enjoy a healthy, well-balanced meal together. With this cookbook, you do not need to cook separate meals for your family and yourself to follow the program and achieve the success of your weight loss goals.

Some of the following terms are found in many of our recipes. For your convenience here are some definitions to help in the preparation of the recipes.

Julienne: Slicing foods into thin matchstick like strips.

Chopped: Cutting food into uniform bite sized pieces.

Grated: Thin shreds of a food. Large pieces of food are rubbed against a serrated surface such as a grater. A food processor can also grate many foods.

Zest: The colored portion of the skin/peel of a citrus fruit such as an orange, lemon or lime. Removing this outer layer of skin can add great flavor to foods.

Diced: Cutting food in to small cubes.

Minced: Cutting food into very small pieces. Minced foods are smaller than chopped foods.

Working the recipes into your meal plan

You may notice that there some ingredients in some of the recipes in this cookbook that are not on your weight loss plan. It is okay to use these recipes! These ingredients are portion controlled and the calories are factored into the exchanges.

In addition, some recipes do not appear to have the same exchanges and serving sizes as the menu plans. For example, a recipe may call for only half a cup of raw vegetables but may count as a whole vegetable serving. When working out the exchanges, the registered dietitians have looked at the recipe as a whole before determining what to count it as. As long as you measure out the portions of ingredients and count the recipes as indicated, these recipes can all be used on a regular basis.

Want to change the number of servings from a recipe? You can convert your favorite "Family Fare" recipe to a single serving or adjust any single serving recipe so it can make multiple servings. Here are a few examples:

A single serving recipe that calls for 2 tablespoons of skim milk and 1/2 cup (125ml) fresh broccoli can be adjusted to make 12 servings. There are 16 tablespoons per cup, so the new 12 serving recipe would have 24 tablespoons or 1 1/2 cups of skim milk. The new recipe would now call for 6 cups of broccoli.

A recipe that yields 12 servings that calls for 1/4 cup (125ml) of juice can also be modified to serve any number of people. 1/4 cup is 4 tablespoons or 12 teaspoons, if changing this recipe to make 4 servings you would need teaspoons or 1 1/3 tablespoon of juice. To make 1 serving you would use only a teaspoon of juice.

Use the following conversion charts to help you adjust any of our delicious recipes.

Have you ever been confused by how many teaspoons equal a tablespoon, or how many grams equal an ounce? With the reference chart below, hopefully, we will answer all those questions about US and metric measurements.

Conversion Chart

1/4 tsp = 1.25 ml	
1/2 tsp = 2.5 ml	
3/4 tsp = 3.75 ml	
1 tsp = 5 ml	
1 Tablespoon (Tbsp) = 3 tsp = 15 ml	
1/4 cup = 60 milliliters (ml)	
1/2 cup = 125 ml	
3/4 cup = 200 ml	
1 cup = 250 l	
2 cups = 1 pint = 500 ml	
4 cups = 1 quart = 1 Liter (L)	
1 ounce (oz) = 28 gram (g)	
4 oz = 112 g	
8 oz = 224 g	
16 oz = 1 pound (lb) = 448 g	

Metric conversions
1 inch (in) = 2.5 centimeters (cm)

The following are flavorings, spices and herbs that can be used to make foods tastier without adding salt:

Beef: bay leaf, horseradish, marjoram, nutmeg, onion, pepper, sage, thyme.

Lamb: chili powder, curry powder, garlic, lemon juice, rosemary, mint, turmeric.

Pork: garlic, ginger, onion, sage, pepper, oregano.

Veal: bay leaf, curry powder, ginger, marjoram, oregano.

Chicken: cumin, garlic, ginger lemon juice, marjoram, oregano, paprika, poultry seasoning, rosemary, sage, tarragon, thyme.

Fish: curry powder, dill, dry mustard, lemon juice, marjoram, parsley, paprika, pepper.

Carrots: cinnamon, cloves, chives, coriander, marjoram, nutmeg, parsley, rosemary, sage.

Corn: cumin, curry powder, onion, paprika, parsley.

Green Beans: dill, curry powder, lemon juice, marjoram, oregano, tarragon, thyme.

Peas: ginger, marjoram, mint, onion, pepper, sage.

Potatoes: dill, garlic, onion, paprika, parsley, sage.

Summer Squash: cloves, curry powder, marjoram, nutmeg, rosemary, sage.

Winter Squash: cinnamon, ginger, nutmeg, onion.

Tomatoes: basil, bay leaf, marjoram, onion, oregano, parsley, pepper.

Ingredient substitutions

If you cannot find…

Sugar Twin® Brown Sugar use Splenda® or other heat stable artificial sweetener instead.

Herbox® very low sodium broth and bouillon then choose a fat free broth with as little sodium as possible. Some very low sodium bouillons and broths contain potassium. Try to choose brands that do not have potassium as an ingredient.

Splenda® use another heat stable artificial sweetener.

- 1 Tbsp flour can be substituted with 1 1/2 tsp of arrowroot starch or 1 1/2 tsp of cornstarch

- 1 clove of garlic can be substituted with 1/8 tsp of garlic powder

- 1 tsp lemon zest can be substituted with 1/2 tsp lemon extract

- 1/4 cup fresh chopped onion can be replaced with 1 Tbsp of instant minced onions

- 1 tsp of dry mustard can be replaced with 1 Tbsp of prepared mustard

- 1 Tbsp of finely chopped fresh herbs can be replaced with 1 tsp dried leaf herbs or 1/2 tsp ground dried herbs

- Egg substitute can be replaced with egg whites. 2 egg whites will replace 1/4 cup of egg substitute.

- Fresh vegetables can be substituted with frozen vegetables.

- Vegetarian Proteins found in any recipe, including those in the vegetarian section can be substituted with animal proteins. Poultry or beef could be used in place of Tofu in a recipe for BBQ Tofu.

- Meats can be substituted for one another.

Sugar Substitutes

Equal®	1 packet = 2 tsp sugar
Equal Spoonful®	1 tsp = 1 tsp sugar
Equal Tablet®	1 tablet = 1 tsp sugar
Splenda®*	1 tsp granulated = 1 tsp sugar
	1 packet = 2 tsp sugar
Sweet 'N Low®	1 packet = 2 tsp sugar
Sweet 'N Low® Brown	1 tsp = 1/4 cup brown sugar
Sugar Twin®*	1 tsp granulated = 1 tsp sugar
Sugar Twin Brown*	1 tsp granulated = 1 tsp sugar

1 packet = 2 tsp sugar
*Heat stable, can be used in baking

Artificial sweeteners are a great way to keep the sweet flavors in your favorite recipes and foods. Most of these are non-nutritive sweeteners, meaning that they have no nutritional value, so they do not contain significant calories.

Steps to reduce sugar in the diet

- Read the ingredient list on labels. If sugar is listed as one of the first five ingredients, the product contains a large amount of sugar as a sweetener.

- Use less white and brown sugar, honey, jam or jelly. Try sugar free jams and jellies.

- Purchase unsweetened cereals.

- Purchase fresh fruits, or choose canned or frozen fruits without added sugar.

- Try to avoid adding sugar to coffee, tea, cereal and fruit.

- Try reducing the amount of sugar in recipes. You can usually cut the sugar by 1/3 in most recipes without compromising flavor. Try introducing spices like cinnamon, cardamom, coriander, nutmeg, ginger and mace to enhance the sweet flavor of foods.

You'll be delighted with your L A Lite Cookbook. We have created the recipes that you want and your family will enjoy! In addition, we have included our clients favorites. This cookbook is great for clients on the program, as a gift for family or friends and can be used to prepare everyday meals or special occasion dishes for a party or get together! **Bon Appetite!**